Parenting in Public

Parenting in Public

Family Shelter and Public Assistance

Donna Haig Friedman

with Rosa Clark, Brenda Farrell, Deborah Gray,
Michelle Kahan, Margaret A. Leonard,
Mary T. Lewis, Nancy Schwoyer, Elisabeth Ward

Illustrations by Sarah Haig Friedman

Columbia University Press
NEW YORK

Columbia University Press

Publishers Since 1893

New York   Chichester, West Sussex

Copyright © 2000 Columbia University Press

Library of Congress Cataloging-in-Publication Data

Friedman, Donna Haig.

  Parenting in public : family shelter and public assistance / by Donna Haig
Friedman with Rosa Clark [et al.]; illustrations by Sarah Haig Friedman.

    p. cm.

  Includes bibliographical references and index.

  ISBN 978-0-231-11105-8 (pa)

  1. Homeless families—United States. 2. Homeless families—Government
policy—United States. 3. Shelters for the homeless—United States. 4. Social work
with the homeless—United States. 5. Family social work—United States. I. Clark
Rosa II. Title.

HV4505 .F75 2000

362.82'83—dc21   99087067

∞

Casebound editions of Columbia University Press books are printed on
permanent and durable acid-free paper.

Printed in the United States of America

c 10 9 8 7 6 5 4 3 2 1

p 10 9 8 7 6 5 4 3 2

Contents

Acknowledgments

A community of persons with considerable generosity, wisdom, and expertise enabled this book to be brought to completion. I offer these acknowledgments as an expression of my deep appreciation for the contribution each made to this work and for the innumerable ways each has touched my life, both personally and professionally.

The program directors, frontline staff, and mothers, who participated in the study upon which this book is based, were tremendously generous in their investment of time, energy, and thoughtfulness during our interviews. They trusted me to listen without judgment and to try to understand the world through their eyes. I was awed by the complexity of the situations and emotions each person shared in response to my questions. My drive to complete this book is grounded in the deep sense of responsibility I feel to honor these persons by telling their stories.

For the past seven years I have had the good fortune of being educated in the realities of family homelessness by women and men who have been directly affected and/or spend their lives working to end this tragic circumstance. Their contributions of time and energy in educating me and in providing technical and emotional support along the way were, and continue to be, significant. They include: Davina Anthony, Edward Chase, Kelley Cronin, Mary Doyle, Elyse Jacobs, Fran Jacobs, Stasia Lopopolo, Ruth McCambridge, Richard

Ring, Lissette Rodriquez, Betsy Santiago, Deborah Stone, and Julia Tripp. I want to thank particularly the eight women who joined me in writing *Parenting in Public*: Rosa Clark, Deborah Gray, Brenda Farrell, Michelle Kahan, Margaret Leonard, Mary Lewis, Nancy Schwoyer, and Elisabeth Ward. I have been deeply transformed by my associations with these women, especially as we worked together to craft this book.

During the early stages of this project Marty Wyngaarden Krauss, Carol Trivette, Carole Upshur, and Constance Williams worked as a team of experts to assist me in learning each step of the research process. Alice Grebinger painstakingly and expertly transcribed the audiotaped interview material. Our talks over coffee as we exchanged scripts for new tapes were always enlightening. During the final stages Ellen Bassuk and Constance Williams carefully reviewed the manuscript and provided me with timely, incisive feedback. Their insights have significantly enhanced the shape and substance of this book. The work of several persons was invaluable in ensuring that the final manuscript was in good technical shape: Kathleen Rowan, Michael McPhee, and Matt Vasconcellos. I am also very grateful to John L. Michel, associate executive editor and Alexander Thorp of Columbia University Press for their steady and affirming editorial assistance, as well as to Susan Heath, manuscript editor.

Financial support for the research was provided by the Merck Scholars II Program and the Frank and Theresa Caplan Endowment for Infancy, Early Childhood, and Parenting Education Fellowship, The Heller School, Brandeis University. The J. W. McCormack Institute of Public Affairs, University of Massachusetts Boston, provided resources for completion of the book. The scope of this research and book project was directly affected by the availability of this financial support. I gladly accept the social responsibility that receipt of such resources places upon me as a social policy researcher and writer.

A network of colleagues and friends provided unconditional personal support as I carried out the research and completed this book. I will be forever grateful to each of them and count myself very fortunate to be part of their lives: Randy Albelda, Jim Canavan, Mary Ellen Colten, Judith Francis, Phyllis Freeman, Cindy Frodie-King,

Amy Glass, Mary Grant, Consuela Greene, Samara Grossman, Oscar Gutierrez, Michelle Hayes, Mary McCann, John McGah, Jim McNulty, Pam McQuide, Dolly Ntseane, Bill Silvestri, Vickie Steinitz, Michael Stone, Sandy Topalian, Elaine Werby, and Robert Woodbury. My mother, Sylvia, my brother, Dave, and my sisters, Peg and Betty, provided valuable moral support, especially as the book was nearing completion. I am most grateful for their understanding and encouragement.

I have disguised the identities of mothers, staff, directors, and shelter agencies throughout the book in order to protect their anonymity.

The two persons whose lives were most directly affected by my completion of the book and whose support was unflagging were my husband, Steven, and my daughter, Sarah. Sarah, a writer herself, read early drafts of each chapter and never failed to get to the heart of the matter in her feedback. She also created the book's illustrations. Her integrity and sense of social justice are the bedrock of her spirit and intellect. I have learned so much about being a writer from her. Steven, also a writer, has been tireless in his steadfast love, confidence in my abilities, wise insights, and patience throughout the past seven years as I carried out the research and wrote this book. Having been both a researcher and author, he was more aware than I of the personal sacrifices we as a family would face once I began this journey. He was also intimately aware of the intensity with which I approach my work. Nonetheless, he traveled with me as a loving companion from beginning to completion. In addition he provided me with direct and concrete technical help on the last strenuous lap of the journey. I am most grateful for the gifts of Steven and Sarah in my life.

To all of these persons, to Mary Ann Allard, and to my father, Tom, I dedicate this work.

Parenting in Public

Prologue

Fourteen percent of all renters in the United States, 5.3 million households, are living in a "worst case housing needs" situation.[1] They are paying more than 50 percent of their income for housing or are living in substandard housing. Beginning in 1983 the federal government began cutting the number of new housing vouchers it funded each year. By 1995 the country's low-cost housing stock was so limited that only about two out of every five families in the United States who had extremely low incomes—that is, less than 30 percent of the area median—were able to find housing they could afford. Most of this limited supply of low-cost housing was the result of government assistance in the form of subsidies or public housing.[2] Between 1995 and 1998 Congress, for the first time since 1977, denied funding for any new rental subsidies,[3] a striking reversal in our country's long history of attempting to meet the objective we set for ourselves in the Federal Housing Act of 1949—that is, to ensure "a decent home and suitable living environment for all Americans." No wonder that the growth of family homelessness in the country coincides with the federal government's retreat from keeping up with the demand for housing assistance. In study after study, access to housing assistance prevents families, no matter what their personal situation or psychological needs, from losing their housing and falling into the pit of homelessness.[4]

Congress continues to decrease the country's stock of low-cost housing through policies that, on the one hand, are improving the livability of public housing developments by mixing families with a range of income levels, and on the other hand, do not require a one-to-one replacement of units affordable to families with the lowest incomes.[5] As a result, between 1996 and 1998 the federal housing assistance waiting lists increased substantially. On average, in 1998 to 1999 the few housing assistance waiting lists still open across the country included the names of over twenty-five thousand households per waiting list. Without housing assistance, families across the country have to pay on average more than 75 percent of their already low incomes for market rate rental units, and in some parts of the country, their entire incomes must be spent on such housing.[6] When families have to "wait" for housing assistance, their family lives are not standing still. They still need a place to live. They still need to do everything any other family has to do to keep its members sheltered and functioning. Housing is basic.

Renters are in the worst housing situations. In the booming economy of the end of the twentieth century, homeowners in general tend to have higher incomes and are able to purchase mortgages at the prevailing low interest rates.[7] The fastest growing group of households with worst case housing needs is renter family households with children in which one or more adults are working.[8] These are the same families who have been targeted in this country's welfare reform efforts. Indeed, many of these families have voluntarily left the welfare rolls and ventured into the paid workforce. In 1996 "welfare as we knew it" was radically transformed when the sixty-year federal entitlement to cash assistance (Aid to Families with Dependent Children [AFDC])for families living in poverty ended. Although state variations in welfare reforms are numerous, most are designed to encourage parents who are poor to connect with the paid workforce. Many of these welfare experiments have precipitated new connections between government, the private employment sector, and nonprofit organizations. They have tapped a deep belief and abiding conviction among all United States residents, regardless of class, race, or ethnicity, that work is a core element in enabling a person to feel some sense of worthiness as a contributor to community life.

However, we now know that income from paid employment is only one part of what families need to move out of poverty and to thrive. We now know that income from a full-time, minimum-wage job is insufficient for enabling a family to pay market-rate rents almost anywhere in the United States—rural, suburban, or urban areas alike.[9] The growing income inequality gap in the United States provides a partial explanation for this troubling fact.[10] The wealthiest 1 percent of households in the country have profited from the current economic boom and in 1997 held assets equal to the remaining 95 percent of households. In fact, the median household income in 1997 was $11,700, lower than it was in 1989.[11]

We also know that to combine good parenting with working well is a very difficult job under the best of circumstances. Witness the abounding literature on the hardships faced by women with ample incomes who try to balance work and family commitments.[12] Carrying out these two tasks in a way that works for both children and parents is nearly insurmountable if the tasks are confounded by meager wages and unsteady work opportunities; by transportation hurdles such as the use of public transportation to get children to child care and parents to work on time; by difficulty in finding affordable and high-quality child care that is available during parents' actual working hours; by difficulty in accessing affordable and consistent health insurance and money for prescriptions; and by practical obstacles to getting children to the doctor, such as work commitments and transportation snags. Family circumstances are even more untenable if mothers and children are at the receiving end of physical, emotional, or sexual violence;[13] if they are living in a "worst-case" housing situation, with no access to publicly funded housing assistance; or if they are indeed without housing and are living in tenuous housing doubled-up with friends or relatives or in a temporary shelter. These extremely stressful circumstances are exacerbated further if the treatment parents and their children receive when they reach out to friends, social service agencies, and government brings humiliation, punishment, and isolation.

Parents who are poor, in particular single female parents, have always been held to a higher parenting standard in the United States than have those with higher incomes. Surveillance of the parenting behaviors of those with low incomes is possible because of these families' unavoidable reliance upon a public assistance program that has been riddled from its inception with stigmatization of its beneficiaries.[14] This reality is clear when one looks at what has become a largely unexamined, but fully matured, family shelter service system in the United States. The intricacies and impacts of these realities for mothers, frontline staff, and program managers are explored in detail throughout this book.

The quality of families' lives and of their encounters with human service workers when they seek and receive public assistance matters. Under the best of circumstances, the experience can have a powerful, long-lasting, positive impact on the lives of children and their parents and can be pivotal for their future. Because the well-being of children is inextricably tied to the well-being of their parents, whether parents experience a sense of efficacy, of competence, of positive connection with others matters. These objectives are integral to the family support model of connection between helpers and families that my coauthors and I explore in the following chapters.

We have attempted to bridge the gulf between two parallel movements operative in the United States at this time, that is, on the one hand, an increasingly stigmatizing and shredded public safety net for families with children who have the lowest incomes and, on the other hand, an asset-oriented social movement whose proponents are working toward ensuring that neighborhoods in the United States are providing families of all shapes and sizes with the resources they need to work well and to care for their children well.[15] We have written this book for the purpose of bringing the contradictory elements of these two parallel social movements into sharper focus and, by bridging these two universes, pointing a way for making progress as a nation in addressing the intractability of family homelessness.

Overview

The in-depth case studies I carried out in five shelter programs in Massachusetts, and my phone interviews with fifty-five shelter directors, provide the primary substance for this book. In it, I tell you what I saw, what I thought, and what mothers, frontline staff, and shelter program directors told me about giving help and receiving it. The written reflections of my coauthors offer another window for understanding the themes covered in each chapter. They provide fresh and current viewpoints regarding shelter life and the complex help-giving and help-receiving labyrinth. These perspectives move beyond the simplistic arguments I hear in welfare reform debates—and the simplistic understandings I had when I began the study. As a reader, you have the benefit of four voices throughout the book, that of a researcher, mothers, staff members, and program managers. Solutions to the quandaries of supporting parents in shelters are harder to grasp than I had originally expected when I began this study. We as a group of writers attempt to tackle these troublesome issues very directly throughout the book.

Chapter 1 offers an overview of the book's core arguments and theoretical framework. Chapter 2 describes the impact of shelter environments on families' lives and parents' care for their children. The physical environment of shelter programs can have a significant impact on the quality of families' lives in a shelter. Chapter 3 examines the struggles and dilemmas of mothers, frontline staff, and directors as they negotiate with each other in the face of the sometimes competing needs of parents and their children. Chapter 4 explores the diverse programmatic and help-giving approaches managers and staff use to create safety and order in their shelters, in particular the shelter rules. Chapter 5 examines the contentious issues related to whether services for family members should be standardized or tailored to each family's unique desires and needs. Chapter 6 explores divergent values related to self-sufficiency and community building, as they affect families' lives in shelter settings. A congregate shelter setting offers families the possibility of experiencing a sense of belonging and connection with others. Whether shelters ought to foster these connections is controversial.

In the last two chapters, we come full circle and connect key issues from the core of the book to recommendations for public policy and human service practice. My coauthors and I hope that our combined observations and reflections will inform readers and add depth, substance, and optimism to the policy and practice discourse regarding families in need of public assistance in the United States.

I

Parenting and Public Assistance

The scream started again today
a slow silent scream of frustrated anger
Today, I wailed at the wall of officialdom.

Smug, smiling, filing-cabinet face,
closed to my unspoken entreaty,
social justice is my right
Don't dole it out like charity.

Robbed of independence, dignity in danger
I stood dead locked, mind locked.
Helpless in his sightless one-dimension world

I walked away

My mind screamed a long sad chaoin (cry) for the us and
damned their "social welfare."

—Cathleen O'Neill in M. Daly

The most fundamental parenting task is to provide for children's basic needs: safety, shelter, food, clothing, and medical care. When government intervention is needed to assist parents in fulfilling these most basic tasks, parents lose autonomy. Their family lives become subject to public scrutiny and criticism. The public stigmatizes these families for being poor, linking their poverty to personal deficits. They are parenting in public. Families who are homeless are desperate for public assistance and ostracized for their dire circumstances. With my eight coauthors I was motivated to write this book to counter these pejorative views of poor people, particularly impoverished families. We believe that poverty is the predictable result of imbalances in our society's economic structures and arrangements, not a result of parents' personal deficits.

We use the Massachusetts family shelter system as a microcosm to explore the impact of help-giving approaches as they are experienced by mothers and service providers. This book explores what happens to mothers and staff in settings that adopt and resist a prescriptive and deficit-oriented ideology. The book is based upon my research and policy work with the family shelter network over the past six years. The study, in which I put family shelter staff and environments in Massachusetts under a microscope, took place between 1993 and 1996, at a time when welfare reform was center stage on the public agenda.

I became interested in doing this study after working as a consultant with an agency in the Boston area that operated several family shelter programs. The agency hired me to assist staff in designing an early intervention program for the homeless families they served. Having previously worked in the early intervention field, in which strength-based, consumer-driven practices were considered the standard for effectiveness, I was shocked by the level of oversight that seemed to be the modus operandi of this agency. For example, case managers regularly told parents when their children were to be in bed and meted out punishments when parents did not follow their rules. Often, the staff members were younger than the parents they were chastising; many were not parents themselves.

Curious to understand how common such practices were and, if they were common, how they got to be that way, I began to reach out to others in the state's family shelter network to learn about the system. Through a series of interviews with key informants, including some of this book's coauthors, I learned that, while rules and regulations of the sort I had seen in this one agency were common, state officials and leaders in the field thought that helping practices and program approaches varied considerably among the programs in the state.

The foundation upon which the Massachusetts family shelter system was built is reflected in a 1986 document, written by fourteen family shelter program directors, articulating the principles that guided their programs' helping practices with families. They emphasized family strengths, access to resources, community building, and advocacy for changing the conditions in society that caused families to become homeless.[1] When I began the study in 1993, little was known about the extent to which programs continued to operate from these guiding principles. My initial experiences working with a family shelter agency suggested that these principles had been abandoned. I wanted to find out if that was true and to learn about shelter programs' help-giving approaches, especially as they affected parents' roles with their children when they were living in a shelter. I wanted to understand why at least some programs had reverted to a deficit-oriented, noncollaborative, paternalistic approach or were unable to implement the principles articulated in the 1986 document.

I was transformed by what I saw and heard from mothers, staff, and program directors. I witnessed courage in action. I witnessed mothers and staff members struggling to rise above and overcome obstacles not of their making. I listened to stories from mothers who were grateful for the sensitive interventions of shelter staff in their families' lives. I also heard from mothers who felt humiliated by demeaning program practices and interactions with staff. I learned about the difficult dilemmas staff members and program managers struggled with as they attempted to balance the sometimes competing needs of all those who resided in their shelters. Their stories were compelling and eye-opening.

My coauthors are a gifted group of experienced colleagues. Some are mothers who have lived in family shelters, and some are frontline staff members and program directors who work in and manage these shelters. Each of the women who joined me in writing this book brings considerable expertise to the table. Using the research as a foundation, the substance of this book reflects our combined experience in addressing family homelessness in Massachusetts. We propose an alternative policy and practice framework that runs counter to the prevailing punishing and stigmatizing cultural trends.

Six key principles characterize the emerging family support approach that we promote in this book. This approach builds upon other family support movements[2] but focuses to a greater extent on families who do not have a home of their own, have few resources and social support networks, and have been stigmatized and marginalized as a result of their reliance upon public assistance. The principles we promote here inform the broad context of human service work, including the quality of relationships between families and service providers, the design of program policies and services, the quality of service environments, and the public policies affecting human services. The model we propose is based upon the assumptions that all families must have the economic means to meet their basic needs; that all families have strengths and aspirations; and that when parents are supported in realizing their hopes, children benefit. Using this framework, human service workers act to ensure that families receive individualized support, have maximum control and choices, have avenues for becoming collaborators in the decision making process, and have opportunities to move successfully toward their unique aspirations.

The key principles of the emerging family support approach are:

- Poverty and its effects are best understood by viewing the world through the eyes of those who are poor, those who are most directly affected. Macrolevel analyses of poverty, while valuable, fail to take into account the practical realities of poor families' lives, the impact of unrelenting stress on families' lives, and the devastating impacts of stigmatizing and demeaning human service practices and policies.
- Human service work is most effective when consumers have a significant role in decision making and governance. With this approach, not only do parents have a role in determining which services they will use, they also have a role in determining program and public policies that have a direct impact on their lives.
- Strengths are the starting point for relationship building and service planning. Every parent has capacities and aspirations that, when tapped, sustain resilience, energy, and hope. These strengths, along with realistic options for securing a steady and adequate income, are the family's avenue out of poverty.
- Mutuality characterizes effective relationships between human service workers and the people they serve. Respect is at the core of the relationship. These parties treat each other as equals, and hold each other accountable.
- Respect for the centrality of the parenting role is essential in all interactions between human service workers and parents,

even when human service providers must step in to ensure children's safety.

- A belief in our common bonds as humans, helper and help-receiver alike, is essential for breaking down class, racial, and gender barriers that perpetuate poverty and the marginalization of people who are poor.

Creating policy and providing services according to these principles is exceedingly difficult. The principles fly in the face of the prevailing attitudes and ways of working in many human service arenas in the United States, in which the corporation's or institution's interests hold sway over the best instincts of workers and clients.[3] Demeaning, paternalistic[4] attitudes have been codified in federal and state legislation, and in government contracts with the nonprofit organizations who carry out the state's work with families in need of public assistance and emergency assistance. With my coauthors I take issue with the negative assumptions upon which these laws and policies are based.

Local welfare and other human service workers, like family shelter staff and managers, are caught in the middle of the debate. They may find ways to counteract the paternalistic stipulations in their contracts with the government or fall prey to an insidious process of control and power that, in the end, serves to disempower both them and those they serve. I learned through my research that, while agencies must deal with these requirements and embedded ideologies, they can actively resist the pulls to become deficit-oriented and prescriptive in their relationships with parents. Many do resist.

The structure of the book itself provides a clear example of this model. We collaborated in a way that honors the unique experiences and insights each of us brings to the table, without regard to rank or station in life. Three reflections, one written by a mother, one by a frontline staff member, and one by a program director, follow each chapter. Half of the women who contributed their reflections to this book have been homeless with their children, have lived in a family shelter, and have had to rely upon public assistance to help them when their families ran into difficult times. Several of these women have also worked as shelter staff members or program directors. The other women have managed or worked in family shelter programs. All the contributors are visionary leaders in the onerous work to end family homelessness in Massachusetts. All are insiders in the struggle to eliminate poverty and its effects. Their views of the causes and effects of poverty are grounded in their lived experience and the knowledge they have gained in their work with hundreds of families struggling to make ends meet. Readers may decide to read the reflections as they complete each chapter or to read them after completing the rest of the book. Chapter 7 is written in the form of a conversation and is the product of a tape-recorded group reflection in which we pondered the meaning and significance of what we have learned from our work together on this book.

The research grounds these reflections and our experiences. The study I conducted with family shelters in Massachusetts included phone interviews with fifty-five directors, representing 95 percent of the state's publicly funded programs. Over 80 percent of the directors also completed a mailed survey. I also conducted face-to-face interviews with ten frontline staff members and thirty-nine mothers. Half of the mothers were former and half were current residents of family shelters. In conjunction with the face-to-face interviews, I immersed myself in five programs whose directors differed in their beliefs about help giving. Two were led by directors who espoused paternalistic beliefs and three were led by directors who espoused family support beliefs. The influence of these belief systems is evident in the ways shelter programs in Massachusetts set up the physical environment; handle privacy in shelter environments; deal with shared responsibility for the care of children; involve parents in the creation and review of shelter rules; standardize or individualize services; and manage ties among families and staff. We explore these themes throughout the book.

Why a Focus on Parenting?

Parenting is a perfect lens through which to explore help giving with families who use public assistance. Parents and their children are the primary recipients of welfare public assistance in the United States.

Welfare policies across the country focus on the need for recipients to join the paid workforce as a means of ending their economic reliance on the government. The presence of children in these families is what complicates the policy making. Our policies need to provide realistic avenues for parents to both work well and parent well. As public assistance policies are implemented by welfare workers, shelter staff, and other human service workers, both parents and children feel the effects, beneficial or not.

Support for parenting is extremely complex and critically important for the growth and development of the next generation. Children's sense of self and sense of competence is directly tied to that of their parents. When parents are stressed, children feel the effects and are less able to develop a sense of security and curiosity about themselves and the world around them. Supporting parents in their roles as parents is exceedingly difficult for human service workers under the best of circumstances. When parents are dealing with the devastation of being without a home for their children, their sense of inadequacy, shame, and fear is heightened. Family shelter staff and program managers face enormous challenges in their efforts to find effective ways of enabling parents' sense of themselves to be healed and restored. Not only are parents and children extremely stressed in these settings, but the residential physical environment itself demands that the needs of all children and parents be balanced with the needs and preferences of individual family members. If, under these circumstances, shelter staff and program managers can find effective ways of supporting parents and children, then surely welfare workers and other human service workers can be empowered to do so as well.

Much has been written about family homelessness in the United States. The literature includes macrolevel and microlevel analyses of this social problem. However, as a country we have little information about the ways in which our public assistance practices and policies have an impact on mothers' care for their young children. This book attempts to fill this gap by providing a comprehensive portrayal of one state's system of congregate family shelter, as well as detailed, in-depth observational and narrative accounts of family life and parenting dilemmas in shelters as experienced by mothers, staff, and managers in diverse programs. In addition, by design, the book reflects a dynamic collaboration among those most directly affected by homelessness, those who provide service, and those who conduct applied public policy research.

What we have learned is instructive for other human service arenas along four dimensions. In particular, we highlight:

- effective ways for human service workers and their clients to relate to each other;
- the organizational features and program policies conducive to positive assistance for parents and their children;
- community and neighborhood-level underpinnings needed to enable parents to support their children in their own homes; and
- the public policies that are essential for buttressing effective human service work and for reducing the systemic conditions that exacerbate poverty and its effects.

Family Homelessness and the Family Shelter System

Families are the fastest-growing segment of the nation's homeless population. As the welfare rolls have declined, family homelessness has been on the rise in the United States. Families now make up 38 percent of the country's homeless population.[5] The growth of this social problem is, simply put, a consequence of inadequate financial, housing, and social resources for low-income families in our country.[6] In the wake of increasing numbers of homeless individuals and families in the United States, a shelter industry has developed, increasingly incorporating an array of social service supports into programs, in addition to providing homeless men, women, and children with emergency shelter.[7] As providers interact with increasing numbers of families and as federal and state policies have shifted, family shelters have become comprehensive family service centers with codified rules and regulations. A new institution has been born, with a full-fledged workforce and mature but largely unexamined service approaches. In Rossi's words, "emergency" shelters have become the "bottom layer to local housing markets."[8]

When family homelessness was "newly discovered" by the media and government in the early 1980s, emergency shelter was a transient fix for what was hoped would be a temporary social problem. Public sentiment reflected both sympathy for families and outrage that an affluent United States society could allow families to go unhoused.[9] Federal and state policy makers focused on developing more housing options for poor families and providing emergency shelter as a temporary solution. As the public has tired of the problem,[10] as the economic conditions for poor people have worsened in general, and therefore, as policy solutions have failed to provide a quick fix for family homelessness, policy approaches have reflected beliefs that homeless people are dysfunctional[11] and have included mandatory social services as a condition for homeless families to receive access to public shelter.[12] The "emergency" shelter system has become a permanent part of the human service landscape and is increasingly being looked to as the last remaining thread of the social safety net.[13]

Many low-income families do not become homeless. Those who do have fewer sources of support. In addition, their kin and friends, those whom they call upon for help, also have limited financial resources.[14] Public assistance in the form of housing subsidies and "welfare-as-we knew it" (i.e., AFDC), along with a high school diploma, more people to call on for help and support, and fewer conflicted relationships protect low-income families from becoming homeless.[15] Contrary to popular stereotypes, parents who have lost their housing actively seek, use and exhaust every other option before they ask for shelter from the government. Typically, they rely upon a series of extended family members and friends for temporary housing. Many move in with three or more other households before they seek emergency shelter.[16]

These dislocations are highly stressful for both children and parents and exacerbate the effects of the trauma of impoverishment.[17] Children lose valuable connections with their friends and belongings. Their school attendance suffers and their continuity in learning is interrupted with every school or day care change. Parents also lose connections with friends and family and, if working, may have to quit their jobs. In addition, during these dislocations children and parents typically suffer stigmatization, humiliation, and ostracism from those within their communities and others they reach out to for help.[18]

In the face of these devastating events and circumstances, seeking emergency shelter or other public assistance is a parent's demonstration of tremendous courage. She is making a choice to keep her family off the street. She, as a worthy citizen, is making a claim on behalf of her children and herself for some part of the country's public resources. She is saying "No," however tentatively or strongly, to the internal and external critics of her character and her mothering.[19] Making the decision to seek help to care for her children, no matter what kind of humiliation comes in its wake, is a choice to hold on to her parenting role, a choice that becomes a source of strength for survival and transformation.[20]

When parents and their children knock at the emergency shelter door, they are traumatized and in a state of shock as a result of the devastating events they have just experienced. Unfortunately, at times residing in a shelter adds to the trauma.[21] In many parts of the country, children and their parents share some of the living spaces with others either in dormitory or barrack-style settings or in smaller, congregate settings in which each family has a cubicle, partition, or room of its own.[22] In some places, families have beds in shelters that house single men and women with serious alcohol, drug, or mental health problems. In many parts of the country, parents and their children have to leave the shelter during daytime hours.[23]

The quality of the shelter experience matters greatly. This point is my core argument. A positive shelter experience, however short or long, can help family members to recover from the losses and stigmatizations they have suffered. To recover from the trauma and to move out of homelessness with optimism and hope, children and their parents need and deserve a safe and caring shelter environment and experience.

Family Homelessness in Massachusetts

In Massachusetts policy changes and cutbacks in federal and state housing, income support, and homeless assistance programs during the 1990s have had cumulative impacts on the poorest households in the state. As a result, homelessness in the state has grown.[24] For example, federal housing assistance for Massachusetts households decreased by 11 percent from 1994 to 1996. Funding for the state's rental assistance program decreased by 62 percent from 1990 to 1996. Federal funds for fuel assistance decreased by 49 percent in the period from 1994 to 1996. Funding for food stamps decreased by 32 percent in the same period. Federal and state funds for prevention of family homelessness in the state decreased by 64 percent in the period from 1990 to 1996. A smaller pool of housing subsidies and federal housing policy changes contributed to increased lengths of stay for families in shelters. For example, in 1986 families were in and out of emergency shelters within a matter of weeks. In 1997 families lived in emergency shelters for four to six months or longer. In other parts of the country the length of time families stayed in emergency shelters varied considerably, from a few days to a matter of months.[25]

By 1998 the refusals and barriers for obtaining ways into shelters and out of homelessness had intensified. In addition, in Massachusetts, after 120 days of living in a shelter, homeless parents with school-age children had to meet a twenty-hour weekly work requirement, as well as mandated weekly targets for seeking housing. Most homeless families use welfare, that is, Temporary Aid to Needy Families (TANF), and in Massachusetts are currently subject to twenty-four-month time limits on welfare receipt. The first Massachusetts families, including some who were homeless, reached their time limit and lost all cash assistance in December 1998.

Massachusetts family shelter models.   Massachusetts currently operates four program models for provision of publicly funded family shelter. They are: nonspecialized, congregate programs; specialized congregate programs; scattered site programs; and transitional shelter programs.[26] A congregate shelter setting is the most common family shelter program model in the state. Its distinguishing program feature is that families share some of the physical living spaces. For example, each family may have its own bedroom but share eating or kitchen facilities with other families. Or, the physical setup may include partitions between each family's sleeping area rather than a separate bedroom for each family. Between 1993 and 1999 the number of publicly funded nonspecialized congregate programs in the state decreased from fifty-eight to forty-five. However, the number of families receiving shelter each night increased slightly during this period, from approximately 450 to 475. In 1999 approximately eighty families lived in specialized congregate shelters for homeless mothers (and their children) with substance abuse difficulties.

Other program models with shorter service histories in Massachusetts than congregate settings are scattered site and transitional shelter models. A common distinguishing feature of these two program models is that each family lives in a private apartment setting. This physical feature provides a shelter alternative for large families, two-parent families, families with adolescent males, and families with health problems. These two program models differ from each other along an important program dimension. Scattered site programs are designed for families whose length of stay will be shorter than a stay in a transitional program: the focus is on shelter as an emergency measure. Transitional shelter programs are designed to allow families to engage in a more long-term process of vocational and educational skill development: here, the focus is on shelter as an intervention. By January 1999 over 300 families resided in scattered site programs each night, an increase of 13 percent from 1994; approximately 175 additional families were involved with transitional shelter programs.[27]

Congregate and scattered site programs were originally designed to be emergency shelters. That is, the primary objective was to temporarily house homeless families and to assist them in accessing and retaining permanent housing as quickly as possible (a short-term process of one to three months). Specialized programs for parents with alcohol or drug addictions and transitional shelter programs were designed with the primary objective of assisting parents to overcome personal difficulties that had interfered with their ability to retain permanent housing (a long-term process of six to twenty-four months).

During the years when I was carrying out my study, families were staying longer in emergency shelter settings than was originally planned or expected. In 1994 the average homeless family with young children in Massachusetts actually spent five to six months or longer in a temporary emergency family shelter setting. This slow movement out of emergency shelters resulted in the periodic swelling in the number of homeless families being sheltered in hotels or motels in Massachusetts. The state's response to the growing population of homeless families was to restrict eligibility for family shelter further and to eliminate the use of hotels and motels as options when family shelters had reached capacity. That is, in 1994 the administration barred the following groups of homeless families from state-funded shelter: those who became homeless for nonpayment of rent in subsidized housing; those who had a family member accused (not convicted) of criminal activity; those whose children had not been living with them for the past six months; and those who had left their housing after they received an eviction notice but before the sheriff actually arrived at their door to physically evict them. These policies were successful in reducing the numbers of families counted for official purposes as homeless. Advocates contend that the actual numbers of homeless families in the state has increased; however, they struggle with documenting the need, since an unduplicated count of those who use shelter and those who request but are denied emergency shelter is not available. The most current estimate indicates that at some time during 1997 the number of homeless families in the state was approximately ten thousand, double that of 1990.[28]

During those years agencies sheltering families in the state saw themselves as more than places for children and parents to simply sleep and eat during their search for stable housing. They operated, and continue to operate, to a great degree as family multiservice centers. Almost universally, participating programs provide case management, basic life skills training, housing search and placement, and limited emergency transportation services.

When I was surveying programs, most congregate family shelter programs were small in capacity, serving from four to twenty-two families; nearly three-quarters of the programs served fewer than ten families on any given night. In 1991, a U.S. Department of Housing and Urban Development (HUD) national evaluation report recognized Boston family shelters for being "small, family-like" settings that provided families with both direct and indirect access to a wider array of supports than did programs in other cities.[29] The family shelters in Massachusetts continue to be smaller in capacity than those in other parts of the country.[30] The typical congregate shelter setup is one in which each family unit has a private bedroom; other living spaces (kitchen, dining room, lounge, bathrooms) are shared in common with the other resident parents and children. In 1994 over one-third of the programs excluded adult and/or adolescent male family members from living in their community settings. Others also excluded families in which parents had active substance abuse or severe mental health difficulties.

In 1994 these shelters appeared to be the primary avenue for homeless families to obtain low-cost permanent housing. This trend has continued. For example, in 1997 families leaving shelters were more successful in obtaining housing subsidies than those who sought help from homeless prevention programs in the state.[31]

The directors I surveyed tended, as a group, to view families as resourceful but negatively affected by barriers and obstacles outside their control. These directors did not appear to have adopted the punitive mentality, characteristic of the "get tough" welfare reform framework, which blames families for creating their own difficult circumstances. In addition, the directors tended to espouse helping practices that emphasized family strengths and parents' roles in deciding which services they wanted to receive.

For the most part the families residing in these settings were headed by single mothers with preschoolers, a total of 901 family members (341 mothers, 27 fathers, and 533 children).[32] Seventy-nine percent of the children were six years of age or younger; 54 percent were three years of age or younger. Although many mothers were young, nearly 40 percent were over twenty-five years of age. A majority of mothers (80 percent) had limited educational experience (high school degree or less). A large proportion of these mothers were African American or Latina (30 percent and 25 percent, respectively), disproportionately higher than in the statewide population.[33] Almost without exception, programs served families with diverse ethnicities.

The Congregate Setting: Parenting in Public

In congregate family shelter settings, that is, settings in which homeless families share some of the living spaces with other families, parents and children open themselves up to a remarkable level of professional oversight in exchange for the help they receive. The result is that almost all the family interactions take place in full view of other unrelated families and of service providers. This community setting is complex for several reasons. First, the most intimate interactions between family members take place within view of other parents, children, staff members, and directors of shelter programs, who ostensibly have easy avenues for surveillance of parents' behavior. Second, parents and children must negotiate the smallest details of daily living with other families who, at first, are strangers. For the most part, this involves wrestling with values and norms related to cultural and familial differences. Third, to gain entry to the shelter setting, parents must also agree to follow rules, rules that govern many aspects of daily living, including the care of their children, as determined by help-givers rather than by themselves.

In short, shelter staff have complete access to the texture of families' lives, their goals, and their vulnerabilities. In the course of a few days, a staff member may have met individually with a parent to discuss her service plan, led a parenting group in which the same parent talked about interactions with her child, intervened in a family crisis, and gone on a field trip with the family and others. Little about family members' interactions with each other and with other families is hidden from staff view. Likewise, the competencies and vulnerabilities of staff members are within "public view." They don multiple "staff hats" to interact with parents and children as individual counselors, group leaders, crisis interventionists, and friends.

Time and physical boundaries that exist between service providers and clients in other human service settings are not present in these shelter environments. On the contrary, both mothers and staff in family shelter settings have multiple opportunities to witness each other's personal strengths and shortcomings. They have a unique opportunity, not as readily available in other human service contexts, to connect with each other on a person-to-person level, in addition to a professional-to-client level. Both mothers and staff are vulnerable to being tremendously hurt or supported by each other's treatment. Within this context, they have to come to terms with the inherently complex power dynamic that exists in their relationship. Social exchange theory offers a useful lens for understanding how these relationships might work.

Conceptual Framework: Social Exchange Theory

Power and Affiliation

The principles of power and affiliation operate beneath the surface of relationships in a shelter.[34] Parents are totally dependent upon the programs for a roof over their children's heads. Managers, providers, and parents have to contend with the uneven power dynamic this highly unnatural set of circumstances creates as they attempt to develop compatible and trusting affiliations with each other and among families.

Social exchange theory defines power relationships as those existing when one party has resources the other party highly values and is unable to access through other avenues.[35] The dependent party in this relationship has little to offer in return, although dependent persons try to reciprocate (i.e., to create an even balance in what each party gives and receives). Without reciprocation, the dependent party is at a disadvantage, indebted to the other. People will try to create an evenly balanced relationship of exchange, even when they are in a position of relative dependence.

The dependent party is willing to conform to the demands of the powerful if the expected outcomes seem worth the personal costs of the investment. The dependent party will continue to conform to rules and norms set by those in power if these expectations are met or exceeded. Social exchange theorists propose that these conditions contribute to group cohesion and shared group norms between and among the dependent parties and those in power.[36] On the other hand, dependent parties begin to resist the powerful and become aggressive and angry if expected outcomes are not met, if other benefits that encourage positive affiliations between and among the powerful and powerless are not forthcoming, and if no other alternatives exist for gaining access to needed resources. Under these circumstances, dependent persons can respond by coalition building (teaming up against the powerful), by direct confrontation, or by indirect acts of resistance.[37]

Emotional bonds between people hold currency in explaining certain social exchanges.[38] For example, people will make allowances for friends that they do not make for lesser acquaintances. Such affiliations take time to develop. They are built upon trust and mutual exchanges of affirmation and are an expression of shared values. Reciprocity is an essential feature of affiliation between and among persons.[39] Affiliation or positive emotional bonding between those with and without power is nurtured when those in power exert their influence through fairness, affirmation, and generosity, rather than through force.

Social Exchange Theory Applied to the Family Shelter Context

When a family knocks at the family shelter's door, they have exhausted all other options for shelter. In social exchange terms, the program has a resource essential to the family's well-being. From the program's perspective, the greatest leverage for gaining a commitment from the family to comply with organizational and group norms exists when families first arrive. Maintaining order and predictability within the shelter setting is a value prized so highly that help givers are willing to ask parents to give up some of their autonomy as parents in exchange for living in the shelter.

From families' perspectives, they are most desperate for the resources the organization has to offer at their point of arrival. They may be willing to give up some of their autonomy (e.g., agree to obey rules; agree to follow program norms for child rearing) in exchange for the security of having a place for their children and themselves to live and the possibility of gaining access to affordable housing more quickly than they would otherwise. For both parties, the value of security supersedes the value of liberty.[40] Families have little to offer at first in exchange for shelter and service support other than compliance with organizational and group norms. This compliance is not inconsequential, however. A noncompliant family can upset the applecart considerably in a communal setting.

Parents in Massachusetts may find that they and their children are in fact safer in the shelter than they were living in their car or moving every few months from the home of one friend or relative to another. They may find that by being in the shelter they are gaining access to permanent avenues out of homelessness and poverty. If so, giving up autonomy as a parent may feel like a worthwhile tradeoff. As time

passes, the presence of other benefits, related to the quality of relationships with staff and other families, may become more important
in affecting parents' feelings regarding their loss of autonomy, especially if their stays last longer than they had anticipated. Such sec-
ondary benefits, conducive to developing affiliation, are those that are
likely to be available in family support settings (e.g., friendship with
other mothers, avenues for being affirmed for their unique skills and
competencies, and having a role in determining their own service
plan).

The costs for programs to develop these other positive benefits for
families are worthy of consideration. For example, programs risk losing some control over organizational and group norms by including
families in service planning and program evaluation activities. The
potential exists for families to use such openings to develop coalitions
that aim to balance the power between the program and parents as a
group. Program managers would need to believe that taking the risk
of giving up some authority would be worthwhile in the long run,
that parents would be more satisfied, more congenial with each other,
more compliant with group norms, and less stressed, and that children
would thereby benefit and the program would be more effective.

Program managers would also need to believe that conflicts with
parents could be resolved more easily if they allowed parents to have
significant decision-making roles. For example, if shared power was a
reality in these settings, parents would have a sense of efficacy in their
relationships with staff—that is, they would be confident that their
views were taken seriously. They would expect to engage in adult-to-
adult interactions with staff members. In other words, parents and staff
members would be holding each other accountable for following
through on their commitments. Under these circumstances, the relationship would rest on a solid foundation and could withstand difficult challenges. The strength of the relationship would be tested to the
greatest extent when conflicts between parents and staff involved sensitive issues, such as a staff member being so concerned about a parent's care for her children that the staff member felt obliged to intervene, or a parent being so upset by a staff member's undermining of
her parenting role that the parent felt compelled to report the incident to the director. In settings in which power relations were bal-

anced and connections between and among people were strong, room would exist for handling conflicts and for making occasional mistakes without jeopardizing the stability of the relationships.

Parents might become angry and unwilling to continue to comply with organizational and group norms if they found that shelter living lasted longer than expected and other affiliation benefits related to the help-giving process were not available. Such benefits are not integral components (by definition) in prescriptive and deficit-oriented program types.[41] Under these circumstances, families would risk being thrown out of the program if they expressed their distress aggressively or did not comply with shelter rules. They might seek alternatives such as teaming up with other parents or with sympathetic staff to pressure for programmatic change. They might use indirect forms of resistance, such as minor rule violations, verbal agreement without follow-through, decreased investment in the shelter community, or subtle complaints or criticisms of staff and other parents. For example, parents might keep to themselves or avoid the shelter and staff as much as possible. They might miss scheduled meetings with their case manager. They might take out their frustrations on other resident parents or children.

Staff might interpret these indirect acts of resistance as evidence of parents' lack of motivation and personal deficiencies, reinforcing the continued absence of affirming relationships and opportunities for parents to influence program operations or to demonstrate their competencies. I believe that this negative snowball effect is more likely to happen in program settings that lack explicit mandates to understand parents' hopes for their families, to match their service supports with these desires, and to offer opportunities for parents to experience positive connections with others and an affirmation of their strengths.

Social exchange theory also informs the puzzling findings cited in other studies of family shelters regarding the common use of shelter rules.[42] Rules may actually operate to increase the level of trust families have in the program's use of its power. That is, specific guidelines provide a measure of objectivity to a host of routine interactions among families and staff members. Ideally, they serve to increase the likelihood that families will be treated fairly by program staff. For example, all families are subject to the same restrictions, counteracting the temptation for staff to use favoritism with families who are more compliant, more friendly, more likable, and so forth. This is an example of a circumstance in which a one-size-fits-all approach might work. Although families might find the multiplicity of rules a very difficult aspect of shelter living, their affiliations with staff and other families would be strengthened through staff members' impartial enforcement of rules rather than discretionary preferences. Giving families an active role in devising program policies, for example, could mitigate the negative impact of rules and regulations. As a generous use of power, it might also foster positive affiliations between parents and staff.

The Emerging Family Support Paradigm

Generous uses of power are compatible with the emerging family support principles advanced throughout this book. Each of its tenets describes a dimension of positive relationship building between those with power and those who are dependent, in which the expectations and priorities of dependent persons are listened to and become a focus of service intervention. Responsibility for reaching expected outcomes is shared, reciprocity and affiliation are nurtured, and strengths of dependent persons are affirmed. Those with power and those who are dependent treat each other as adults and hold each other accountable for the actions they have agreed to carry out in their work as a team. This type of relationship, I believe, strengthens a parent's self-esteem and confidence in her parenting abilities. Expected benefits for staff and programs adopting these helping approaches would likely be satisfying relationships with families, a sense of effectiveness and competence as help givers, and fewer problematic interactions among families and staff in the communal setting.

In contrast, deficit-oriented, paternalistic models of care pay less attention, by definition, to helping processes that affirm strengths, that use collaborative approaches for decision making, and that build a sense of affiliation with and among those without power. At its extreme, a paternalistic model characterizes help-giving approaches in which those in power impose their will on those who are dependent. Under these circumstances, those in power can hold dependent persons accountable for their actions but cannot be held accountable in return. The interpersonal dynamic set in motion is one that resembles parent–child relationships, one that I believe undermines a parent's self-esteem and confidence in her parenting abilities. More anger and resistance can be expected from parents living in family shelter settings using this model of help giving than from those living in shelters that use a family support philosophy.

Reflections on Chapter 1

Reflection: Mother, Brenda Farrell

As I reflect on chapter 1, I find myself saddened and confused as to why our society and the policies that govern us continue to blame the victim—in this case poor women and their children—and unapologetically advance policies that only serve to further alienate us as a community. Welfare reform and its "pull yourself up by your bootstraps" mentality has never been a cure for poverty or homelessness, yet we ignore the failures of the system and place stricter requirements on families who are by design unable to achieve success.

Financial security for families' transitioning from welfare to work has never been the goal of welfare reform. Many states play a numbers game with the goal of simply decreasing caseloads. I question the wisdom of a government that believes decreasing caseloads and declining numbers is proof that welfare reform is working. The "one size fits all" cure for poverty reflects a total disregard for poor families and their children.

Even with a booming economy the number of poor continues to rise and hundreds of families fall through the cracks of an almost nonexistent safety net into homelessness. This tragedy argues for the need to develop programs that treat people as individuals. We should be supporting families to identify their unique struggles and reduce barriers that may prevent them from achieving the goal of financial stability. This would ultimately decrease caseloads and decrease episodes of family homelessness.

Instead, families are often treated with contempt and disrespect by society, the media, and the "system" that was originally set up to address their needs. The numerous rigid and time-consuming requirements of the new welfare reform laws make it nearly impossible for any family on TANF to comply. These hurdles are more difficult for families who are under the increased stress of being homeless.

Advocates for a system of rewards and punishments put homeless families in a "less than" category, somehow at fault for their homelessness. When my children and I were homeless, I often felt that I was a being treated much like a cow being herded through a maze to slaughter, no choice of my own, only one path to follow. Whether I liked it or not, whether I needed the particular service or not, move ahead, follow the herd or my children and I would be run over by the forced stampede behind us.

The "blame the victim" mentality was so reinforced each step of the way that many homeless mothers I met, as well as I myself, felt that we were to blame for our homelessness. I needed support to take a step back and realize that as a single mother with one income I was unable to support myself and my two young daughters. The high cost of housing and child care were simply out of my reach. Without an education I, as many other single parents, would never be able to earn a wage high enough to raise my children alone.

The many programs that I sought help from were unable to help me. Many families facing homelessness today face a bleak future. Affordable housing, so crucial in preventing and essential in moving families out of shelter, is almost nonexistent. Shelters are full, and families simply have no place to go. There is a gridlock in the system. In fact, emergency temporary shelter has in many ways become transitional housing. The increased restrictions on eligibility for family shelter continue to close the door to shelter for more poor families. These eligibility requirements often undermine families' efforts to become self-sufficient. In 1998 a single mother with one child who was working full time at a minimum wage job earned too much money to obtain shelter in Massachusetts. Too poor to afford a home, yet too rich to receive emergency shelter. Clearly these policies directly contradict to the "go to work" message families on welfare are receiving from the state agency that administers shelter and welfare programs in Massachusetts.

Families seeking emergency assistance (EA) shelter cannot simply knock at the door to ask for help. Instead a family must apply at the local welfare office and be put through a series of tests to be deemed EA-eligible. Families must prove beyond a reasonable doubt that they are homeless. If a family is found to be-EA eligible, the family is not guaranteed a shelter room. Some welfare offices use scare tactics to keep eligible families out of shelter, such as telling a family that the only space available is hundreds of miles away.

The relationship between families seeking shelter and the administering state agency in Massachusetts is not a partnership; it is paternalism at its worst. This lack of partnership often carries over into the shelter program itself, leaving parents feeling helpless. Families often need advocates just to get into a shelter. Families are often denied shelter for "rendering themselves homeless." The idea that families are rendering themselves homeless is offensive to families forced to live in often demoralizing programs.

In congregate shelters, families are forced to have every move watched not only by staff but also by other families. Frequently, families have no place to be alone and they are subjected to a barrage of rules and mandated meetings. Very little value is placed on the parent, the rights of parents and their parenting skills. Little consideration exists for the stress of living under a microscope and having their every move evaluated.

Although many shelters offer a variety of services for families, I found many of the mandated programs, meetings, and workshops to be useless. These workshops were not what I felt I needed to help my family overcome homelessness. However, my opinion did not matter. If I did not attend the meeting, I was threatened with losing my family's room.

Homeless families customarily have to attend several meetings per week, including parenting, budgeting, and nutrition classes. I found all of the above insulting. To me it was simply more reinforcement that I was a failure and that simply being poor implied that I was not intelligent or a good parent. The one-size-fits-all approach to solving family homelessness simply doesn't work. There should be programs that cater to individuals' needs and that work together with the parent to develop a plan of action.

The abuse of power was perhaps the most disturbing part of my experience and has left the deepest and longest lasting scars. The feeling of hopelessness and lack of power that I felt reinforced a feeling of spiraling ever deeper into a system of programs that were not meeting my needs. This devastating experience has driven me to continue my work to help eradicate family homelessness in Massachusetts.

The social exchange theory that defines power relations as those existing when one party has resources that the other party highly values and is unable to access through other avenues goes one step deeper with homelessness. As a homeless parent, not only do you value the shelter roof over your head, you truly need it to survive. This puts you at the mercy of the provider. I disagree with the idea that the dependent party is willing to conform to the demands of the powerful. I felt I was *forced* to conform for the safety and well-being of my children. I humbled myself and felt humiliated many times for the stability of my children.

Finally, I firmly believe that the state must reflect and take responsibility for its actions. Decreasing prevention programs by 64 percent in Massachusetts has led us to a shelter system that is ready to collapse, as programs are full and waiting lists have built up for entry into shelter. No room exists in the system for families to move forward. The front door continues to close as the back door remains locked. Most important, there is no oversight of the programs themselves, no input from the families as to how well the system works, and no quality controls on how families and their children are treated. Until we reach a point where programs treat people as individuals, homeless families will continue to live by the "luck of the draw" and receive help based on the beliefs of the provider rather than on the individual needs of the families.

Reflection: Executive Director, Nancy Schwoyer

For the last twenty years the family shelter system has been necessary in our society because some families are too poor to afford housing. The 1996 welfare reform legislation was the codification of dominant social attitudes and opinions about the causes and effects of and cures for poverty in the U.S.—namely, that people are poor because they don't try hard enough.

So, we have a shelter system, and we have welfare reform. That is a fact. I cannot deny that the welfare system needed changing. But the debate on the reasons for welfare reform shifted from views of the welfare *system* as deficient and in need of overhauling, to a view of welfare *recipients* as deficient and in need of discipline and regulation. Simply stated, if people are poor because they are deficient, and people are homeless because they are poor and therefore deficient, then it is no surprise that the policies, practices, and programs of the shelter system focus on "reforming" people who have made themselves homeless. The policies and practices of local housing authorities, and state and federal housing programs, are crafted to ensure that only the "reformed" get into shelters and benefit from their resources.

As a country, we now have a set of public policies and practices that support the myth of the American dream—namely, "if you work hard enough, you will enjoy the fruits of this land of milk and honey." This may mean "pulling yourself up by your own bootstraps" so you can be self-sufficient. The myth of the American dream results in a cultural discomfort and even rage at the policy and practice of people being entitled to cash benefits, food, and health insurance—the safety net that was created in response to the depression of the 1930s.

In this first chapter Donna Friedman makes it clear that she believes people are poor and even homeless in our country because there are structural deficiencies in our society, not because people haven't tried hard enough, or because of other personal deficiencies. The limitation of space allowed for this response does not permit an adequate analysis of the causes of poverty and family homelessness in Massachusetts and in the U.S. at this time in history. However, I believe it is where the reader of this book needs to begin, i.e., to look at what has happened to jobs and housing and urban and suburban development since the end of World War II, and particularly in the last twenty-five years.

If we agree with Friedman's thesis—and I do—that people are homeless first and foremost because they are poor, we will understand and support her proposal that the theories of family support and social exchange provide us with appropriate processes for improving life in family shelters. But I would also argue that these two theories are subject to practical distortion if we believe the primary function of shelters is to be multiservice centers and, therefore, that the primary role of shelter staff is to be a "caregiver." As an educator I am more comfortable when these two theories are grounded in a pedagogy rooted in social analysis and social change rather than in theories of social work rooted in the understanding of social workers as extensions of mental health workers. If shelter providers assume we are *primarily* caregivers, then a great deal of effort goes into "how" we give care and into the relationships within the shelter. If, on the other hand, we understand ourselves to be facilitators of change, then our energy is focused on an agenda rooted in the causes of homelessness and the solution to it—housing for individual families, housing for everyone! I believe theories of social exchange and family support are important theories to inform the kinds of relationships we need to have for "humane" social change that is rooted in a belief in interdependence, mutuality, and co-responsibility.

In my eighteen years of living and working with homeless families, I have found the pedagogy of Paulo Friere, the Brazilian educator, invaluable. Friere's pedagogy begins with engaging those oppressed by poverty and oppression in an analysis of their situation. In his book,[1] Friere explains that real social change happens when the oppressed understand *where* they fit in society, *why* they are where they are, and *when* they together learn the necessary skills to change the situation. While a tension exists between the oppressed and those with power, because the latter have resources of land, money, education, position, etc., that the poor do not, Friere challenges the "powerful" to take a hard look at society and to understand it from the point of view of the "have-nots" and to work with the oppressed to change the unjust or inadequate structures. In other words, Friere's pedagogy, unlike the theories of welfare reform, does not teach the poor that they need to change themselves so they can *adapt* to unjust, inadequate systems. It offers them the opportunity to create the kind of life that the "marginalized of society" want for themselves, their families, and their neighborhoods. It provides the skills needed to create social policies that are fair, equitable, and just.

I believe that those of us who operate family shelters in the social context of welfare reform have to be very clear about our beliefs and

assumptions about the causes of and solutions to homelessness. If we
are convinced that families are homeless because they are poor,
because they cannot afford housing, then our practice as shelter
providers will be grounded in respect for the families in our shelters
and belief in their capacity to be participants not only in the life of
the shelter but also in the life of the communities of which they are a
part—town, neighborhood, school, etc. In this book, Friedman calls
what I am proposing "the family support framework." The foundation
of the framework as I understand it, and as it is applied to the social
problem of homelessness, is the conviction in the words of Friedman
that "homelessness is the result of poverty, inadequate availability of
affordable housing, and low wages." I believe this conviction must be
the foundation of the processes and programs in family shelters. For
me this conviction shared among staff and homeless families is what
makes sense of the social exchange theory and the family support par-
adigm. And I propose that Friere's pedagogy of the oppressed is a useful tool to use for teaching shelter staff and homeless families the skills
of social analysis. More important than the best self-directed family
life plan is an understanding of social location by the homeless family,
because it shows where the family fits in society and *why*. It also shows
where the "helper" fits and, more often than not, the helper in the
family shelter system is located economically very close to the family
who is homeless. Can we consider that the unjust social systems that
are the root of homelessness in Massachusetts and the entire U.S.
exploit the "worker" as well as the "customer" (the homeless family)?
But that is another essay!

The shelter system has become a part of a much larger social service system. Social workers are the professional providers of the service. I often wonder what Jane Addams, the foundress of social work a
hundred years ago, would make of our family shelters. As I understand
her life and work, she believed the purpose of social work lived out in
the settlement houses was social change. She did help immigrants
adapt to the harsh realities of their new country, but she did so in
order that they could *participate* in it and withstand unjust systems and
change them.

I propose Jane Addams would want shelter providers to make
homeless families feel "at home" and to teach skills of social analysis,

group facilitation, problem solving, and conflict resolution as well as nutrition, parenting, and budgeting. I propose she would warn us about the inadequacy of a social service model that pits the "helper" against the "helped" and teaches people to *adapt* to the unjust systems that are the root cause of their homelessness. Finally, I think she would challenge us to understand the world in which we live, to know those who control it, and to be clear about where we fit in the scheme of social reality, so that homeless families, providers, advocates, and even policy makers will respect each other and work together to make a more civil and just society where, of course, everyone has a home!

Reflection: Family Life Advocate, Mary Lewis

As family life advocate and case manager, I am now a "frontline" worker in a family shelter serving up to seven families, three in a congregate setting and four in off-site units. I have been a social worker in the field since 1972, so I have had to wrestle with the question of how to give help in the most respectful manner possible while working in various settings. The central question for me is how I reconcile the values of the program funders with my own values regarding help giving. As long as I can do the tasks required while not compromising my own framework and value system, I can function authentically as a helper. In order to do this, I must first clarify my goals and develop a framework to guide my actions. Once this is achieved, I will be better able to do the required tasks in a manner that is comfortable for me.

In any relationship or community that we join we must make a certain amount of compromise. Communities of all sizes require adherence to their rules, norms, or expectations. This compromise is an essential part of the community's organization and operation. We find this throughout history (for example, the Mayflower Compact and the U.S. Constitution) and within all relationships (for example, marriage vows) and groups (for example, self-help groups such as Alcoholics Anonymous [AA]). What makes the helping relationship open to abuse is the depth of need or desperation that the one receiving help finds herself in. Lack of options or choice increases a person's need or sense of desperation. Therefore, when working with a home-

less family it is imperative that I as a help giver am aware of my power
in opening up doors that lead to increased growth and autonomy or
closing doors in ways that restrict growth, inhibit autonomy, and lead
to further disempowerment, disillusion, and shame.

Four ideas are the foundation for my way of giving help:

- The importance of separating poverty from the kind of problems we all share, human problems such as fear, anxiety, and
  worry;
- The "centrality of motherhood," the importance of the life-
  directing force of the "mothering relationship";
- The concept of resistance;
- The belief in the framework of mutuality as an important
  element in the helping relationship.

Poverty robs or blocks a person's ability to access the resources necessary for her family's needs. These resources include safe affordable
housing, adequate food, a safe family life, solid education, employment
that pays an adequate wage, good health care, and appropriate child
care. Without these supports a family is not able to fulfill societal
expectations of self-sufficiency and self-support. These are systemic
needs, not only personal issues.

Homelessness is an economic problem. All of us suffer from personal problems regardless of our age, race, spiritual belief, economic
status, or location. I often ask homeless mothers with whom I work
whether they would rather be dealing with their problems while living in their own home or in a shelter. Overwhelmingly, they respond
that they would prefer to be living in their own home. It is often difficult, but it is critical to separate homelessness from unique personal
problems. This separation is difficult because the healing from and
dealing with the personal problems may be an essential step toward
obtaining a job, an education, or housing. Therefore, people link personal and financial problems as if they are one and the same. If the
separation is not made, then as a worker I can begin to confuse the
economic problem of homelessness with personal difficulties and
become more judgmental in my thinking about families' situations. I
will then begin to view all homeless parents as less able to care for

themselves and their families. I will be less able to recognize the homeless parent's strengths and individual needs.

Homeless and housed families are the same in their wanting the best for their children. Homelessness itself creates problems and certainly can reawaken problems that a family may have already learned how to solve. When a homeless parent accesses shelter for herself and her children, she is doing so in the face of great shame and marginalization. The message is clear. According to one mother, "People definitely think we're not good enough mothers, just for the fact that we're homeless, we're not good mothers."[2] This blaming stance allows those in our society who have "made it" to distance themselves from those who have not. Most homeless parents have heard society's message that they have "messed up,"[3] are undeserving and dysfunctional. They have lost everything. The one thing they hold onto is the importance of themselves as mothers. It is a core identity and they fiercely defend it. It is important that as a help giver, I understand and honor this driving force. It is a force that drives people to ask for help and agree to compromises that promote the image of themselves as faulty mothers and dysfunctional people, in order for their children to receive the stability and shelter that they need. Some of the compromises might not be "bad" or "harmful." In fact, they may lead to services that the parent wants. It is the manner in which the services and the requirements of shelter are enforced that makes a difference for many families.

Due to this "centrality of mothering," the parent may also make choices that we do not understand. Some of the choices may have negative societal implications. However, as a help giver I must first understand the goal from the perspective of a mother before I can help her develop other options that may produce fewer negative effects. (I use "mother" here and refer to parents as "her" since over 95 percent of the heads of households that I work with are women.)

How does a mother cope? How does she hold back all the negative images that both she and society at large hold about her? She resists. I use the term "resistance" in the political not the psychological sense. The psychological sense means a blocking or hindrance of movement toward health. Resistance in this sense is a negative adaptation. Resistance in a political sense, on the other hand, means an acting out against a dominating power. In this sense resistance can be the act of

protecting something that is a core part of ourselves. It is a fending off
of the negative (real or perceived) judgments of others.[4] A homeless
mother resists, fights against both the real and perceived negative
images of herself.

If we view a parent's reaction through the framework of resistance,
we may be able to understand her actions and attitudes as protecting
something that she as a parent perceives as a threat to her children, rather
than viewing her behavior as difficult and oppositional. For example, a
mother's resistance to bedtime rules, even though she has shared with
her case manager her desire to have some time for herself and to get her
family into a routine, can be seen as her resistance to a perceived message that she needs someone to tell her how to mother and, therefore,
that she is not good enough. If I become just the "rule enforcer" then
she and I fall into a power relationship—one that she must resist. However, if I can first understand her resistance as meaningful and important
to her and connect with her unspoken but powerful need to be a good
enough mother, then we have a chance to create a relationship built on
respect and mutuality rather than on hierarchy and power.

Mutuality in a relationship means that both the mother and I are
affecting each other and being affected by each other. I am open to
the influence that she brings. I am no longer expert and mother to
the client; rather, I am a partner in her effort to find and establish the
goals that she has for her family. This mutuality helps to lessen the
familiar power dynamics that often separate people. "Rational mutuality can provide purpose and meaning in people's lives, while the lack
of mutuality can adversely effect self-esteem."[5]

In my role as social worker in a family shelter, I find it imperative
that my beliefs and values are clear. The building of a respectful relationship needs trust and understanding and takes time and persis-
tence. As a worker I need support and continuing education so that I
don't fall into the easy trap of separating myself from and sitting in
judgment on the families I am trying to help. A group of homeless
mothers who were asked what they think help givers need to do or
learn gave a profound answer. The women: they said that workers
must take time to ask rather than assume, listen rather than direct and
respect rather than judge. If I do this through the framework that I
have presented, then as a help giver I have a better chance of doing

the work required of me in a manner that is consistent with my belief system. The closer my actions are to my values, the more positively I am able to view myself, my job, and the mothers with whom I work. This framework may not be the one held by funders, but it is one through which I am able to provide the services and perform the tasks required by those funders. By clarifying and maintaining my own belief system, which includes respect for the dignity of people and an appreciation of the impact of poverty on people's lives, I am able to create a space that will foster growth and autonomy for both those with whom I work and also for myself.

2

Family Shelter Environments

Homelessness is a severe trauma. It stays with you the rest of your life.
In the two years I was homeless, the main thing that was reinforced
within me
was that I was not worthwhile,
that I did not belong, not only to the community,
but maybe even to humankind.

—Zenobia Embry-Nimmer

Linda[1] is putting Brian and David to bed in a room they share
with Susan and her two-month-old infant. Linda and her
preschool sons have lived in this shelter for almost four months.
Brian and David no longer sleep through the night. When
Susan's baby wakes up, the boys awaken and are ready to play.
Typically, it takes several hours and considerable patience for
Linda to quiet the boys enough to get back to sleep herself.
Linda and Susan are at odds with each other over making their
shared bedroom arrangement workable.

The physical environment of shelter programs can
have a significant impact on the quality of families'
lives in a shelter. In some parts of the United
States, families live in open dormitories with homeless individuals.[2] In
Massachusetts mixed dormitory settings for families are not an allowable option for publicly funded shelter programs. Rather, some shelter

settings provide a separate apartment; others provide a bedroom, bathroom, and kitchenette; most provide a separate bedroom for each family. A few others necessitate families having to share bedroom spaces with other families. This chapter will explore a range of controversies related to the physical environment of family shelters and its impact on the well-being of children and their parents.

The debates are innumerable. How comfortable should family shelters be? Wouldn't families be tempted to stay longer in shelters that are warm, homey, and comfortable? How much privacy should families ideally have when they live in a family shelter? More private space for each family results in fewer families being sheltered. More private space for each family can also reduce their access to minute-by-minute support from other families and staff. Some might say more privacy for families interferes with the ability of staff to oversee family interactions: mothers I have spoken with consider more privacy a definite benefit, while many staff view it as a definite disadvantage. What about families having an ability to lock their rooms or secure their belongings? What about room inspections? Should staff be able to inspect families' rooms unannounced or under any circumstance? How do families actually survive sharing a kitchen, a bathroom, a dining room, and living room with other families for the many months they are living in a shelter? These are families who are, at first, unrelated strangers. How can these spaces be kept clean? The health and safety of children, in particular, necessitates that eating and bathroom spaces be kept clean. How do families survive living in one bedroom for so many months? Finally, what about the presence of adult male and adolescent male family members? Some congregate family shelters exclude these male family members from their programs, others do not. Why? And what is the impact on women and children of each of these common program practices?

The Big Picture: Background on Family Shelter Environments

When natural disasters, such as hurricanes or tornadoes, strike a community, federal, state, and local organizations mobilize into action to provide swift relief for those affected. Schools and armories become temporary overnight shelters for large numbers of community residents, men, women, and children alike. Concerned citizens ensure through their donations that disaster victims have food, water, clothes, and other basic necessities of life. Presumably, emergency responses to such natural disasters are needed for very short periods of time. Emergency shelters for homeless men, women, and children in the United States were originally set up with this short-term, natural disaster framework in mind. That is, homelessness, especially for families with children, was viewed as a social problem with a short lifespan: shelters would be a necessary but temporary solution. Tragically, "emergency" shelters have become acceptable "homes" for parents and their children, who are now living in these settings for longer periods of time, six to ten months on average in the United States.[3] For very young children this amount of time constitutes a significant portion of their infancy, toddler, and preschool years, a period of life that is pivotal for their future growth and development. The well-being of children and parents is deeply affected by the quality of the environments in which they live.

The Impact of Family Shelter Settings on Children and Mothers

Key studies of shelter settings and their impact on children in the past two decades have contributed to public attention and outrage regarding public policy approaches to solving family homelessness. Kozol's landmark exposé of the inhumane living conditions to which homeless families were subjected is the most well known.[4] Over a two-year period, he befriended a small number of families living in Hotel Martinique, a hotel shelter for homeless families in New York City. He vividly chronicled the tragedies ordinary children and mothers endured at the hands of impassive, greedy hotel owners and an overwhelmed welfare system.

A few years later Grant documented the negative effects on all aspects of children's well-being—their eating, sleeping, playing, learning, sense of security, and so forth—from living in these same hotels.[5] Cooperative and mutual baby-sitting relief among mothers was a lifeline for the families living in the shelters he studied. In these settings, each family had one private room; families shared bathroom spaces; children had no floor space for crawling or playing; and rooms were equipped with refrigerators but included no cooking facilities. A preschool child care program was available on site on a first-come, first-served basis for resident families.

Berck's and Walsh's qualitative examination of shelter living through the eyes of children documents the shame and stress children experience when their families are homeless.[6] Berck conducted interviews with thirty children and adolescents living in hotel, barrack, and family-style shelters in New York City. The views of these young persons underscore the importance of the structural features of a shelter setting. The barrack shelters had no physical partitions between beds. Every aspect of daily living took place in public. Although being homeless and living in any type of shelter is stressful, the children and adolescents living in barrack settings reported violations of their sense of security from the lack of protection and privacy. These young people described emotional states of fear, hypervigilance, shame, and lack of trust in the people around them. The young people whose families had a private bedroom were much more positive about their shelter experience. Children described feeling a sense of safety and solidarity with others in these settings, even though the amount of private space for families, the programmatic approaches for regulating daily routines, and the provision of service supports differed among sites.

Walsh interviewed children living in a hotel/motel or a congregate family shelter in Massachusetts.[7] Most of these children were tremendously ambivalent about shelter living. They portrayed family shelters as stressful settings in which children and their parents have to conform to innumerable rules that impose a regimen on most aspects of daily life—that is, meal and snack routines, shower use, chores, TV, radio and phone use, and so forth. One teenager deplored the impact of shelter life on her mother's autonomy. She referred to home as a place in which "my mother doesn't have to do what other people tell her to."[8] However, they also expressed gratitude for having a place to live, the freedom from fights between their parents, and the friendship opportunities shelter living offered them and their parents.

Molnar conducted a review of shelter programs that specifically provide services for homeless children in New York City.[9] She documented the negative effects of shelter living on mothers' sense of themselves as parents and on their emotional well-being: "Mothers are constantly monitored. They must check in and out. They must verify their baby-sitting arrangements. Caseworkers are always prying into their lives. . . . Teachers know all about their children. They have little privacy. . . . They become depressed, withdrawn, and angry" (p. 91). She recommended that shelter programs support the family as a unit (parents and children together) in meeting the goals they have for themselves. She identified peer support for parents as an essential component of any effective program for homeless families but indicated that this feature was universally lacking in the programs she reviewed.

Other researchers note anecdotally that mothers are typically subject to criticism from other mothers in shelter settings.[10] Boxhill and Beatty, in a qualitative observational study of forty families living in a night shelter in Atlanta, chronicled the negative effects of "public mothering" on parents' sense of themselves and on their relationships with their children.[11] Boxhill described the lengths to which some mothers went to create a private family space when they were caring for their children in such a public setting—for example, transforming a bed sheet into a tent big enough for a mother to talk quietly and privately with her infant and toddler.[12]

Hemminger and Quinones carried out a qualitative study with 55 percent of the families who had resided in the Wellspring family shelter in Gloucester, Massachusetts, an effort by the program itself to evaluate its work with families and to make programmatic changes based upon what they learned from the parents and children they had served.[13] This program describes its philosophy as being grounded in the values of "mutual respect, cooperation, and empowerment."[14] Ninety-six percent of those women who were interviewed continued to live in their own homes with their children after leaving Wellspring. The parents' views on the impact of living at the shelter reflect considerable ambivalence. On the one hand, many expressed deep appreciation for the nurturing and attention they and their children received from staff. "My daughter was only a baby, but I think that she was touched by a certain love that has made her beautiful inside. She received a lot of attention, more than she would have received otherwise."[15] On the other hand, they resented the amount of unsolicited advice they received from staff about caring for their children: "You get a lot of inputs and comments from other people, that you don't

want to hear. He's my son. Nobody wants to hear, 'Put a jacket on
your kid.' Nobody wants to be told."[16] Ironically, parents recommended that the shelter childproof the environment. The hardest
aspects of living at Wellspring for these parents were having to deal
with so many rules and giving up their autonomy (the subject of
chapter 4 of this book) and sharing living spaces with so many others.
The benefits they identified included learning many skills related to
parenting.

Congregate Family Shelter Settings in Massachusetts

Shelter capacity.   Congregate family shelter programs in Massachusetts tend to be small in capacity, smaller than those reported in studies of other shelters across the country.[17] When I carried out this
study, the number of families residing in the state's congregate shelters
each night ranged from four to twenty-two. The average number of
families sheltered in programs was eight. Over two-thirds of the programs sheltered nine or fewer families each night, while the other
third sheltered between ten and twenty-two families.[18] Programs varied to a greater degree with respect to the number of children residing in shelters at any one point in time. On average, fifteen children
resided in Massachusetts' congregate shelter settings on the date I surveyed directors. The range varied from a low of five to a high of
thirty-eight children. The average number of persons—mothers,
fathers, children, and teens—residing in shelter programs was twenty-
one family members. The lowest census for a program was eight; the
highest was forty-nine persons. Given the high number and the
young ages of children residing in these shelters each night, directors
bear a serious responsibility to create policies and promote practices
that will ensure that all the children and parents will be as safe and
healthy as is possible while they are living communally.

Private, common, and child play spaces for families.   Most often, each
family had a private bedroom space. Many programs were attempting
to provide families with additional private areas. In a small number of
programs, no private space was available. All programs reported that
they had private bedrooms for at least some of the families living in

their shelters. Many also provided each family with a private bathroom, kitchen, dining space, or lounge/living room space. Typically however, families shared the bathroom, the kitchen, the dining space, the lounge or living room, and the child play space with other families. Almost universally, a child play space was part of these programs' physical environment.

Type of bedroom arrangements. I asked directors to describe the bedroom spaces in their shelter. In only a few programs, some or all families shared their bedroom spaces with other families. In three of these programs, a curtain or partition provided a physical separation between families. Over half of the programs provided larger families with more than one bedroom space. Only a few programs reserved certain bedroom spaces for specific types of families. The vast majority of programs provided families with a bedroom door that could be locked. A few programs severely limited family control over others' access into their bedroom space. The most extreme example of such practices was voiced by one director: "No locks, the families are not allowed to do that . . . fire reasons and because we don't think it's appropriate. Locks wouldn't give us (the staff) access to the bedrooms. We get donations from people visiting. That's why they make their beds." In this program, the staff regularly escorted visitors, potential donors, through the families' bedroom spaces. Families had no direct channels for protecting their belongings or their dignity. This practice raises serious questions about the program's basic respect for families, given that no provision was made for families to have a private space for storing or arranging their belongings, an issue of critical importance according to the homeless women Liebow befriended.[19]

In summary, congregate shelters for families in Massachusetts tend to be smaller in capacity than that reported for other programs in the country.[20] Many programs have found ways to set up their environment to enable families to have more than a bedroom in private. However, more commonly, families living in these shelters share most of their living spaces with other families, thus necessitating that they negotiate the smallest aspects of daily living with "strangers." Under some circumstances, individual families even have to share their bedroom spaces with another family. In addition, parents and children in many shelters are with each other "round the clock," unless children are involved in child care or school programs.

Program approaches for sharing living spaces.   Certain program policies specifically address the ways in which families share common living spaces and negotiate their daily living routines with each other in these shelters. These program policies were devised to bring order and predictability to routine transactions between and among families and staff. Any family members who have chosen to share their living space with others for a period of time understand the significance these details of daily life can have in affecting their sense of well-being. That families living in congregate settings are sharing spaces with "strangers" and staff members, some of whom have different ethnic traditions, and that families are living on the program's turf, serves to magnify the complexities of life for family members.

Directors and staff members described their programs' policies in many areas of daily living and told me how they thought these ways of organizing daily routines were working. Mothers also had definite opinions regarding how the setup worked for them and their children, what they liked and did not like. I observed and participated firsthand in some of the communal activities taking place in five shelters. The following sections weave together what I was told and what I witnessed.

Mealtimes.   Nearly half of programs paid for the food for all three meals. Many directors said that families could buy food if they wished, but that they encouraged families to save their food stamps while they were living in the shelter. One program strongly urged families to turn over 50 percent of their food stamps to the social worker for safekeeping. These vouchers were returned to families when they exited the program. Families in over one-third of the programs purchased their own food for all three meals; the program provided food assistance if needed. The remaining programs routinely shared food-purchasing responsibilities with families. Typically, families bought their own breakfast, lunch, and snack foods, while the program bought food for the evening meal. Two programs required families to make a contribution toward the cost of food.

Preparation of a community meal occupied the time and energy of families in nearly half of the programs. For all but one of these programs, parents rotated cooking responsibilities for the evening meal only; in the other program, they also rotated responsibility for preparing breakfast. A few programs organized food preparation by including this task in staff job responsibilities and/or by enlisting volunteers or a food service company for this task.

Only one program used a teamwork approach in which staff, parents, and volunteers prepared the communal evening meal together. The director enthusiastically described the benefits of rotating cooking responsibilities among mothers: "They alternate in cooking the evening meal. . . . It is a happy time. They work in teams to cook the evening meal. They alternate the teams. The family gets to share the duties with all the residents. They get to know each other and learn from each other." This director placed a high premium on finding ways of building a sense of connection among mothers and children in this shelter. This orientation came through at a later point in our interview when he told me a story about moving the TV from the communal living room to the dining room. He described an intervention that was an imposition of the director and staff members' values and went beyond simply ensuring safety and order in the shelter. He and his staff had made a conscious decision to have the TV located in a room in which sitting for long periods was uncomfortable, as a means of cutting down the amount of time mothers and children watched TV at night. This environmental change worked, according to his and his staff's values. After making the change, he told me, mothers and their children talked, laughed, and shared stories with each other at night in the living room, without a TV in their midst.

In contrast, another director emphasized the learning mothers gained from cooking for others: "We're trying to teach *all the mothers* (my emphasis) independent living skills, so the dinner preparation becomes a chore for the mother to learn how to plan a menu, and shop, and cook . . . to be able to do this in her own apartment." I deduced from her comments that she assumed every mother who came into her shelter needed to learn these skills, that she did not recognize differences in mothers' competencies and in their desires to take on such a responsibility. This program's policies were directed toward mothers with a low level of homemaking competence. I wondered how mothers in this shelter, in particular those who had

thought of themselves as good cooks, food shoppers, or meal plan-
ners, might feel about being viewed as women who needed help with
such basic daily tasks as learning how to buy and prepare food.

These two examples illustrate that programs with similar policies—
that is, mothers rotate cooking for shelter residents—can operate with
very different objectives and views regarding families' strengths or
deficiencies.

Nearly half of the programs had a schedule for all three meals in the
shelter. Only two programs had no set mealtimes: "It's according to
their individual family schedule. Each family prepares their own
meals. They buy their own food, have their own storage area, and
refrigerator and table," one of the directors said. "Families make their
own meals, any time they want. They have to coordinate amongst
themselves." Only about a quarter of directors described their policies
regulating families' access to the kitchen or pantry areas in the shelter.
Three directors indicated that these spaces were open twenty-four
hours a day. The remaining directors described practices restricting
access to some of the kitchen and pantry areas: "There are times the
kitchen can be used, 6:30 to 8:30 A.M., 11:30 A.M. to 1:30 P.M., and 4:30
to 7:00 P.M.," and, "they have supper at 5:30 P.M., there's no cooking
after 7:30 P.M., but you can use the microwave after that." Many mothers I interviewed in shelters with these restrictions were vociferous
about the terrible position these rules put them in with their children.
They were torn at times between meeting their children's needs—for
example to have a milk bottle warmed up or to have a snack—or following the shelter rules. Staff and mothers alike indicated to me that
resolving these dilemmas caused mothers considerable anguish.

For the most part, those programs in which families ate meals as a
community rather than in separate family units, had set mealtimes. In
nearly two-thirds of programs, families ate the evening meal communally. The number of families appeared to affect the kinds of policies
programs devise: "We have a schedule. Duties rotate. While parents
help to prepare meals, there is baby-sitting during cooking, food
preparation, and cleanup. There's a first and second lunch and dinner,
because we have sixteen families." A few programs required families to
be present for a 6:00 P.M. dinner, Monday through Thursday. I wondered how families managed to comply with this directive, given fam-

ily members' typical outside commitments, such as school, work, social service or medical appointments, and children's after-school activities.

Cultural differences among families also presented some challenges to mothers, staff, and directors. Indeed, one director told me that she had eliminated the communal meal due to these complications: "We had a communal meal at one time, with cultural differences and people's tastes, it wasn't working at all." Another director described her approach for dealing with these differences: "Celebrations (fiestas) including ethnic dishes are a monthly event." Another director expressed her frustration that family norms are so negatively affected by shelter life: "Cape Verdean families . . . in their own homes, they put a pot on the stove and let it cook all day. They eat when the spirit moves them, but how do we do that here in the shelter?"

Keeping the common spaces clean.   The final policy area specific to communal living has to do with cleaning and maintenance of the family bedrooms or units, as well as the common areas in the shelter. Every director I spoke with described the program policies for household chores. In nearly three-quarters of the shelters, parents were responsible for cleaning the common areas and their own bedroom or private living space. In a small number of programs, staff and parents shared responsibility for cleaning the common areas. In even fewer programs, staff cleaned the common areas or the program hired a maintenance service for this purpose. Most commonly, parents were assigned a daily chore by staff. Parents took turns assigning chores in a small number of programs. Most used a rotation system in which each family took a turn at each chore on a rotating basis.

Directors of ten programs told me that shelter staff were responsible for checking that parents had completed their chores satisfactorily, dynamics characteristic of relationships between parents and children. The following comments reflect the ways these practices work: "The (residents) have chores checked twice daily; those are assigned weekly. The chore is checked between 9:30 to 11:00 A.M., and 7:00 P.M. to 12 midnight. The parents come to the staff and say, 'My chore is done. Could you check it?' "

In contrast, other programs attempted to minimize the parent-child dynamic in staff members' relationships with parents. For example, families in another program assumed the responsibility of checking chores: "A chore monitor (a guest) assigns chores each week on a rotating basis. It's decided at the house meeting. Staff used to check chores. Now guests do that. Guests do all the monitoring. Staff would say if there was a problem." A few programs address this issue by using a teamwork approach. One director put it this way: "People are responsible for their own rooms. Each person, including resident staff, take a common space, one hour per week, which we do together. These jobs get rotated. Both staff and residents take care of dishes together, usually one night per week." Another program that used a teamwork model for meal preparation also used this kind of approach for cleaning the shelter space: "The residents share the common areas. They work in teams."

Directors of ten programs told me that shelter staff inspected the families' rooms or units daily, twice weekly, or weekly. In contrast, another director described her "hands-off" policy: "Everyone has the same chore for a month. There are fewer chores because each family has its own living unit. We don't require that they keep their units clean. We got rid of inspections. We don't enter their unit without permission, unless there's suspicion of some illegal activity or a visitor staying over or something like that."

The most stigmatizing and humiliating practices I heard about were described by two directors who added chores as a punishment for parents violating a shelter rule. "First time is a warning and a 'job jar,' all those things you don't do every day, like taking cigarette butts out of the rock garden. You have twenty-four hours to do it," one director told me. A job jar is a container holding multiple slips of paper on which are written unpleasant cleaning jobs. The parent picks from the jar to learn which job he or she must carry out.

Accommodating male adult and adolescent family members.   Over a quarter of programs in this study excluded male adult and adolescent family members. As a result, some families had to separate in order to receive shelter. That is, adult and adolescent males had to obtain shelter with friends or relatives, seek beds in the state's shelters for singles, or find a place to sleep on the street. Some families with adult and adolescent males may have received shelter as family units in the state's scattered site shelters. The vast majority of congregate family shelters did allow male family members to live in their shelters, including four of the five shelters I studied more deeply. However, congregate family shelters in Massachusetts are gendered settings. More mothers than fathers and more female staff than male staff live and work in these settings. Directors of programs who had found a way to include male family members matter-of-factly described the accommodations they make: "There are males and females in the building. They must be dressed outside their rooms." And: "Men and women are assigned chores equally. For household chores, it's easier for everyone to be treated equal. All husbands should learn to cook, and women to pick up the yard." Others described some of the difficulties they encountered by allowing males into their congregate settings: "When we have only one male parent in the house, it's hard. We are one of the few shelters who accept fathers. The whole relationship of congregate living changes. He usually feels he can't go to anyone for support, because he's a guy, he should be in control all the time. Men have a very difficult time reaching out to other residents for support. They are more likely to go to staff. It's like a rooster in a henhouse. No one understands the male end of parenting, the dual role type of stuff. All our staff are female right now." And: "There was an alienation of a male head of household (with three children). No matter what this man did he could do no right with the five women in the shelter. The entire group judged him right from the start. It was very difficult for him to stay here because of the pressure placed on him by the peer group. I talked with each person individually. There was an overall lack of respect for him as a single male parent. Maybe it wasn't because he was male, but it affected his parenting and his job from being in this environment." And: "A lot of couples break up in the shelter, and they get back together after they leave." And: "Sometimes there's a problem with a mom and dad with the other women all vying for his attention, as he was the only male at the time. We don't get a lot of two-parent families. When we do, staff will groan. It always becomes an issue. With a single dad, it's not as tense. It's the competition among the wife or girlfriend with the other three women in the shelter for the attention of the one male."

The Shelter Space Sets the Stage for "We" or "Other" Relationships

I had an opportunity through my visits in five shelters to witness the diverse ways in which shelter programs were set up; how they put their policies into operation; and how their programmatic approaches affected the children, parents, and staff who lived or worked in these settings. During my six months of immersion in these five programs, I was amazed by the tremendous diversity among them with respect to their physical configurations, the value systems of staff and management, their programmatic approaches for organizing daily routines in the shelter, and the resulting atmosphere that pervaded each program. Some emphasized the differences and boundaries between staff, parents, and helpers as "other," thus adding to parents' sense of humiliation and isolation. Some stressed the similarities and connections between staff, parents, and helpers as "we," thus emphasizing their common bonds as humans and attempting to ameliorate parents' sense of self-blame for their homeless circumstances.

The Refuge (the "Ranch")

This shelter program, housing sixteen families each night and referred to as the "Ranch" by one of the mothers I interviewed, was on a campuslike setting that housed several other programs, including a day care center operated by the shelter program's umbrella agency. The director's office was in a building separate from the family shelter. The building that housed the administrative offices had a large conference room, the group meeting place for staff. I carried out several interviews with staff and mothers in this room. The first time I used the room, the chalkboard was full of notes that seemed to be listing the feelings mothers and fathers might have (e.g., fear) and ideas about respectful ways of treating families. The family shelter was neither homey nor institutional-looking, simply "tired"-looking. The lower level had a large, carpeted community room with walls full of colorful cartoon characters, a small indoor kid's gym, a lounge and TV area, and a few staff offices. A pay phone, used by families to make personal phone calls, was on the wall just outside the door to the community room. On the second floor were families' bedrooms, a bathroom, a communal kitchen, and a communal eating area. The third floor had another large bathroom, another staff office, and several more large bedrooms, shared by two or more families, those with the fewest children. Throughout the shelter, posted signs were written in both English and Spanish, the primary language for a majority of families in this program.

One afternoon I went to the shelter building to have dinner with the families and staff. I arrived at the shelter around 5:00 P.M., not sure where to go. Following the directions a staff member gave me, I knocked on the locked outside door. Rosa, a Latina staff member opened the door, welcomed me, and suggested that I could wait for dinner with the families in the community room. I eyed an empty spot on the couch next to Sue and her preschool son, Jim; another mother was sleeping on an adjacent couch. The sleeping mother's eight-year-old daughter, Annie, and two-year-old son, Hugo, were also present. At Rosa's urging, Sue moved her feet so that I could sit down. Within seconds, Hugo jumped up on my lap and plastered his body on my chest as he sucked on his bottle of milk and watched TV with the rest of us. *Power Rangers* was on. Hugo had cornrow braids in the top of his hair, an adorable kid. He also had chicken pox.

Hugo's older sister, Annie, was watching him and mediating for him when Jim wanted to use Hugo's toy. At one point, Hugo got down off my lap and fought with Jim over his toy. Jim got very upset and was working himself into a temper tantrum. His mother tried to subdue him with words, to no avail. She threatened his having to go to their bedroom. That didn't work either. She wrapped her legs around his legs and her arms around his arms, so that he was physically restrained. Annie tried to mediate. At one point she asked Hugo which toy he wanted. Then she told Jim he could have the other toy. I was very impressed with her skills with her younger brother. However, this didn't work either. She also tried to take the toys up to their room. When she did, her mother roused enough to tell her, "No." Annie then went over to the adjoining sitting area, looking very angry. After a few minutes she came back and sat down on one of the easy chairs to watch TV. Feeling at a loss for words, I asked Annie what grade she was in. She said, "Second, but I should be in third."

Jim and Hugo went over to the playgym, and quickly got into a fight. Sue removed Jim from the area. He responded by having a full-blown temper tantrum. Annie tried to help by going upstairs to get some milk for Hugo, an action that violated the shelter's rules. A few minutes later she returned and announced that she had been caught and couldn't do it. Two more preschool children entered the community room and headed for the playgym. One of them asked me to come to play with him. I had met him earlier in the day when I interviewed his mother. Within a few minutes I was playing hard with four active preschoolers. Each wanted a lot of attention. At one point I looked over to the lounge area and realized that all of their mothers, with the exception of Annie and Hugo's sleeping mother, had left the room. The kids really liked my oohing and aahing over their acrobatics. Two of the children tried to sit on my lap at the same time. I felt a bit overwhelmed.

Dinner was not ready until 6:30 P.M., much later than usual. Local college students were due to arrive by 7:00 P.M. to play with the kids. The children and I played a game called "owl's eyes," which involved getting nose-to-nose with each child. At one point Hugo was trying to drop what I thought was a piece of candy from his mouth into my mouth. I asked to see what he had in his mouth. It was a toy, not a piece of candy, as I had thought. I mentioned this to Annie, his sister. Earlier, I had noticed that Julie, one of the preschool kids, had a small felt marker cap in her mouth, an object small enough to swallow. I took it out of her mouth and threw it away in spite of her protest. I realized how quickly I had assumed a child supervision role, in the absence of their mothers.

Rosa announced that dinner was ready, so we went upstairs. Hugo's mother got up from the couch. She said she had a very bad headache, that she had had a head injury, and bad sinus problems, and hadn't slept the night before as Hugo's chicken pox had kept him and the rest of the family awake most of the night. In the kitchen Sue settled Jim in the only high chair. She gave him his food, fixed herself a sandwich, and then settled herself at a table across the room from him. The evening meal, roasted chicken and french fries, was set out in large platters on the stove counter by the cooks, Lanetta and Rosa. Dinner was served buffet style. Rosa and the mothers pitched in helping each other with their children through the whole dinner.

Lanetta's oldest child asked me to sit next to him. I offered my help to Lanetta who was struggling to fix dinner plates for her preschoolers while holding her infant. She did not respond directly but did allow me to hold the foil under the chicken while she pulled off two pieces. I was back at the table before she was. Her son told me he was hungry. I told him that his mom was about to bring his food over, which she did a minute later. Once we were all seated, I realized that none of us had juice. I offered to get juice for everyone at our table. Lanetta was drinking a Pepsi. Other mothers criticized her for this when she left the room a little later. This shelter had a rule that if you bring in food or drink from the outside, you're supposed to bring enough to share with others.

Within a few minutes the college students arrived. All the kids ran off to play downstairs, except for Lanetta's two preschoolers. She was out of the room. When I, being ever ready to jump in and help, asked them if they were done, Rosa told me that only the mother can tell their children to leave the table. She called Lanetta, who came in and let them join the other children downstairs. As you can see, I would have had a hard time, if I worked in this shelter, holding back from taking over for parents. On the one hand, they might welcome the help, but on the other hand, I would inadvertently be setting up a situation ripe for resentment and misunderstanding.

During the course of the next hour, the mothers and Rosa engaged in a low-key, easy-going banter. All of the mothers were Latina, as was Rosa. They sometimes spoke to each other in Spanish. In Rosa's presence, Hugo's mother expressed admiration for Rosa who worked the 3:00 to 11:00 P.M. shift at the shelter and was also enrolled in college as a full-time student, taking six courses at the time. Hugo's mother then talked about how she had prevented herself from getting ahead in life by becoming a mother at age fourteen. When Sue and Lanetta left the room, the other two mothers began to complain about them. One was critical of Lanetta's way with her children and her unwillingness to share her Pepsi. The other, a pregnant woman, complained about Sue taking up so much space in the bedroom they shared. This type of gossip is not unlike what happens around kitchen tables in suburban homes or around water coolers in office settings. However, in these shelter settings, in which families live in close quarters and have no choice regarding who they share living spaces with, the ostracization that may result from such gossip can have serious consequences for those who become its target.

Hugo's mother said that she wanted syrup for her waffles. Rosa went to the store room to get it for her. When Hugo's mother was finished using the syrup, she ran her finger along the top, licked her finger, and closed the bottle. Also, two of the mothers talked about the cockroaches in the shelter. We saw some in the kitchen. I killed one at their request, being the only person to have shoes on, as they were all wearing house slippers. Annie, Hugo's sister, came into the kitchen to get juice. She picked out a cup from the cupboard, looked at it, and said that it wasn't clean. Rosa suggested that she wash it out. I was concerned about how easily health problems could spread in a shelter, as a result of all that I had seen throughout the afternoon and evening. I left a little later, feeling a deep sense of appreciation for the willingness of the staff and mothers to let me into their world for this short time. I had witnessed the mutual respect that flowed between Rosa and each of these mothers. I was impressed with Rosa's unflappability, her low-key attention, humor, and support of both the mothers and the children, and her clarity and sensitivity in gently stopping me from usurping the parents' roles with their children.

The Gathering Place

The urban neighborhood in which this shelter was located was full of large houses in need of repair. Some were boarded up. The shelter itself was a large, somewhat run-down mansion. The large glass- and wrought-iron door was locked when I arrived. No parking was allowed on the street without a visitor pass. The director told me, "The city didn't want us here, so they gave us only a few visitor permits for parking. And they tell the cops to come by here frequently, just to keep letting us know that we aren't wanted." This was a stigmatized program, an "undesirable" in the neighborhood. Apparently, community members thought that the program threatened rather than contributed to the well-being of the surrounding community.

On my first visit, I was greeted at the door by Julia, the child advocate, a young Caucasian woman. She welcomed me warmly. All the families and other staff were in a housing search meeting in the shelter's first-floor lounge/dining room. Julia showed me into a front parlor, a newly renovated, beautifully furnished room. Several large piles and boxes full of donated clothes and small appliances littered the floor, the leftovers from Christmas. Julia was in the process of sorting the donations and writing thank-yous to donors. She had just started working at the shelter a month earlier. In her first month she had fixed up gift packages for each family's Christmas. Because many of the gifts were already wrapped, some parents got gifts for their children that did not fit their ages. Next year, Julia indicated, she would have mothers do the selecting of gifts. I asked how it was for the families to be the receivers of so many donations at Christmas. Julia said, "Some mothers are ungrateful, some are grateful." She intimated that they should be grateful even if they couldn't use the gifts.[21]

Within a few minutes, the director came into the room. He had been director of the program for two years. His office was a large room with high ceilings, next to a large staff room that housed four desks. On the door of the staff office was a sign, Keep Children Out Of The Office. As I looked around, I wondered how staff conversations with families or phone conversations about families could be handled with privacy. Later, after speaking with mothers who talked about how hard it was to supervise their children at all times in the shelter, I also wondered how a mother could meet with a staff person in the office and supervise her children at the same time.

The director took me on a tour of the shelter. In general, the place seemed somewhat run-down with a few exceptions, the child playroom and front parlor. The child playroom was located in a cold and drafty basement. The room itself, bright and warm, had been renovated with funding from a corporate donor. The door to the room was locked, and the toys in cabinets were locked. The child advocate said that she locked the cabinets because if she did not, the toys would be left all around. She arranged for tutors to come into the shelter during the week. They used this room. She also used this room to take care of children when the mothers were in mandatory meetings. She seemed very proud of how she had set up the room. I wondered to myself how the room would be taken care of if she had involved the parents and children in setting it up. The first floor lounge/dining room area had three couches set around a large TV. Two big tables were placed next to the walls adjoining a large kitchen. Some mothers and a father were visiting with each other in the kitchen when we passed through. All but one of them were smoking. One of the mothers was holding her sick infant who had chicken pox.

On the second floor were five bedrooms, one in the process of being renovated. All the doors to the bedrooms were closed. The director told me that he did not want to intrude upon families' private space by showing me their bedrooms, an action that I supported completely. He talked about how some families damaged their room space. For this reason, staff carried out daily room inspections. There were more bedrooms on the third floor, along with a little alcove under the stairwell to the attic that had a rocker and table. Some parents sat in this space when they waited for their children to fall asleep at night.

I came back to this shelter many times over the next two weeks. One evening I joined the families for supper. While I was there, Terry, one of the fathers living in the shelter with his family, was talking with Beth, the staff person on duty for the evening, about an excess of donated bread that had been left at the shelter. He suggested to her that they donate it to a home for seniors down the block. With her approval, he delivered the bread. He was back in ten minutes with a story to tell Beth. A small group of elder women were sitting in the living room of the home for seniors. "One said to me, 'What are you doing here, you son of a bitch,' " he said. He told the woman it was bread. She asked him if there was any garlic bread, to which he responded in the affirmative. She said, "You're okay then." Terry and Beth got a good laugh out of the story. Terry worked at the shelter part-time doing community service, while living at the shelter with his wife and children. Later, I talked with Terry while he was holding one of his infant twin sons. The baby's twin brother was upstairs in bed with the flu. In fact, Terry wasn't feeling too well. He had a rash all over his arms and face. "That's one problem with this place. One person gets sick and it goes through the whole house," he said.

Shortly thereafter, I went into the kitchen where a number of parents were gathered, both men and women. Adult and adolescent male family members were allowed to live in this shelter. Terry's wife introduced me to a man who was hanging out in the kitchen. I assumed he was a father from another family. I found out later that he was a visitor who had been banned from the shelter by Julia. The other parents and a school-age young girl expressed irritation with Julia about this. The kitchen area was a very bright and comfortable gathering place. Staff members were uniformly upset that parents gathered in the kitchen so often. In an effort to break up the comradery among families in this shelter, parents were prohibited from visiting with each other in their private rooms. In addition, an influential staff member was trying to find a way for each family to have its own dinner table. Not surprisingly, many families resisted these pushes by staff to keep to themselves.

The evening I visited, Yolanda, a young African American mother, was in charge of cooking the meal for eleven families. Beth, a Caucasian staff member, was her helper. In this shelter families were required to be present for the evening meal. Beth explained to me that usually a second parent helped by taking care of the cook's children while he or she was cooking. For some reason a staff member was stepping into this role tonight. Yolanda was preparing baked chicken, stuffing, and vegetables for dinner. Beth had made the sauce they would pour over the chicken. I asked Yolanda if she had cooked for so many people before. She said she had, and was more composed about this challenge than I would have been if I were in her place. She and Beth appeared to have a very relaxed and relationship. At one point Beth was feeding Yolanda's adorable three-month-old daughter, who was reclining in an infant seat. I stood alongside Beth, admiring the baby. Beth said that she had never fed a baby this way, that she longed to hold the baby while she fed her a bottle. Yolanda had asked her to feed the baby that way. Beth was honoring but not liking the mother's wishes. Yolanda was very affectionate and loving with her baby throughout the evening.

The interactions among most families in this shelter appeared to be pretty friendly. Some parents were talking and joking with children from other families, and parents were exchanging stories with each other. One Asian family, sitting off to themselves in the dining room, were not part of this exchange. All of the family members visiting in the kitchen, with the exception of Yolanda, were Caucasian. Beth quietly announced that the dinner was ready. She invited me to help myself by going through the buffet line. She apologized for the craziness. I was puzzled by her comment and asked what she meant. "Well, there is so much activity," she responded as she passed the table around which the parents had been gathered. "This makes me crazy. This table is dirty." Yolanda sat in the dining area on a couch with her baby. I sat near her. Beth pointed around the room and said, "We try to get each family to sit with their own family, but it doesn't work." The Asian family was sitting alone. Two children from another family were sitting without food. Beth told them to go upstairs and get their mother. When the mother and the two children came downstairs, they appeared to be outcasts. The mother gave Beth an Alchoholics Anonymous schedule book and said, "I'm not the only one around here who can use this." The comradery among some families appeared to exclude others.

Yolanda told me that her infant was a miracle baby, that she had used cocaine until her sixth month of pregnancy. A friend had been with her during the labor and delivery. She was very scared during labor but thrilled that the baby came out okay and was now a month ahead of schedule in her development. Her baby was cooing and smiling and had a very easy going temperament. Yolanda had two other children, a set of three-year-old twins who were living with her mother. She did not want them exposed to the swearing or other negative behaviors of the children living in the shelter. Beth interrupted our conversation and told Yolanda that she needed to help clean up.

After dinner, eight-year-old Eddie asked Beth if she would play a game with him. She said it would have to be after she had checked parents' completion of chores. He asked how long that would take. She responded by saying that it depended upon whether or not the parents had done their chores right. "If they don't, then I have to show them how to do it." For the moment, Beth and Eddie were joined as allies, pondering the deficiencies of parents in the shelter. I wondered about the effect of this alliance on Eddie: What would he be thinking about his and other parents' competency and authority?

Beth told me later, when we were by ourselves, what she had learned in her few months of work at the shelter. In school she had studied group dynamics. She had seen all of it in action among the families, such as scapegoating and the roles different parents took.

"Work here is hard, because you are always on. There is no place to go for privacy. Someone is always saying, 'I need,' " she said. "We are trying to find better ways to deal with the lack of privacy in the office." These were stresses mothers had described to me as well. We chatted a little while longer before I left. I thanked the parents who were in the living room for being so open in welcoming and allowing me, a stranger, into their midst. Terry said, "Thanks."

Room at the Inn

On a spring day, I arrived for a two-day visit at this shelter. The building stood out as I drove up. A huge sign celebrating a million-dollar building fund-raising campaign rested on the front lawn. Upon seeing this building, I realized that I was carrying in my mind a stereotype of a family shelter, institutional and unpleasant looking, and that this program's exterior did not fit my preconceptions. It was a lovely, well-maintained, antique inn. A very welcoming staff member answered my knock on the door, and showed me to the parlor. The whole place was beautifully decorated. No prohibitions or Staff Only signs were on the walls, only some messages about conserving water. The home felt like an old country inn. The rooms were full of sturdy antique furniture, very homey, warm, and comfortable. The part of the building that housed staff offices, a child playroom, and education center had just been dedicated at a celebration ceremony. As a result of what the program learned from families through a follow-up study with former residents of the shelter, the agency had raised funds to create and staff the newly built education center.

A sunporch with very long wooden tables served as the place in which staff and families all ate lunch and dinner together. The aroma of cabbage soup and homemade bread filled the air for hours before lunch. On my first day in this shelter, no families were present for lunch but most were present for dinner. All the staff working in the building stopped what they were doing to have lunch together. I felt very at home here right away. The atmosphere was both peaceful and exhilarating. I felt the contagious energy that comes from being with men and women who believed in the value of their work. It felt like an atmosphere in which creative thinking and teamwork would be nurtured.

After lunch the director took me on a tour of the building. Out of respect for families' privacy, the only area we did not go into was the family bedroom area. Three families lived in this main building and shared the kitchen, dining room, bathrooms, and living room in common with other families and some of the staff who lived on-site. Three other families lived in "scattered site" apartments in a building several blocks away—small, separate apartments, with a shared bathroom. As a result of conscious planning, the program sheltered small numbers of families in the main building and emphasized other program and advocacy activities at the state and local level focused on having an impact on the structural causes of homelessness. Their programs included the shelter, an education center, and a lending and technical assistance program to aid families to start their own businesses. Their education programs were open to low-income families from the community. Staff from this program were active with local community groups in developing affordable housing and economic opportunities for low-income families. The child playroom and the education center were bright and inviting. Tables and equipment in the education center were set up for a class, to be conducted later in the day by a volunteer who was one of the first female graduates of an engineering program in the Boston area. The class was focused on assisting women to learn how to do home repairs.

The place was full of community volunteers with tremendous expertise. Volunteers or staff prepared hot lunches and suppers, not resident parents. If a mother wanted to cook, she could. The director said that one of the mothers was working up to the challenge. She was collecting recipes. I thought how different this was from other shelters I had visited, in which families were required to take turns cooking for large groups of families. This shelter's system seemed to be more respectful of a person's readiness to take on the challenge, as well as her interest in the task; it seemed more respectful of diversity.

During the tour we went outside to the garden and playground. One of the little children came up to the director, who gave her a big hug. They talked about the child's upcoming birthday. The director asked the little girl what she wanted as a gift for her birthday. She replied that she wanted a pair of shorts. I thought to myself how modest this request was compared with birthday wish lists of most other children I had been in contact with who were neither homeless nor poor. Every time I saw a staff member near a child during my time at this shelter, I witnessed her saying something very complimentary to the child, using affectionate words such as "sweetpea," or outright talking about one of the child's special qualities or skills. I witnessed staff members giving hugs to mothers as well and affirming their strengths. At no time did I witness any judgmental comment made by a staff member about or toward any mother or child.

On my second trip to this shelter, I arrived a few hours after a group of families had returned from an overnight at a housing authority elsewhere in the state. Periodically, housing authorities in the state open up their waiting lists for families seeking a Section 8 housing subsidy. When I carried out this study, homeless families had priority for Section 8 openings.[22] Families who obtained federally funded Section 8 certificates had to find landlords willing to rent to them using the housing subsidy. If they were successful in finding an apartment and a willing landlord, families paid up to 30 percent of their income for rent, while the federal government reimbursed landlords for the remaining portion. These certificates were and are extremely difficult to obtain. The waiting lists were and are very long. When waiting lists opened up, a common practice among family shelters in the state was to organize overnight trips for groups of homeless families. They arrived at the housing authority the night before the office opened up and took turns standing in line throughout the night, in the hopes of increasing their chances to obtain applications and get on the waiting list for new subsidies. Families living in this shelter had just returned from one such overnight. The mothers and children were exhausted. At her request, I postponed an interview with one of the mothers who needed time to recover from the stress of this excursion.

On this day I stayed for dinner, which had been cooked by volunteers. Before dinner the staff and families gathered in a circle and held hands. One of the staff members offered a blessing, in which she expressed her gratitude for each person and her hope that the families would receive the housing applications they were seeking. The dinner was bountiful and simple: fish sticks, potatoes, and coleslaw. I noted to myself how different this experience was from another shelter in which the staff were so upset that each family was not eating dinner separately. The staff in that shelter were trying to legislate that parents eat with their own children and that cross-family contacts be limited. Staff did not join families for any meals. In contrast, the atmosphere here around meals was very calm, peaceful, and facilitative of community building. The message seemed to be: "Whoever lives here, while they are here, are family, and they are to be treated with the respect, and as a 'we' with staff, not as an 'other.'" This philosophy, evident in the physical setup of the shelter, permeated the program's way of organizing daily life, including meals and chores. Staff and families shared chores in this shelter. Once a week, they pitched in together to get the job done.

After cleaning up the dinner dishes, which everyone helped with, two of the staff and I had a cup of tea together in the kitchen before I turned in for the night. The next morning I went down to the kitchen early and engaged in a lively conversation with one of the children living in the shelter. This petite, energetic, and talkative seven-year-old was telling me that when she grew up she wanted to be a staff person in this shelter. I told her I thought she would be a great staff person, because she was so friendly and seemed to like talking with people so much. Her mother came into the kitchen then and asked if I had slept at the shelter. I said that I had. She explained that she and her daughters had gone to bed early the night before because they were so tired from the overnight at the housing authority. She said that they usually ate earlier than the rest of those in the house because she was uncomfortable with feeding her children with a large group. I was not surprised to learn about this kind of individualized planning. Staff and mothers had told me many stories describing such practices. Later, while waiting to interview another mother, I listened to and felt the energy in the house. I could hear mothers, who were in a housing search group that took place in the sun room, talking in a very chatty and upbeat tone. Volunteers were caring for their children in the playroom while they participated in the housing search group.

When all my interviews were completed in this shelter, I made my rounds to say good-bye to the families and staff. I came upon a mother and her boyfriend, whom the staff had invited to stay for lunch, who were sitting in the sun room, poring over the mother's bills and papers. I left feeling very good about this place and the ways in which this staff interacted with families. The atmosphere was one of calmness, productive activity, and respectful relationships. In my last interviews with families, I heard their complaints with some of the rules and regulations, but all had identified ways in which they had felt very supported living in this shelter.

The Great Divide: Them and Us

This shelter was a large, Victorian-style structure, located in a rural part of the state. No name was on the building. The inside of the building was modern and bright. The entry into the building led to a "staff only" area, two staff offices, one for the executive director, and another shared by four to five staff. A bathroom in the hallway, beautifully decorated, had a Staff Only sign on it. When I arrived at the shelter, the executive director and a number of staff members were present and working in the staff office. Only one staff member made an effort to introduce herself to me. She asked me to sit on a chair in the hallway to wait for a mother I had arranged to interview. She offered me coffee. The executive director walked past me several times without greeting or introducing herself to me. The reception I received from this crew felt very cold, more so than in any of the other shelters I had visited.

At one point the director, obviously upset, yelled out to one of the staff in the office across the hallway, "What's going on in this wing. Shouldn't you take care of it? It sounds like children jumping on furniture." The staff person quickly went into the "family" part of the shelter, came back, and, looking rather sheepish, stuck her head into the director's office. Then she closed the door that separated the staff area from the family part of the shelter. A few minutes later a young mother came into the hallway. She told the staff person who had offered me coffee that she needed to get into the utility closet, which the staff person had to unlock. She asked, with a sense of apology in her tone, and in the presence of four staff members, if she could use the paper towels that were in the staff bathroom. I sensed from her nonverbal behavior that she felt one-down in relation to the staff.

After interviewing one mother, I left to meet another woman who had previously lived in the shelter. When I returned to interview a third mother, the director said to me, "Have you been hiding in the shelter all day?" I was taken aback by her manner in greeting me, not a hello or welcome but a rhetorical question with a touch of sarcasm. The mother I had arranged to interview showed me into the child playroom where we talked together. We walked into the family part of the shelter, in which ten families shared the living spaces. Each family had a bedroom. Large families occasionally used two bedrooms. Families shared bathrooms, large living and dining room areas, and large kitchen spaces, with room enough for every family to store its own food. The child playroom was spacious, bright, open, and full of stimulating toys and play materials for children. I learned that children six and older could come into this space any time. Younger children needed to be accompanied by a parent. In this shelter, parents were required to take turns assisting the child advocate in caring for children when their parents were attending the eight weekly mandatory meetings. The space in this shelter was modern and bright, but the atmosphere was tense.

That evening I attended a house meeting, facilitated by a staff member, Louise. We met a few minutes before the meeting was to begin, and Louise filled me in on her plan for the session. She was very friendly in greeting me and welcoming me into this aspect of her work with families. She told me that she did not permit personal fights between people in the meeting and did not allow shelter bashing. She said that many times parents would bring up issues in a whining way, complaints without solutions. She said that one of the dryers and a dishwasher were broken, that residents had issues with this. And that there were issues about people not cleaning up after themselves. There had been a problem with destruction of furniture, not treating it like their own. So the program had instituted a new requirement. The person whose chore it was had the responsibility for not only cleaning an area but also fixing and maintaining it. She said that she thought this was a good idea for people to learn because they have to do this in their own homes. I naively asked if the program goal was to promote people taking more ownership for the place. She responded by saying that she wanted the families to be more responsible and seemed to imply that they were on the whole rather irresponsible. Earlier, in my interview with Louise, she had explained how the shelter was kept clean. Daily chores were assigned to parents and checked by staff. Louise told me that many parents didn't know how to clean. She said she was satisfied with the shelter's practice of assigning extra chores to parents who violate shelter rules. They have to pull a slip of paper from a "job jar."

I had just spent the day interviewing four mothers who had uniformly provided me with vivid examples of ill-treatment they had experienced in this shelter. Each was very angry about the ways in which staff treated them as "less than." I wondered to myself how, at such a young age, twenty-six-year-old Louise came to be so comfortable with judging the families she worked with and so comfortable with assuming such an authoritarian role. I also wondered if the anger people felt about the ways they were treated by staff affected their ways of caring for, or not caring for, the furniture and the space. In the house meeting a parent raised the issue of the appliances that needed to be fixed. Louise said that there was no money to fix them. One of the fathers asked about the money the shelter gets from the state each month. Louise explained that the state did not always pay its bills on time. The tone of the interaction between the parents and Louise was reminiscent of parent-child communication. I felt very uncomfortable witnessing parents' lack of efficacy in affecting their circumstances in the shelter and their childlike dependence upon this young staff member.

The Safety Zone

This shelter, a large, three-story house, was in an urban part of the state and served primarily African American and Latino families, many of whom had lived on the streets and had survived serious family disruptions and violence. When I arrived, Rosalita greeted me at the door and welcomed me into the large staff room that doubled as a common living room. While I waited to meet with Rosalita and Jean, I observed them speaking in Spanish with a mother who was filling out a form. There was levity and warmth in their banter. At one point the mother, with a smile on her face, tried to teach Jean the correct way of saying something in Spanish. They both laughed at Jean's attempts to repeat the mother's words. The mother's six-year-old son was also sitting on the couch near me. He seemed to be practicing the

English words he was hearing. In a feeble attempt to make conversation, I asked him if that is what he was doing. He told me that he knew how to speak English. I replied by saying that I could tell he did. He asked for a book from Jean. She got it ready for him and then asked his mother in Spanish for permission to give him the book. The mother nodded assent. I was very impressed with Jean's sensitivity to the mother's parenting role.

When the mother and her son left the room, Rosalita, Jean, and I met. They wanted to know why I was doing the study. I told them about my curiosity regarding how communal living worked for parents and staff and related this topic to my own experience as a mother. Jean responded that this kind of study could be helpful in getting programs to improve. She and Rosalita agreed to participate. A few minutes later a little preschool girl came into the room wearing a ballerina costume. Jean and Rosalita oohed and aahed over her, and she seemed delighted.

In this building each family's room was like a studio apartment, with an efficiency kitchen, a closet, a bathroom, and beds. In the program's companion building families shared a common kitchen, bathroom, and living room, but had a private bedroom with their children. Both sites accepted male adult and adolescent family members. Jean and I walked over to a building a few blocks away that housed more units for families and staff offices. On the way she asked me about where I lived, where I was going to school, and where my daughter was going to school. I was very conscious of my privileged position. Both my daughter and I were attending private universities. Jean muttered something to herself about that and then said, "I'm really glad you are doing this study. It seems important."

A few days later I returned to the shelter to begin interviewing mothers. I arrived while a house meeting was going on. Rosalita asked me to sit on the bottom of the hallway stairs until the meeting was over. I could overhear conversations on recognizing and reducing children's and mothers' stress levels. The leader was very upbeat and affirming in her language: "You all have come up with some great ideas today about how to reduce stress, like music and dancing." There was a lot of talking and participation from the mothers. When the meeting was over, Jean introduced me to several mothers with whom I arranged times for interviews. She then showed me the child playroom, where I would be conducting some of the interviews. Stairs to the playroom were located off the living room. The child playspace was very bright and inviting. When I saw it I became aware of the fact that no children were around, in contrast to the other shelters I had visited. In this program children participate in day care to enable parents to go to school and do their housing search more easily.

The atmosphere in this shelter felt very congenial and relaxed. The mothers seemed to have friendships with each other and appeared to be less stressed than the mothers I had talked with in some other shelters. That the children were in day care during the times I spent in this shelter might have skewed my observations. As it turned out, I saw very few children in this shelter. Mothers and staff preferred to talk with me when children were in day care.

I returned another day to interview a mother who lived in the program's second building. I had to show identification to get into this building, which provided temporary housing for large numbers of men, women, and children. The shelter program used rooms on a floor in this building to shelter five families. The mother, Gloria, told me that the families in the shelter share a bathroom with people with mental illness who live on another part of the floor: "They make the bathroom nasty." I had used the bathroom before our interview began. Someone had used the sink without cleaning up after herself; little hairs were spread throughout one of the sink basins. The rest of the space seemed well taken care of and pleasant.

The physical environment has a powerful impact on families and staff in family shelter settings. The physical setup sends a message to all who live and work in these spaces. The environment can foster mutual respect or it can exacerbate inherently unbalanced power dynamics between families and staff. Cold, institutional-looking spaces and physical reminders of the differences between families and staff undermine the building of trust and communicate a lack of respect for families' worthiness. Well-taken-care-of and homey spaces send a message to staff who work in these settings that those who work and live in them are worthy of being well treated. Respect for families' boundaries and protection of their belongings are essential in building trust and ensuring safety.

No mother I spoke with wanted to live in a shelter. Families longed to be in their own homes. The comfort provided by the warmth and privacy in some settings I visited was a factor in enabling mothers and children to regroup and to recover from the devastation and stress of the turbulent journey they had survived prior to shelter entry. Agency leaders and staff have to struggle with difficult tradeoffs in their deliberations regarding the amount of privacy each family has available. More privacy for each family limits the number of families who can receive shelter. However, families are living in these "temporary" settings for long periods of time, months not weeks. The quality of the environment for both children and their parents deserves the attention of directors and of staff. Program funders also need to provide programs with adequate resources to ensure that these settings are safe and decent places for children and their parents to live.

Following this chapter are three personal and powerful reflections on these issues, one written by Deborah Gray who lived in two different shelters with her children, a second written by Rosa Clark who also lived in two shelters with her son and who has worked as a shelter manager and staff member for over eight years, and a third written by Michelle Kahan who directed two family shelter programs in Massachusetts.

Reflections on Chapter 2

Reflection: Mother, Deborah Gray

My children and I had the experience of staying in three different shelters during two periods of homelessness. Our first experience was in a city in another region of the country, where the shelter system for battered women and their children was in its beginning phase of development. In order to provide safety for myself and my children, I had to leave my home. After a relatively uncontested divorce, we experienced an escalation of jealous rage, stalking, and harassment. Months of terrorism, vandalism, and break-ins to our home took their toll on my nerves and I finally was forced to make the decision to go into a battered women's shelter. I was devastated. I was in a state of shock and couldn't believe that I had to rely on someone else to provide shelter for me and my then three young children.

My whole family was living in one room. Granted it was the biggest room in the house, but it was barely big enough for the five beds, a crib, and one large dresser. My children previously had their own room, a large backyard to play in, and a screened-in porch with their own bathroom. We had to adjust to sharing the room with several different mothers who each had one small child and didn't seem to stay more than a few days. We were considered lucky by some of the other women because we had a bathroom. In fact, we weren't the only ones using the bathroom since the roaches had taken up their residence in there also. I remember crying so hard and so long until I had no more tears. I was working at a full-time job and my children were in school and preschool pretending like we were living with friends. I eventually had to take leave time from my work to maintain my sanity.

There were many types of women living there, some with active substance abuse or alcoholism issues, some with other mental health issues, some with batterers looking for them. One woman came through who made sexual advances to some of the children and young mothers. The noise level was generally high. There were several overactive and out-of-control children of different ages.

It was a lot to deal with and very difficult for us to dig out of the gloom and depression. Depression renders one very fatigued. Sleep seems to be the best escape, unless you are plagued with nightmares. Rest becomes a luxury that a parent cannot afford. Some shelters do not allow women to be in their room during the daytime hours and would not take kindly to catching them in the room lying down.

We were responsible for cleaning our room and bathroom before the 10:00 A.M. daily inspection. We also had house chores and cooking schedules. Separate cliques had formed before I arrived, making it hard to get to know the other women. The physical environment added to the depressing atmosphere. The dirty walls, rugs, and furniture set the tone for the doom and gloom. It was in a huge old mansion not far from downtown. The roaches and mice appeared to be more at home than the guests.

The next time we were homeless was when we moved back to Boston. My relatives pleaded with me to stay with them until we could get settled, but they didn't understand how difficult it would be for me and my now four children to live in a three-bedroom apartment with them and their eight children. They didn't understand the subsidy system or how having a place, any place to stay might jeopardize the transfer of my subsidy from the other state. I checked around the shelters and found one that had enough room for us and we moved in the next day. It was a battered women's shelter with a confidential address in a great location. I felt a little more comfortable there, although still concerned that the batterer would actually follow us up here. We had a huge bedroom on the top floor of a beautiful townhouse in the mid-to high-rent area. The furniture was clean and beautiful and we had our own bathroom with a sunken tub. We were only allowed eight weeks to stay there, and before our time was up we moved into another family shelter. This shelter was in the midtown section in a very busy building. We had two small adjourning rooms with a large shared bathroom and a small kitchen. The laundry was across an extremely busy street in a highly populated area.

Sharing space was not always easy. The hardest spaces to share are the kitchen and bathroom. Most families have their own customs, habits, and beliefs. I was brought up with the understanding that if nothing else is up to par, you still keep your kitchen and bathroom clean. Hygiene became a very important priority. Walking into the same wet shower behind someone else whom you don't even know became a concern. In the battered women's shelters we were lucky to have had the biggest rooms with private bathrooms. The family shelter, which had a congregate bathroom, was very difficult to deal with. It was cleaned up in the morning around 10 or 11 A.M. That meant that by late afternoon and dinnertime, the bathrooms caught heavy traffic. They were usually filthy by 8 P.M. after the children were bathed and ready for bed. I despised having to use the bathroom and the showers at night. No one ever admitted to making a mess. The morning was another high traffic time, but the bathrooms were not cleaned until 10 A.M.

The kitchen was locked during certain hours and we were served dinner from a half-door in the hallway. We had to line up at the window and wait with our plates, bowls, and cups. I felt like I was in a prison lineup. Sometimes the children did not want to eat the food provided, so parents would go out and buy something for their children to eat. I was a vegetarian when I came to Boston, but being in shelters for eleven months, I gave it up. The food was sometimes salty, too sweet, or very starchy. In the battered women's shelter, we took turns cooking dinner for everyone. Some people cooked their ethnic dishes, but many children will not eat unfamiliar foods. Some women just could *not* cook. We had burnt food one night. I cooked a seasoned-baked chicken and packaged flavored rice dinner one night with cornbread and they all wanted seconds or thirds. I certainly made friends after that simple meal.

In our first experience living in a battered women's shelter, we had four beds and a crib. One woman who shared the room with us, and did not have a child with her, was really detached, she didn't talk much. She really didn't seem interested in us at all and she didn't help clean up. She was only there for a few days, but the impact of her despair was very strong. Our other roommate had a toddler, she was there for almost two weeks. It seemed that most women need a little time and space when they first come to the shelter. Trust is a precious thing and you learn to give it a little at a time as you feel your way around; testing, watching, and observing. Her son kept waking up my children during the night. I had to go to work and they had to go to school and child care. I didn't feel much like socializing, myself, especially since we were only going to be at the shelter a short time; but since I had to "be" there, it seemed to make sense to search out a friend. I helped another woman with her son by sharing some of my ideas about parenting and talking with her about my experiences.

When we first arrived at the battered women's shelter in Boston, I heard tales about how staff would use their keys to come in your room and take food stamps or money from your safety box. It was in the closet bolted to the floor—but they kept a key! I can understand the need for staff to have access to the rooms, but families need to be able to lock their doors and feel some kind of sense of security. Room inspections are one way of keeping the shelter clean but they should not be intrusive, such as unannounced looking through drawers, suitcases, bags, etc. Unannounced inspections should be done only with valid evidence of unlawful possessions or activities—or if the family had not checked in before curfew. My children were four, six, and eight at the time. My two girls slept in the adjourning room's top bunk and my son had the bottom bunk. One of the children struggled with enuresis (bedwetting), a very embarrassing difficulty. To get some privacy, the girls dressed and undressed in the closet. Hidden soiled clothes in the closet were not a pleasant surprise. Patience was the "TEST."

I became friends with a couple of parents and had a respectful relationship with a few others who kept their distance, but we helped each other out at times. The staff would talk about other women and in some cases stir up rift and confusion among us. They decided it was not a good idea for us to get together in the lobby and watch TV or a video. They (staff) would pick through the donations that donors would give for the homeless families and take those things they wanted for themselves.

After they picked out what they wanted, they would let us sign up for a slot to go in the room and pick out what we wanted. One time they spread all the clothes out on the floor in the playroom and let us all line up at the door. We had to wait until they opened the door and it was like a stampede in Filene's basement. I resented the feeling of having to pick through the leftovers, even though we didn't have many clothes with us in the shelter. The way staff set this up seemed to be some kind of "power trip." On the other hand, at Christmastime we were overwhelmed with gifts of toys for the children. Each family got a supersized garbage bag full of new toys and stuffed animals. It was wonderful in a way, but it also felt like such a waste to overcompensate with toys. I would have preferred a voucher to buy what I felt would be appropriate for my children. On a positive note, after moving out of the shelter, I maintained friendships with two of the parents I had met there.

In several emergency situations I left my children with two parents in the family shelter. Our children were close in age. We could depend on each other as backup. Close to the time when we moved out, I began taking groups of kids to the playground to help break the monotony of being in the shelter. More and more kids wanted to go with me, but their moms were not agreeable.

If families who are not under pressures of homelessness need time apart, imagine what it must be like for those families who are forced to live on top of each other in a shelter. One woman had to take a room in the basement of the townhouse because her son was almost fourteen years old. She was told that when he turned fourteen she would have to find some other place for him to stay. The family shelter had a rule that no children could use the elevator without a parent or even go to the bathroom unsupervised.

There was a children's play space in the family shelter, but it was only available at certain hours on certain days. Volunteers would come in to do activities with the children two times a week. And sometimes on Saturdays they would take them on field trips. This was the best part of our stay there. You can't imagine how a parent looks forward to those few hours of quiet. It was not easy for the volunteers to deal with all the children of different ages and abilities at one time. Some children were sent back to their rooms because they were overexcited and couldn't control themselves.

While being in the shelter, I realized that this was a time I could focus on nurturing my children. We had all been through a very difficult time that led up to us becoming homeless, and while I was working hard to keep my sanity, I had tried really hard to keep routines as familiar as I could for the children. They actually said they had a good time in the shelter. We spent time talking, reading, playing, and walking. We had routines when we were in our own place, but having a set bedtime curfew in the shelter helped them to get their sleep schedules back on track. After being in our own apartment for about six weeks, my son complained about not having fun. "I wish we could go back to the shelter so we could go places and have fun in the playroom." He really enjoyed the company of other boys and the child care volunteers who played with them and took them on field trips. On the other hand, I'm happy to be in a place of my own. I now feel a sense of privacy and safety, and the autonomy to make decisions for myself and my family without the intrusion or control of others.

Reflection: Mother and Staff Member, Rosa Clark

As I sit here today dictating my reflections, I have to admit that it probably took me so long because it means having to revisit some feelings I would rather not think about. The feelings that I'm revisiting bring me back to having a family, having my first child, having my first apartment and to the relationship that I was in at that time with a man who could not cope with being a father. I was probably also going through postpartum depression now that I think back to it, and I had a good friend of mine who I just called one day and said, "Please you have to come and get me out of this situation, out of this relationship," and that was how I ended up at Project Hope.

As I remember, coming through the doors of Project Hope, I immediately sensed a feeling of relief. People were welcoming, people were smiling, people hugged me, and I felt the beginning of a sense of safety and warmth. For me, my experience at Project Hope was one of safety. I felt a lot of warmth, you know, and it may have had to do partly with the way I was welcomed into Project Hope, the care that people gave to me. They opened their arms and they opened the doors to me and my nine-month-old son. I am a Hispanic woman. I was twenty-three years old. When I came to this country, I was fourteen years old, so I came with much more of a sense of my own home back in Honduras, where I did not challenge rules. A sense of entitlement was not even in my vocabulary. When I came into the shelter, I was so grateful for being given the opportunity just to get out of the situation I was in and pleased to be in a place where there was a lot of care, which I experienced on a day-to-day basis.

At the beginning I isolated myself in the room, and I think it had to do more with feeling abandoned, not by the system but pretty much abandonment by my mate because he could not deal. He was twenty-three also, and he hadn't been brought up on how to be a father or how to respond to me. I was very vulnerable and he just couldn't deal with that. He was more dealing with his stuff, what was going on with him. So, isolating myself in my room gave me some time to bond with my first son, who at that time was nine months. I kept my room immaculately clean. I spent a lot of time just organizing it and cleaning it and arranging my things to feel comfortable with my baby. I had one room and one bed and I had a dresser and I had my baby's crib and I had a lot of things to stimulate him. As I think back to that room, it was a place where I could have my private time and mourn the ending of a relationship but also begin building a new one with my child. At the time I was at the shelter, a lot of couples there were Hispanic. Little by little I began to leave my room and get more involved with the happenings around Project Hope. I am a person who likes to clean a lot, and I like to cook. I didn't know if people had chores that they were supposed to do. I just found myself cleaning things, trying to help out. It was like I'm living here, this is ours, and we have to take care of it. There wasn't anything that I wouldn't have done.

Remember, I wasn't much into structure, and I did understand that there was a curfew. I didn't have anywhere else to go but to be at Project Hope, so curfew was beside the point for me. I didn't really care about that. I did feel like if I wanted privacy I could go to my room, and this was back quite a few years ago so the shelter system wasn't as developed as it is now, so that rules were not a problem for me. They really didn't affect me in any way, shape, or form. I wasn't in tune with whether it affected other families. I just know that we got along well. We all did what we were supposed to do. I was just pretty focused on myself but also got kind of tuned in with some of what was going on around me. My stay at the shelter was about four months, and during that time I made some friends. I got to know the staff, and it was quite a positive experience. I have been and will continue to be forever grateful. That is the only way that I could see the situation for me. Because I was in need and someone or many people were there to help me. I was at a low point in my life, my self-esteem was down. People cheered me, people were thanking me for things that I did and how I looked out for the shelter.

I remember that there was one person who was doing some child care. I remember her knocking at my door. The first time I remember her knocking at my door on the third floor, I was a little withdrawn. It was the beginning of my stay. She asked if I wanted to bring my son into the day care and I said, "No, no, we're okay." And I don't know if part of it was because I wanted to just spend time with my baby or part of it was having to come out and confront another situation, whatever, but Mary Ellen was her name. I'll never forget her. She was a beautiful person. She had such a low tone of voice, you could sense the realness in her from the first time I met her. She had a beautiful smile on her face. There was a warmth about her. She continued to talk with me and let me know that if I wanted to bring him in to the child care, he could play a little bit and then I could have some time to myself. So I understood her reason behind it, and after probably about a week, I said, "Okay I'm going to give it a try." And I did, and it was beautiful because I got to go in the day care. I got to see my son play on the floor, and he was more stimulated, and I was able to play with him; and then little by little as I let the wall down, I could trust Mary Ellen with my son. I did leave him, and I saw what a genuine person she was. So that was a good thing for me to trust her. I didn't see it as her forcing me or invading my privacy, not at all. I guess for me it was trusting people and believing that we're all good people. She's real and the people that are in the shelter are all real, and they're caring and they're doing this because they want to help us. So for me privacy was not really an issue.

In closing out these reflections, there was no point in the time I was in the shelter that I felt like I was being taken advantage of or felt like if people were leaving me out of any type of decision making, or people were not sensitive to my needs, or that the frontline staff used their power in any way to humiliate me. I think I learned a lot about people who do this work and their commitment to it. Along the way, like everything else, shelter systems have gotten bigger and more people are coming into it. Now it's different. My personal experience was very gratifying and I learned a lot, and for that I am appreciative.

Reflection: Program Director, Michelle Kahan

Previously, as director of a few different types of shelter programs, and currently, as a consultant to various programs serving homeless populations, I have had the opportunity to experience and witness shelter living in divergent physical settings. The first shelter I worked at provided each family with their own living unit, complete with kitchen, bathroom, living room, one bedroom, and a locked door. The shelter building was comprised of five of these units, four of them serving families of various sizes, and the fifth converted to staff offices and shared living spaces. While the building was not always in prime condition, each family benefited from private spaces within which to conduct their lives. During my tenure there, we expanded this small, homey program to encompass an additional ten scattered site apartments of between two and four bedrooms that the agency rented on behalf of homeless families. The units were scattered among the various neighborhoods served by the agency. Families placed in these units were provided with the same services as families living in the shelter building; they benefited from increased independence and privacy, yet had fewer opportunities to share in community support.

After several years, I left this program to direct a battered women's organization. This agency also offered a shelter program, at a secret location for safety purposes. The shelter was located in a three-story building, a converted two-family house. The first floor offered a recently renovated communal kitchen with two stoves and refrigerators and a walk-in pantry; a large dining area; a small living room; two children's play areas; several storage closets; and a hot line office used by staff. The second floor was comprised of six bedrooms, two small bathrooms, and a tiny enclosed porch that served as a library. The third floor, really a converted attic, housed the agency's offices and a storage area for donated clothing. The program was considered an eighteen-bed shelter by its primary funding source. In practice, that designation translated into families sharing small bedrooms. Sometimes a mother with one or two young children would live with a pregnant or single woman (singles and families live together in Massachusetts battered women's shelters, unlike in the state's nonspecialized homeless shelter system). Or a mother and her four children, boys and girls aged five to fifteen, would share one small room. There was one bathroom available for every three rooms. As the program was usually full, privacy was rarely to be found anywhere in the cramped, dingy building. Families in this program cooked and ate their meals independently, unless they chose to join together for a special dinner.

As director of this shelter, I was confronted daily with a myriad of problems resulting from communal living. Cleanliness was always an issue, with residents and staff having varying standards. As the women did not have keys to the rooms, or locked space in which to store their belongings, accusations of theft were constant. Bedtimes were chaotic; one child would be just about asleep when another would begin to cry. As a practitioner of the family support philosophy, I resisted getting involved in many of the trivial arguments. I encouraged residents to work out their difficulties with one another and to recommend systemic policy changes that would decrease the level of conflict. I also struggled with a decision around shared rooms, finally restructuring the environment so that each family received their own living space, with one room reserved for up to two single women. Despite the obvious benefits for residents, this decision was difficult. As there is always a shortage of beds for domestic violence victims, I worried that women in dangerous situations would be denied shelter due to this policy. In the end I realized that we could not adequately help families in such a contentious living environment. As a newcomer to this crowded environment, I was amazed at the level of conflict. I had not realized the advantage provided by the physical space at the homeless shelter where I had previously worked. The lack of privacy at the battered women's program was appalling to me. I knew that if I were a resident, I could never survive under such circumstances, no matter how great my need for a safe place to live.

Shelters are incredibly stressful, chaotic living environments. Families end up living in them only after exhausting all other options. As stated in the quote at the beginning of this chapter, homelessness can be traumatizing. Negotiating shared living is always difficult, even in the best of circumstances. In designing shelters, it is critical to respect the different talents and histories each resident will bring to the environment, while devising a system that can fittingly serve the whole. Spaces for private, family interactions through which parents can retain their independence and self-respect are vital to ensuring that both adults and children survive this trauma without lasting negative consequences. I often hear advocates who do not share the family support philosophy postulate that shelters should not be too comfortable. These advocates fear that if shelters are too comfortable, then they would be serving as hotels and families would have no incentive to leave. I have never met a shelter resident who did not feel stigmatized and shamed by the experience of homelessness. Shelters are not hotels, by any means. Families living in them are well aware that their situation is not permanent and that they must follow rules and meet requirements in order to remain in the shelter.

Recently I visited a transitional living program for homeless families. Consumers of this program come from the agency's shelter, graduating to more independent living and privacy. While in the shelter program, the young mothers have their rooms inspected for cleanliness daily. After moving to the more independent program, their rooms are inspected only three times per week. They receive warnings for rule violations such as unmade beds and dirty dishes. I shudder to think what would happen if one of the agency's staff came to my home for an inspection. It seems to me that the value of a transitional living program comes through its ability to develop independent living skills. As long as I pay my rent, I don't have to prove that my bed is made. Why should the residents of this program be required to do so? How does that requirement better prepare them for independent living?

3

Parental Rights and the Protection of Children

Africans believe in something that is hard to render in English.
We call it "ubuntu botho."
You know when it is there and when it is absent.

It speaks about humaneness, gentleness, hospitality,
putting yourself out on behalf of others, being vulnerable.

It recognizes that my humanity is bound up in yours,
for we can only be human together.

—Nobel laureate Bishop Desmond Tutu, South Africa

Diana is loudly yelling at Anna, her twenty-two month old daughter, in the family shelter's child care room. Anna looks terrified. The other preschool children, their parents, and a staff member stop what they are doing, staring in stunned silence at the enraged mother and frightened child.

The most common program model utilized across the country to shelter homeless families is one in which families share living spaces—that is, congregate living—and are therefore faced with the challenge of caring for their children in "public view," within eyeshot of shelter staff and other unrelated families. Interactions among families and staff members in these settings are indicative of public policy debates regarding the role of the community in ensuring children's safety while protecting the freedom of parents to care for their children according to their own norms, values, and wishes.

Program policies governing who is in charge of child rearing are at the heart of the most complex aspects of help giving for parents when families are living in congregate shelters. This chapter examines the struggles and dilemmas of program directors, frontline staff members, and mothers as they negotiate with each other in sharing responsibility for the care of children. On one level this involves determining program policies that address many aspects of children's daily routines such as: when they go to bed, how they are supervised throughout the day, how child discipline is handled, and how staff members will intervene when they witness a scene in which they believe the child is being harmed by a parent's actions. On another level this involves figuring out moment by moment how to deal with the innumerable vicissitudes of life with large numbers of mostly young children[1] in shared living spaces from a diverse range of families who are, by definition, in distress. Given that the most powerful predictor of child well-being is parental stress,[2] successfully navigating these dimensions of families' lives in shelters matters, if the well-being of children is to take center stage for all the adults involved.

Shared responsibility for the care of children is a reality in these settings. Directors and staff of shelter programs must ensure that every child and parent in the shelter is safe from health and other risks and has some minimal level of calm and predictability in the environment. In addition, directors and staff are legally and ethically responsible to act quickly and decisively when they witness situations that they perceive as emotionally or physically harmful to children, even when their actions interfere with a parent's autonomy.

Alice, the staff member who told me the story this chapter began with, described how hard it was for her to decide how to intervene with Diana who regularly screamed very loudly at her two children. In addition to its effects on Diana's young daughter and son, Alice also worried about children from other families feeling unsafe as a result of witnessing this mother's yelling. She told me that she asked Diana to take a private walk outside with her. "We had a conversation, and it was a really positive experience. I think the timing was just right. . . . I said to her that I felt real uncomfortable about the way she was yelling at her son. . . . I feel like I'm intruding just by being there with you and your child, yet there is nothing I can do because this took place in the middle of our program. . . . I asked her to consider that [her yelling] made other people feel uncomfortable, that her voice was really loud, and her tones were really demeaning and angry."

Alice told me that a few months after this conversation took place, she noticed that Diana was talking to her child, not yelling. She told Diana of the positive changes she had seen in her son's behavior as a result of this change. In response to my probing, Alice reflected upon her effectiveness with Diana, "I felt great. . . . Professionally, I acted when it happened. I didn't wait three days or a day to talk to her about it. It was going on then. I waited for her to stop yelling, which she did. That is when I went over to her. I knew I was treading on some really private feelings, but the simple fact is that she is yelling at her kids. Whether or not she trusts me, I really need to tell her that."

Diana, the mother in this story, seemed very close to tears several times as she told me about her experience at the shelter and the cir- cumstances that led to her being homeless. She was a very petite, wiry, and spirited twenty-two-year-old woman. Initially, she seemed uneasy answering my questions about the ways in which she and Alice worked together. She had very little positive to say and needed my reassurance that what she said would not get Alice in trouble. Our interview took place in the child care room. She settled her children into some play activities so that we could talk. Her four-year-old eventually got into building blocks; her twenty-two-month-old was unhappy the whole time. Both children were extremely active. Diana was hypervigilant about their wanderings throughout our time together; she was after them in a flash. We had to interrupt the interview after about one hour when the children had finally had it with our talking. We finished the two-hour interview in the evening after they were asleep.

Diana told me that she resented how Alice tried to get her to par- ent in a different way. "I would say that I am raising my children, and I feel that I am doing a good job. I do it by myself, and I told them even before I moved in here, that if you don't like the way that I do something, I don't want you saying, 'you need to change.' . . . I haven't got no problem, but Alice told me that I yell at my kids too much, and that she can hear me yelling at my kids from her office. I said that I don't yell at my kids, I raise my voice at them. . . . Alice has a parenting [class], and it is her opinion or your opinion. She reads out of books and the books don't have life. . . . I tell her that I hit my son. . . . I sometimes spank him if he really needs it. . . . Then after I give him a spanking, I let him know why he got that spanking. I only did it one time since I have been here, and that is good because I have a lot of stress. I have people (friends and family) telling me I should hit them because they walk all over me. I always tell myself that I don't want to hit my kids. . . . Some days I feel so stressed that I take it more out on my kids, not beating them or anything, just like mad at them. Some days are good, some days are not good. I just know that the days that are not good, everybody is on you."

Diana told me that she thought she was close to moving out of the shelter and was simply trying to keep herself from snapping. Although Alice felt she had been successful in helping Diana to change the way she communicated with her children, Diana viewed this "help" as an added stress. Diana thought that her strengths and coping strategies had been neither appreciated nor recognized by Alice. Diana felt humiliated and burdened by well-meaning advice that failed to acknowledge the extent to which she was already making changes in her parenting in the face of external pressures from friends and family to be punishing with her children.

My interview with another mother forced me to confront how hard it would be as a staff member to refrain from intruding upon a mother's role with her child, particularly when my parenting style differed from hers. This was one of the only times, across my interviews with thirty-nine mothers, in which I felt uncomfortable with a mother's way of caring for her child. In this situation, the issues were minor, had nothing to do with safety, and were solely a matter of our having different parenting styles.

The interview took place in a large staff office in the shelter. Before we went into the room, I witnessed Hilda, twenty-four-year-old mother of four-year-old Brian, and two-year-old Jesse, being yelled at by a staff member in the presence of other mothers and children who were gathered in the shelter's living room. The staff member said in a harsh tone, "Have you cleaned the kitchen?" The mother's first comments to me were expressions of anger about the criticism she said she regularly received from certain staff. She, I, and two-year-old Jesse settled ourselves in the staff office. No matter what Hilda did to try to interest her daughter in playing outside the office with another child, Jesse said in a very loud voice, "NO!" The mother was doing very little to give her daughter something to do while we talked. I had hoped to have Hilda's full attention during the interview. So, I did what I could. I gave Jesse a piece of paper and a pen to play with while we talked. Hilda settled herself on the couch. I was considerably uncomfortable with what Jesse was doing throughout the interview: for example, eating all the bananas the staff member had stashed away in a bag on her bookcase, playing with the staff member's belongings on her desk, and touching my all-important tape recorder. When I asked Jesse not to touch the tape recorder, Hilda pulled her away from it. I gave Jesse more paper to play with since she was also pulling apart the audio cassette holders I had set aside. I felt distracted at times by what Jesse was doing, but Hilda did not seem uncomfortable. I thought how hard it would be for me to hold back from usurping Hilda's role as mother if I were a staff member in this shelter. In fact, as you can see, I took an active "parenting" role with Jesse throughout the time we were together. While I believe strongly in help giving that is respectful of parents' unique ways of caring for their children, I fully appreciate how difficult this might actually be in situations with mothers and children in which parenting styles differ.

These two situations reflect the kinds of struggles mothers, staff, and children get into with each other as they live their daily lives in family shelters. In my interview with Hilda and her daughter, Jesse, no safety issue was at stake: Hilda and I simply had different child-rearing styles. My approach was to be extremely vigilant and active in redirecting Jesse's behavior; Hilda described her own style as laid-back and nonintrusive. She told me that she regularly gets accused of not disciplining her children because she chooses to correct her children by talking with them in private rather than scolding them in public. In her eyes, her efforts to save her children from being embarrassed in public are viewed by others as her being too permissive with her children. In contrast, the situation Alice and Diana described had more to do with children feeling safe, not just Diana's children but also the other children in the child care room who witnessed Diana's yelling. In either case, without careful attention, help givers can unwittingly set a cycle into motion in these situations in which a mother feels judged and criticized. Perhaps this is what happened with Hilda as a result of my actions in our interview. Parents' self-esteem takes a nose-dive, and their stress levels increase. The stress and pressure come out when they are with their children; everyone involved pays a price.

Effective Parenting Help

Studies of parenting by mothers while they were living in shelters with their children emphasize the importance of the help-giving environment in affecting the ways that parents respond to their children.[3] Specifically, they recommend that staff find ways to promote the building of supportive bonds among mothers and avenues for mothers to maintain both control and intimacy with their children. They emphasize the need for helpers to enhance parents' self-esteem, efficacy, and confidence in caring for their children. Studies from the fields of child welfare, family violence, maternal health care, child-hood disabilities, and child development[4] all recommend as "best practice" standards an orientation toward identifying and building upon the strengths and the perhaps untapped capacities of families, and collaboratively designing service interventions with families that match their expressed priorities and concerns. These principles are rooted in an ecological perspective[5] that recognizes the inseparable interconnectedness between the well-being of children and their families. The child is part of the family system, the family is nested within a neighborhood and community of formal and informal social networks, and this broader social network is part of a larger society that has an impact upon family and community life. If children are to grow well, their parents and their family must also be thriving.

Mothers and frontline staff members I interviewed identified help with parenting as the most successful area of help giving provided to families while they lived in the shelters.[6] Three factors emerged as being critical in determining whether a staff member's help was perceived as effective: talking with parents in private; using a nonjudg-mental approach; and being sensitive to timing (not reacting in a cri-sis mode, if possible). Mothers I interviewed made it very clear that how staff treated them as parents affected them most deeply. Being homeless in and of itself is devastating, and leads to feelings of failure and self-blame.[7] The one aspect of their lives that they try to hold on to has to do with their children. Helping children to get through the difficulties, keeping the family together, and holding onto a sense of self-worth as parents were core parts of the survival and healing process.

The Context

A metaphor used by one staff member to describe the web of relationships in community settings such as these shelters was that of lots of little children surrounded by parents and many aunts (for some, uncles as well). On average, fifteen children resided in the shelters on any given night, ranging from a low of five to a high of thirty-eight children. Nearly four out of five children were six years of age or younger. Lots of adults were around to tell children what to do and lots of children were mixing it up with each other. In these settings, what one parent does with her child is witnessed by other parents and children. Sometimes parents who are present when an incident between children is happening have to step in and set limits or resolve the situation with children who are not "their own." Cultural differences among families add to the complexity of these shared child-rearing circumstances. For example, only a handful of programs sheltered families representing one ethnic group. The vast majority hosted families from a diverse range of ethnic groups, each with its own rich traditions for family routines, rituals, and approaches to raising children.

In addition to going through the typical growth stages, children are also dealing with and recovering from the trauma of being homeless: they have lost friends, belongings, their own space, and familiar routines.[8] In the shelter setting they are dealing with many new, unrelated adults in their lives. Through it all they experience the effect of their mother's stress. Mothers are juggling an enormous number of competing demands: caring for their children; looking for housing; attending mandatory meetings (in some shelters); and meeting welfare work requirements. The mothers also have to deal with their own personal reactions to the trauma of losing a home and have to find ways to get along with other parents. In addition, they must have enough of a relationship with staff, likable or not, to maintain peace and get the help they need to obtain a house and other resources. The mothers also have to answer to other adults, while maintaining authority with their children, and have to muster the inner resources to do all this, while at the same time assisting their children with the developmental and emotional reactions the children are having to their situation.

Staff members in these settings are charged with the responsibility of building a positive working relationship with each family, likable or not. They have a mandated child protection role. They are in the position of responding to complex family situations, ones in which many family members are recovering from the effects of violence[9] and are extremely stressed, in addition to being extremely poor. Staff members must reconcile their own values and helping styles with the policies of their parent organization and funding sources. Directors are responsible for creating a vision, an atmosphere for community building, and an effective system of service that results in families with diverse needs obtaining housing and moving out of homelessness permanently. They must provide guidance for staff regarding the complex, minute-by-minute situations that come up with family members, as well as direction for resolving the conflicts and crises that inevitably arise. That direction has to be driven by the vision, not by the idiosyncrasies or biases of individual staff members.

Given all these pressures, living or working in these settings is extremely challenging for children, parents, staff, and managers. Navigating these relationships successfully, supportively, and nonintrusively is a challenging venture, more demanding than in other human service settings in which contacts have natural time, location, and other role boundaries and in which the power dynamics are less pervasive.

Program Policies

Child bedtimes.   The overwhelming majority of programs required that young children be in their bedrooms by certain times and/or required that parents stay with their children in their bedroom until the children had fallen asleep. Many shelter directors believed that these policies helped children by getting them onto a regular schedule. They reported receiving feedback from former residents who have continued the bedtime schedule and routines, and who have learned the value of having more regular routines for their children. Directors also described incidences in which parents felt the positive benefits of having time to themselves at night after their children go to bed, an experience directors indicated was new for many parents.

Based on these viewpoints, directors seemed to be making an assumption that the bedtime routines they saw when families entered their shelters were the only ones within families' repertoires. Could it be that most homeless families have had their bedtime routines disrupted as a result of the series of dislocations they have gone through before getting to the shelter? The typical pathway to family shelter is to lose your housing and then to move in with a series of friends and relatives for limited periods of time until you wear out your welcome.[10] For children and parents, this is an experience of being constantly uprooted. Any parent would have difficulty maintaining a consistent schedule with their children under these circumstances.

Supervision of children. Most programs require children to be closely supervised, within arm's reach, by their parents at all times, especially infants, toddlers, and preschoolers. Some programs provide child care during the day or at designated times to enable parents to meet other obligations such as mandatory meetings, housing searches, and welfare work requirements. Some directors saw this supervision policy as one avenue for preventing program staff from inadvertently usurping parents' roles with their children. A tendency for confusion exists when so many adults and children are in the same environment. At times it is hard to know who is watching which child. In the words of one director, "It's a struggle. Because there's five adults living here. There's assumptions, like 'I'm sure someone's watching them.' So much going on where kids aren't supposed to be, and they can't be without their children. It's very difficult for parents to supervise."

Many programs allowed and encouraged parents to work out cooperative baby-sitting arrangements. They typically required parents to gain staff approval for these baby-sitting arrangements. A common practice was for both parents to sign a baby-sitting form in which the parent leaving provided information regarding where she could be reached and the time she expected to return. Program policies restricting baby-sitting arrangements between parents, reported by a few directors, were the result of past abuses in which parents had left their children in the care of another parent and then failed to return until three or four days later. Many directors indicated that they did not allow overnight baby-sitting. They also spoke about the role staff took in assisting parents to say no to another parent when they did not want to have baby-sitting responsibilities and in offering parents guidelines for the selection of competent caregivers for their children. This is actually a more complex process than it may appear to be on the surface. For example, a staff member may be uncomfortable with a parent's ability to care for another parent's children but would need to be protective of both parents' rights to privacy and respectful of one parent's communication with another.

Disciplining children.   Policies regarding disciplining children were perhaps the thorniest ones for directors, staff, and parents to work out. Overwhelmingly, the most common program policy was a prohibition against parents using physical or verbal abuse in disciplining children (sometimes described as no "spanking," "hitting," "yelling," or "swearing"; sometimes stated simply as no "corporal punishment"). Many directors and staff members agonized over interactions with parents about disciplining children. Directors realized how upset parents were with being told by shelter directors and staff that they could not spank or yell at their children when they were living in the shelter. According to the directors, this option left many parents feeling out of control and many children feeling very relieved and safe, at least when they were on shelter grounds.

A negative consequence of this dynamic was children exploiting this tension between staff and parents by testing the limits with their parents to see if their parents were going to spank them and then running to the staff to report on their parents' behavior. Some directors told me that they empathized with parents' distress at feeling so out of control and that they worried about undermining the parental role. Others were cognizant of the limitations of their policies. They assumed that although parents may not spank children in front of staff, they will do so when they are off shelter grounds and very likely will blame their children for getting them in trouble with staff.

Many directors realized that their program policies created significant hardships for parents when they lived in family shelters. However, in their minds the concerns I have already described provided justification for program policies in which parents were held responsible for round-the-clock supervision of their children and in which staff assumed responsibility for setting guidelines and monitoring how parents carried out these responsibilities—including the ways they disciplined their children. Herein lies the rub. To paraphrase the words of many mothers I interviewed: Does becoming homeless mean that I am unable to parent? How am I to explain to my child that I have to get staff approval for getting them a baby-sitter? My children see me being treated like a child. They lose respect for me.

Several directors emphasized the importance they placed on not usurping parents' authority with their children and the extremes to which they would go to back up a parent in front of her children and other families. For example, in some shelters, when a staff person needed to speak with a parent about her interactions with her child, the policy was for this conversation to take place privately. If a parent was obviously having trouble handling a situation with her child (e.g., when a child is screaming, yelling, or out of control), staff were encouraged to offer nonjudgmental, nonintrusive help. "They [the parents] sometimes feel like they are losing control. We try hard for that not to happen," said one staff member. "Discipline is hard. They know they can't lose it with their kids with the staff watching. If there's a problem, [the staff] develop a plan with the parent. Staff will offer to watch the child for twenty minutes while the parent takes a walk."

Other directors described using a very authoritarian approach with parents. That is, program staff blatantly assumed responsibility for telling parents how to discipline their children and directly took over the parenting when and if staff saw fit. This included requiring that all parents in the shelter used one method for disciplining children; providing each parent with a handbook that described appropriate and inappropriate parenting; documenting whether each parent was or was not following the prescribed child discipline procedures; and giving warnings for any improper child discipline. One director, only one, said that she routinely reported every parent to the state child protection agency upon entry into the shelter, whether or not she thought the children were being abused or neglected.

Directors and staff face the tremendously complex challenge of supporting and strengthening bonds among family members; providing a safe and predictable environment for all who live and work in the shelter; and intervening effectively with families when the needs of children and parents conflict, without a clear consensus from the experts.[11] The debate does underscore the need for shelter directors and staff to find ways to enable parents to feel in control with their children regardless of which child discipline policy the program chooses to adopt. Given this perspective, program policies that explicitly take control out of parents' hands appear to be the most problematic.

Stories of Shared Care for Children

Using a family support framework as a standard, successful partnerships are those in which the partners view themselves as a "we" rather than as an "other." These relationships are built on trust, a trust strong enough to weather stress and conflict. In the rest of this chapter, I offer an in-depth picture of relationships between staff members and the mothers with whom they worked. These stories provide a window into the ways in which shelter staff members and mothers handled difficult and complex situations in their relationships with each other as they shared responsibility for the care of children. Some of the helping approaches meet the family support standard. Others are examples of help giving that resulted in mothers feeling humiliated and stigmatized. All these stories illustrate the degree to which staff and mothers in family shelters are treading on sensitive, demanding, and uncharted territory as they try to partner with each other, willingly or unwillingly, to care for children.

Knowing when help is effective is a complicated enterprise. Is help effective when a parent's behavior toward her child changes in a positive direction but she feels humiliated and judged by the staff member's interventions with her? Or, is help effective only if it contributes to a mother's sense of self-worth as a parent and if it helps her to envision herself as a worthy mother? Is help effective only if both parties say it is? Is help effective only if a staff member sees a behavior change? Staff members may not always know what impact they have had, positively or negatively, on a parent's actions, thoughts, or feelings toward her child. However, for their work to be meaningful, staff members need to feel a sense of efficacy in their interactions with families. Are there certain helping behaviors that are effective no matter what? For example, is praise of a mother always a good way to provide support? The following stories will add grist to the mill in thinking about the answers to these questions. In the end, nothing about these issues is very straightforward or simple.

Stories of Exemplary Help Giving

Sensitive offer to help.   Rosalinda was a bright, energetic, twenty-one-year-old Latina mother of two children, ages six and four. This was her second time being homeless and living in a family shelter. The previous episode had occurred when she was a teenager, five years earlier. During the current homeless episode, she and her children had moved in with a series of relatives. None of these moves were permanent. As a result, the welfare department arranged for her to live in a hotel shelter until space was available in a congregate family shelter. At the time I interviewed her, she and her children had lived in the family shelter for four and a-half months. Her room was located in the shelter's house on the first floor, easily accessible to others who often came to her door ready to visit. During the times that I spent in this shelter, I often saw Rosalinda and Susanna, one of the Latina staff members I interviewed, informally talking in Spanish and laughing in the common space across from Roslinda's room. In fact, Susanna was fixing Rosalinda's braids on more than one occasion. Susanna told me that Rosalinda was a good mother. Rosalinda was quick to think of a story in which Susanna had helped her with her children, since that very day such an incident had occurred. One of her sons had accidentally knocked the family's belongings from shelves in the room. Rosalinda said that she was furious with her son and yelled at him, ordering him to pick everything up. "I raise my voice, I really raise my voice." Susanna knocked on her door and asked if everything was okay. Rosalinda told her what happened and said she was okay. Susanna's nonjudgmental presence helped to diffuse and calm the situation. This mother said that she really appreciates the help she gets from Susanna. She told me that Susanna makes her feel as though she really cares about her, as though she is a sister she has never had, and has told her that she deals with her own children in the same way that Rosalinda does. Susanna reported that when Rosalinda is having a problem with her son, Susanna reminds herself whose child this is, not hers but Rosalinda's, demonstrating a deep understanding of the centrality of mothering in Rosalinda's self-identity.

Mutuality in the relationship.   I met Jacqueline in her family's newly acquired rental apartment in Boston, where she lived with her five children and her husband. She was a striking, thirty-seven-year-old Haitian woman with five strapping children, ranging in age from four to eighteen years of age. She and her family became homeless when her husband lost his job and the family could not pay their $1,000 per month rental fee on Jacqeline's nursing assistant wages. This rental charge is typical for two-bedroom apartments in Boston.[12] Their situation worsened when she developed a heart problem and had to take time off from her nursing-home job, one that provided no sick time. After a series of failed attempts to get help, the family was able to receive emergency assistance to pay their rent for three months. However, they had no money to pay for heat and were unable to keep up with their rental payments after the emergency assistance ended. In the middle of winter they were evicted from their apartment and slept in their car for three nights. Jacqueline's youngest son's asthma worsened. The family received help from the police, who directed them to an agency with funds to pay for them to spend a few nights in a room, with one bed, in one of the fanciest hotels in Boston. The family greatly appreciated the temporary relief. Jacqueline told me that the kids were "so happy and crying. I told them, I don't know. Let's take it one day at a time. I talked to them and said we are in a situation, and no matter what happens, Mommy is going to help you and we are going to get out of here." After seven months in a motel shelter, they were finally able to get into the family shelter. Through all this, Jacqueline and her husband managed to get their children to school each day: "I had to get up every morning and dress the kids and get them to school. I had to take a cab to the train station to take the orange line, then the red line to take them to school, and after that I have to go to work . . . for seven months."

After some time in the family shelter, both parents were back to work. Ironically, their combined income became too high for them to continue to be eligible for shelter, even though they had not found affordable housing and had not been able to save enough to move out of the shelter. Tragically, the only way the staff and family could solve this problem was for her husband to move out of the shelter. They had been able to stay together through their family's darkest days. Now that they were receiving public "emergency" assistance, family members had to be separated from each other. This turn of events hurt Jacqueline deeply.

Jacqueline and Susanna told me about their working relationship, in separate interviews. I found that their stories had tremendous consistency. Each talked about the other as a teacher. Jacqueline told me that Susanna helped her to understand her eighteen-year-old daughter's need for independence by helping Jacqueline to see how teenagers in the United States had more freedom than they did in Haiti. This enabled Jacqueline to cut her daughter some slack and improved her relationship with her daughter. "When you are talking, [Susanna] really listens." For her part, Susanna, the mother of two school-aged children, told me that she learned some parenting tips from Jacqueline, among them the value of delegating some household chores to children as a way of helping them learn a sense of responsibility. This relationship demonstrates the positive impact of mutuality between a help-giver and a receiver.

Help tailored to parent's learning style.   Luis, a Latino staff member, introduced me to Lanetta and told her in Spanish about the purpose of the study. Lanetta, a twenty-two-year-old mother of three children, ages three, two, and three months, greeted me at her bedroom door when I arrived to interview her. I followed her as she carried the baby and shepherded her two-year-old daughter down the hall and into the kitchen to watch for her bus. The oldest child was also enrolled in preschool, but was staying home, sick from the chicken pox. Several children had chicken pox during the two weeks in which I was interviewing mothers and staff in this and another shelter. Lanetta had been living in the shelter with her children for five months and had given birth to her youngest during this time. The shelter had become their home and the staff her family. She and her children became homeless due to the children's father's drug addiction. Unbeknownst to Lanetta, he had been using their money for drugs and had not been paying the rent. As a result, they were evicted from their apartment. Lanetta and her partner separated, and the welfare department put the family up in a motel shelter until this family shelter had an opening.

Lanetta and her family were involved with the state child protection agency, and Lanetta talked about her protective services social worker as a supporter. In fact, she seemed to assume that others knew much better than she did about how to take care of children. "All the staff tell me that all mothers who have kids should make sure they are fed, that they are not dirty . . . make sure the diapers are changed because they could get a rash." She was very tuned in to her infant throughout the interview, responding to him each time he cried or fussed. Her three-year-old son, Leonardo, came to the bedroom door several times while we were talking. She spoke harshly to him in Spanish when he did. Lanetta viewed help from the staff, including assistance she received from Luis, as helpful. "I feel that because they are trying to help me and my kids . . . I feel like I'm going to be a mother to my kids."

Luis told me about a particular situation in which he had tried to help Lanetta learn about the care of children. He had noticed that she was not feeding her preschoolers before they went to school. They were showing signs of being hungry. When he talked with Lanetta about this, she said she wasn't feeding them at the shelter because they get breakfast at preschool. He suggested that she check with the children's doctor about what children should eat. "Sometimes she responds, sometimes she doesn't. When she sees me around breakfast time in the shelter, she remembers. Her attitude toward me is very respectful . . . she believes that I am trying to help her . . . sometimes she thinks about what I have to say, and I have seen that she is trying."

This story illustrates the value of tailoring help giving to the individual learning style and needs of a mother. Luis skillfully and nonjudgmentally matched his help-giving actions to that desired by Lanetta.

Active, discreet intervention without judgment.   Joanne, a Caucasian middle-aged woman, worked as a family life advocate in a program that espoused "family support" beliefs. I asked Joanne about past personal or professional experiences that had affected the ways in which she provided help. She said that her help giving was influenced by her own experiences in receiving help. As a foster mother of a troubled adolescent, she and her husband were in touch with a multitude of helpers, many of whom emphasized their flaws: "Our strengths in asking for help and dealing with our son were rarely recognized," she said. "Social workers should all have to receive services as part of their training, part of their personal training. They should have to go in and ask for help. That would make things different." Joanne was determined to start with strengths in her work with families, and as she described situations in which she was providing help to mothers, she consistently gave examples in which she showed respect for the parents' choices, desires, timetables, and competencies, including the following story.

Liz was a thirty-nine-year-old Caucasian woman with three children, the oldest an eleven-year-old son. Liz would sometimes scream at her children as they walked through the shelter. According to Joanne, Liz felt a deep sense of failure as a parent. Her oldest son was often the receiver of his mother's sharp tongue. Other parents had a hard time approaching Liz when she was in a hostile or angry state of mind. Joanne felt compelled to intervene when Liz's children were on the receiving end of their mother's angry words. In response to my question regarding what she did that she found worked, Joanne said that she would take Liz into a private room away from the situation. She would just sit with her for a bit, let her talk and vent until she calmed down. Then, she would say, "This is really hard." There would be tears, and Liz would get in touch with her sadness. Joanne felt that being willing to be with Liz through the whole process was what worked. Liz told me that Joanne helped her by sharing her personal experiences with her own son. "She could relate to what I was going through . . . she was always there," without judgment. This story illustrates the impact of supportively connecting with a mother's desire to be a good parent in the face of her profound disappointment with herself.

Affirmation of parent's importance to her children.   Alice, the staff member mentioned early in this chapter, told me about offering help to Connie, who had reunited with her son, daughter, and husband in the shelter. Due to Connie's drug and alcohol addiction, her husband and children lived in the shelter for four months before they were reunited. Alice was sensitive to Connie's acute and deep sense of shame, the major obstacle in her efforts to reunite with her family and establish herself as a wife and mother again. Alice tried to support Connie by regularly sharing her observations regarding the positive changes she saw in the children as a direct result of contact with their mother, in particular her playfulness with them. Alice described Connie's work in addressing her son's temper tantrums: Connie helped her son to overcome this behavior by using all the supports available, including a parenting class, Headstart, collaboration with his teachers, and personal counseling.

I interviewed Connie, twenty-five years of age, in the family's newly acquired apartment. The apartment was filled with lush greenery, the product of Connie's "green thumb." She was very calm and loving with her adorable three-year-old daughter as we talked. Connie had tears in her eyes as she told me about how her addiction led to her family's homelessness and separation. She was grateful for the help she had received in the shelter. She was not as offended by the ways that staff interacted with parents as were other mothers I interviewed. This story illustrates the positive impact of affirming support in the helping relationship, even in the context of a shelter setting that is directive, prescriptive, and deficit-oriented. In this instance, the staff member and mother were on the same wave length.

The healing role of an apology.   Jesse, a thirty-year-old Caucasian woman with an infant, was fighting an alcohol addiction that led to her becoming homeless. Phyllis, a middle-aged Caucasian staff member, saw her as being without the support of friends or family, a woman who was both angry and isolated. Although Phyllis felt they had a good relationship, she could remember no situation in which she felt successful as a helper with Jesse. "I remember I was afraid of [her anger] in the beginning. Once I overcame that, we really . . . connected. I could tell because I crossed the barrier of her anger. I didn't let that keep me away. . . . Like she had her walls, and I could have stayed outside." Jesse confirmed this barrier in their relationship: "I put up a shield of armor. She had to climb over that wall. She wanted to be helpful. . . . We didn't get along from the beginning to the day I left . . . we were alike, we're both controlling.'

Jesse reported that she connected with the director of the shelter, not Phyllis. The director of the shelter recognized her strengths: "Ann thought I was doing wonderful with my small baby. . . . She recognized my strong will—that I was going through a lot of emotional stress, with alcohol, with his father, with my other children [who were not living with her], with being pregnant . . . that I was holding a lot together. To be so strong-willed and still take care of my child, to stay and not run. She gave me a lot of credit. . . . When she [overstepped her authority with me], she always apologized." This story underscores the impact of personal styles and chemistry in affecting the helping relationship, as well as the importance of having at least one person who recognizes a mother's courage and strength. It also illustrates a mother's readiness to forgive when a staff member acknowledges her shortcomings in the relationship.

Stories of Stigmatizing Help Giving

Surprise public attack.   Fran was a twenty-two-year-old Caucasian mother of two children, ages six and three. I met her in her apartment, located a few blocks from the shelter she and her children had lived in for four months. By remaining in the same neighborhood when the family moved out of the shelter, her daughter did not have to change elementary schools. She and her children became homeless after a series of misfortunes hit her family of origin. Her mother, with whom she had been living, died suddenly. Fran and her children moved in with a series of relatives in two states. No arrangement lasted long, due to overcrowding and family violence.

She moved out of the shelter precipitously, into an unsubsidized apartment, due to the actions of a shelter staff member that left Fran feeling shamed and humiliated. Tina, a Caucasian staff member, had organized a surprise "group confrontation" with Fran, who had been isolating herself and her children from others in the house. At the end of a house meeting, Tina asked Fran to listen while the other mothers, who had been prepped behind Fran's back, confronted her about their suspicions that she was using drugs. Tina told me that this "intervention" had been successful. As a helper, she felt efficacious. Fran, who told me that this was the final straw for her, felt shamed and humiliated by the public confrontation. Tina and Fran were clearly on different wavelengths. Tina's actions had troubled Fran enough to cause her to move out of the shelter before she had secured a housing subsidy, into an apartment Tina considered substandard.

Fran did, however, appreciate what Tina had done for her on other occasions. She maintained her ties with the shelter and was still receiving help from Tina. Fran had the courage to set boundaries in their relationship by moving out of the shelter and using Tina's help in a way that protected her dignity. "She always tried to make herself available to me because she understood a lot of what I was going through. She would even go for walks with me outside of the shelter to help me deal with things that I couldn't deal with inside." Fran told me about a situation in which Tina had helped her to resolve a serious problem with another mother who had screamed at her daughter. Fran said that this other mother was really hard to get along with, "obnoxious and rude." She asked Tina for help on many occasions regarding how to deal with the other mother's behavior toward Fran's daughter. "[The other mother] yelled at my daughter's face and was swearing at her, and really, just being in that situation really got to me," Fran told me. Tina's response was to put the responsibility back on Fran's shoulders for making peace with this woman, likening the situation to one that Fran might have to face later in her own apartment, living near someone whom she didn't like. Tina talked with each mother separately and then mediated a session in which the two mothers cleared the air directly with each other.

In response to my question about how Tina's help in this situation felt, Fran said that, although she was very uncomfortable talking directly with the other mother, it worked. Tina had a different perception about the effectiveness of her actions. She felt very unsuccessful in helping these two mothers to resolve their problems: "I tried everything, but just forget it. They were told to stay away from each other. It was a failure because they could never resolve anything, but I think it was because of their [cultural] backgrounds. There were just irreconcilable differences. Neither side wanted to give at all to the other." In this situation, Tina judged her help giving to be ineffective, while Fran considered her actions to be effective. Once again they were not on the same wavelength.

Oppressive supervision. Louise asked to be interviewed away from the shelter in which she and her two-year-old son, Seth, had lived for the past eight months. We talked together in the home of Seth's grand-mother, which seemed to be Louise's off-shelter home base. Her job, her son's child care, and her own school were not far from this house, which she could use as a stopping pad but not as a permanent resi-dence. Louise was a twenty-two-year-old African American woman with tremendous presence. She was extremely articulate and sensitive to issues of power in her relationships with helping professionals. She had a clear sense of the ways she could take charge of her life in the face of what she considered to be heavy-handed power maneuvers of the shelter staff. She had made plans to enroll in nursing school. Throughout the two-hour interview, Louise treated her young son with great sensitivity and talked about his grandmother as a very pos-itive supporter.

She was quite bitter about the help she had received from Janice, the Caucasian family life advocate at the shelter. The level of disagree-ment between her and Janice ran so deep that Louise simply tried to stay away from the shelter as much as she could. Louise could describe no situation in which she and Janice had resolved their differences successfully. When I asked her about Janice's help in the area of par-enting, she said, "She doesn't have kids . . . they [the staff] don't have kids and they are always voicing their opinions. Janice does consider me taking care of my son fine. She is always saying how well I do with him, how well I take care of him, and how well-hygiened he is and clothed. I always tell her, why shouldn't he be. Just because I am in a shelter doesn't mean anything." She went on to say that the staff assumed there must be some drug problem, or substance abuse, or psychiatric disorder responsible for families becoming homeless. "They dig deeper and deeper, and it is like wait a minute . . . something has to be wrong with you . . . I keep proving them wrong . . . she agrees that I take care of my son very well."

Janice's characterization of her relationship with Louise was very consistent with Louise's version. Janice felt very stuck. She was required by her director to monitor each of the mothers' activities. She described her checking up as a violation of Louise's integrity. She described its destructive effects on her own sense of integrity by using a powerful metaphor from her southern roots: "I am required to do this thing and so I have mixed feelings about that and so stuff comes up the side of my neck. . . . In the South, you say the stuff comes up the side of your neck. What that means is that southern white women can say all kind of pretty things to each other and what we are really saying is, 'I hate your guts . . . and get the hell out of my life.' What happens is we put on a pretty face, but then our actions tell that there is something else going on. So, it's like a hidden agenda and it just kind of oozes out of your body, and that is coming up the side of your neck. With Louise, I want to 'leave her be' because I know that she is doing all the things she needs to do. I don't necessarily agree with the way she does them, but I think she's doing what she needs to do. But, my job requires me to check up on her. So, with my mouth I'm saying that I am doing this because I am required to and all of my conflicting feelings about doing that stuff, and getting my back up against a wall . . . all of it is inside me."

This story illustrates the courage and wisdom of a mother who found ways to care for her son, move ahead with her aspirations, judiciously use the support of family, and deal with oppressive helping practices. It also depicts the negative impact of inhumane agency directives on a staff member's sense of integrity.

Humiliating oversight. Julie, a twenty-year-old woman of mixed ethnicity (African American and Caucasian) and her twelve-month-old son became homeless when their apartment building burned down. After a stressful bureaucratic tussle with two welfare offices, she was able to move into a motel for a week until an emergency family shelter had an opening. I interviewed Julie in her new apartment a month after she left the shelter. She told me how bitter she was about being treated like a child and being treated as someone who was flawed. She reported struggling with self-doubt about herself as a parent resulting from this treatment.

One of the situations she described as being most demeaning and humiliating while she was in the shelter was having to give medications to her child with staff watching and logging her movements. This was the only shelter I visited in which medications were kept in a locked box in the staff office and were doled out under staff supervision. The staff office was a small space shared by four to five staff members. For children to receive medications or any kind of pill, the mother had to ask permission from a staff member to unlock the box. With staff watching, the mothers gave the pill or liquid medication to the child, while a staff member noted in a logbook that this event had occurred. Julie described the humiliating scene: "You go in there for an aspirin, and it was [from staff], 'swallow it right in front of me.' Like when he had an ear infection, so amoxicillin was becoming very familiar and he was living on it almost everyday. [He] had to take the medicine, . . . and he fought taking the medicine . . . all in that office with business people coming in and out, and with people typing, and you are right there, in the middle of all that, trying to put some medicine down your kid's throat."

Later that day, when I returned to the shelter from my interview with Julie, I witnessed this situation actually happening with a mother, her sick infant, and active toddler. Four staff members watched as she tried to give a liquid antibiotic to her infant, at the same time as she tried to keep her toddler from running down the hall. The staff member then logged this event in a book that is kept in the staff office. I wondered how this mother felt with all these eyes, including mine, watching her struggle to give medication to her children. Many of the mothers I interviewed from this shelter provided detailed descriptions of other stigmatizing and humiliating interactions with staff members. The impact of these shaming experiences appeared to be profound.

Imposition of staff priorities. Martha was an energetic, thirty-year-old Caucasian mother of four children, ages ranging from three months to eleven years. She was very lively and articulate throughout our interview. I witnessed her charisma in action with other parents throughout the time I spent in this shelter. Others looked to her for both leadership in speaking out with staff and for a good laugh. She had a great sense of humor. Martha was managing to juggle many roles while she and her children lived in the shelter. In addition to the ongoing care of her children, attending eight mandatory meetings a week, and conducting a housing search, she was also attending nursing school, teaching religious education in her family's church, coaching her daughter's cheerleading team, and volunteering in the community.

Martha and her middle-class family became homeless due to the loss of her husband's job during the late-1980s economic slump in Massachusetts. Unfortunately, her husband was unable to get his own business off the ground. They could not keep up with their mortgage payments with their sole predictable income source being Martha's full-time salary. She worked a full-time job and worked as her husband's bookkeeper and sales and customer service representative during this period. Martha was pregnant at the time. In her sixth month of pregnancy, she developed a problem that required bed rest for the remainder of the pregnancy. She had to quit her job. In spite of both parents' best attempts, the family had no steady income. The bank finally foreclosed on their property and evicted them from their home. "We went from making $67,000 to $7,000. . . . It was like a vicious cycle. One door opens, but four get slammed in your face." Family tensions ran high throughout this difficult period, exacerbating her husband's drinking problem. Martha and her husband separated. She and the children moved from one relative or friend to another but were unable to find a permanent affordable housing situation. Martha described feeling very humiliated by having to be on welfare and living in a shelter. She was very angry about the ways in which she and other parents were treated in the shelter, but she nonetheless remained open to the help staff members gave her.

This highly competent mother of four told me a story about pressure and advice two staff members were giving her regarding how to manage her time better in an effort to enable her to have more one-on-one time with her children. As a twosome, they planned a series of meetings with Martha, focused on this goal that they had in mind for her. Martha viewed these meetings as more of a burden than a help. She felt that her efforts to be active with her children's after-school activities were being criticized rather than supported. In Martha's mind, many of the required meetings in the shelter were not as essential for her as were the commitments she had with her children in the community. Martha was particularly affronted by getting such advice from Sheila, one of these staff members, who was not a parent herself. Sheila, a twenty-six-year-old Caucasian woman, told me how frustrated she was about Martha's lack of openness to her advice, "I'm not sure if it's a matter of trust or pride," she said. This story illustrates the negative effect on a mother's sense of herself and on the helping relationship when a mother is forced to comply with priorities and goals that are not her own.

Making Sense of the Stories

As I interviewed the thirty-nine mothers who were living or had lived in one of the five shelter programs I visited, I was deeply moved by the stories they recounted of the devastation related to becoming homeless. I was awed by their resilience, their strengths, and the ways in which they had made sense of these traumatizing events. Each mother had unique competencies and hopes for their families, with distinctly different past life experiences and expectations regarding what shelter life would offer. Some were newly poor; others had known no economic circumstance other than poverty. Some became parents in their early teenage years; others became mothers in their twenties or at a later age. Some maintained close relationships with a wide range of friends and kin; others had few social supports. Some became homeless as a result of a misfortune such as a job loss, health problem, inadequate income, or a fire; others fell into homelessness as a consequence of an out-of-control chemical addiction. Some mothers appeared to learn by watching and following the actions of staff members they trusted; others learned through a talking and listening process with staff members they trusted. Still others seemed to learn by following clear suggestions provided by staff members they trusted. Some were very outgoing, articulate, and ready to declare their wishes and needs; others were reticent, more private, and less ready to assert themselves with those in authority.

This diversity presents a challenge for helpers in shelters, particularly when the focus of their work together is the shared care for children. Staff must manage the uneasy tension involved in figuring out how to offer supportive and nonintrusive help. They have to find ways to balance the needs of children while respecting parents' roles in their children's lives, essential if the relationship is to work at all. The most promising helping approaches were those in which shelter staff responded sensitively and privately to parents' concerns about their children, when they actively intervened without judgment, and when they were able to resolve child-rearing differences. The most ineffective helping approaches were those in which shelter staff criticized and publicly humiliated mothers. Staff members need ongoing support, supervision, and training to enable them to deal with the vicarious stress they absorb as they become part of families' lives in shelters and with the complicated situations that arise between parents and their children each day in these settings.

Unlike other nonresidential helping settings, the contacts between helpers and mothers in these settings have no natural time and space boundaries. Helpers and mothers are thrown together whether they have compatible personalities or not. Having at least one person to turn to during residency in shelter was a commonly referred-to safety valve for many mothers. A minimum of one comfortable, trusting connection did not guarantee a smooth journey for the family and staff but it did provide mothers with a safe avenue for relieving stresses that are inherent for all families living in communal settings.

The mothers I talked with were hungry for good help. They were willing to forgive staff members for indiscretions, if staff members admitted to their mistakes and were human with them. Mothers' advice to other mothers was clear: if staff are heavy-handed in the use of their authority and untrustworthy, keep to yourself. For those who felt connected and trusted staff, their advice to other mothers was to be open. Mothers' and staff members' stories underscored the importance of reciprocity in their relationships, which reduces indebtedness in the relationship. If mothers feel as if they are the only ones benefitting from the relationship, receiving help will carry too high a burden and price. Indebtedness leads to closedness in the relationship.[13] Some of the staff I interviewed talked about what they had learned from the mothers in their shelters, what they were getting from the relationship, and how they communicated these insights to the mother. A recognition of parents' assets and strengths is required for such reciprocity to exist.

Staff, mothers, and directors are part of each others' lives, whether they like it or not. Staff and directors may pour themselves out going the extra mile to help someone. However, they may not see what happens and may not know in what ways they have had an impact on families' lives. Mothers may not be able to change the ineffective and humiliating behaviors of some staff or of other mothers. Everyone may feel somewhat out of control.

Clearly, institutional supports and constraints have an impact on the behaviors of individual staff members. Some bureaucratic requirements negate family support principles and limit the extent to which an individual staff member can foster mutuality in the helping relationship. However, as indicated by the stories and program policies described in this chapter, a proactive institutional strategy for operating from family support principles is essential.

In the next section, Deborah Gray, mother, Mary Lewis, staff member, and Michelle Kahan, program director share their reflections on the themes covered in this chapter.

Reflections on Chapter 3

Reflection: Mother, Deborah Gray

Parenting can be one of the most challenging aspects of one's life. There are tremendous pressures applied from all sides—society, family members, schools, your partner, and even from yourself—to live up to others' expectations. It's one thing to have to deal with all these pressures in the privacy of your own home, but think again about how it must feel to have to make decisions and be consistent and clear about how you want to raise your child under the auspices of virtual strangers in a public shelter.

Parents usually feel that staff, like the social workers who placed them in the shelter, have already formed preconceptions about homeless parents. They act like you are a "bad" parent, like you must have done something wrong. You must not know how to make good decisions, and you definitely don't have any parenting skills. Some staff take over the role of the parent, leaving little room for discussion or negotiation. Of course, not all staff can be lumped into a pile and stereotyped as "off-the-wall," but most of my encounters with, and observations of, staff interacting with parents and children in shelter leave much to be desired. The burnout rate of social workers runs high, and the transient population they are dealing with in shelters may tend to blur the lines of objectivity and the need for human dignity.

Children in shelter, just as any other children who have moved and lost things, need to feel a sense of protection, that there are standards of conduct and structured daily routines to assist them in adapting to their new surroundings and perhaps to people who are familiar to them. It is understandable that the parent is responsible for her child, but let us not forget that the parent has been through a traumatic experience also, which has landed her in the position of being without a home. Rather than approaching the parent with an adversarial attitude, it appears to me that staff would do well to attend some diversity and sensitivity training sessions to better equip them to interact with families in crisis.

Cultural differences in child rearing and disciplinary methods become an issue in shelter. One culture may promote a certain attitude about how to raise children, while another may disapprove of that method—for example, holding a baby too much, spoiling them, not giving them everything they ask for, letting them disrespect their parents or other adults. No culture has 100 percent agreement on one method over another, but some predominant behaviors are evident in ethnic and cultural groups. While spanking, which I define as a pat or two on the bottom, is not the only way to get a child's attention, it is an acceptable method in many cultures. Spanking is "not allowed" in shelters, nor are any other forms of rough or rude behaviors toward children. So what is a parent to do, if spanking or yelling is the only method they know? Living in a shelter with clear rules of conduct and respectful interaction modeled by the staff can become the turning point for a parent who has been existing on the edge with her children in tow. This can be the perfect setting to help her get on track and pick up some new parenting skills by example. I do not mean to imply that staff should be complacent, permissive, or phony. I am however, making a plea for respectful treatment and nonjudgmental attitudes that can set the stage for building and maintaining healthy relationships.

When my children and I arrived in Boston, we had to stay in shelters until the housing subsidy was transferred from out of state. The shelters here were strict and seemed to have no problem finding out who was making waves and thus terminating their stay. My four young children and I had two adjourning rooms that just fit four bunk beds, a crib, a small dresser, kitchen table, and four chairs. The rule was "no children allowed in the hallways." The very long hallways were very tempting as places for young children to run and scream. In the intake interview I was told that if I couldn't control my children, DSS [Department of Social Services] would be called to open a case on me. I didn't even know who or what DSS was! The other mothers had no problem sharing horror stories about DSS taking women's children away and the long battles they had to fight to try to get them back. Certain mothers seemed to be singled out as troublemakers or as if they were just trying to "get over" (i.e., misuse the system, manipulate the staff, or get more than they were entitled to). They would be given three strikes, some less than that, and they were gone. Staff rarely interacted with us, except to give out the food, make us sign the monthly vouchers, and tell us about what our children were or weren't doing. I witnessed many an outburst of temper and angry bouts between certain staff and parents. Holding a torrent of emotions and bad feelings inside with no way to express them or deal with them properly was a constant battle.

Parents in shelter have many outside influences pressing down on them. The anger has to go somewhere. Perhaps shelters could offer stress-management sessions to help parents deal with the anger. An asset-based approach to helping parents in crisis can prove very effective, rather than using the deficit approach or assuming that parents have negative intentions. I remember the phrase, "Keep Hope Alive!" It picked me up when I felt myself sinking too low. The negative attitude of a staff person can bring down the best.

The shelter I was in discouraged mothers from getting together. We were not allowed to visit each other after a certain time at night. There were only supposed to be few women in the lobby at one time unless a lecture about drugs or safe sex was taking place. We formed our own little support groups to help encourage each other. We had to sign and turn in a baby-sitter's form to leave our children with another mother. We had to call in and tell the staff person on duty if we wanted another mother to get our children off the school bus and bring them upstairs. I guess the shelter was trying to protect the children, but they made it very difficult for the parents to do basic tasks like housing search, shopping, and laundry. Some parents clearly needed firmer structure and rules to help them care for their children's needs, but many parents are just caught in a poor situation, and know very well how to care for their children.

Everyone needs a break at some time. The stress of parenting in public puts significant pressure on mothers and children. My coping strategy was to take my children outside as much as possible. We went for long walks, to playgrounds, on bus rides, to museums—anything to get out and let loose. Near time to move out of the shelter, I began to take some children from other families with me to the playground about a block away from the shelter. It made all the difference for the children to get out and run and play and laugh.

Reflection: Program Director, Michelle Kahan

My introduction to the world of homeless family shelters was as a program director in a shelter with a "family support" philosophy. From the shelter residents and my colleagues, I learned a great deal about managing the complexities of working and living with families in crisis. When I began, we had the luxury of three full-time staff to assist four families. One staff member assisted the residents in attaining permanent housing; another served as their family life advocate, providing advocacy, referrals, and counseling; and I dealt with the administrative aspects. None of us were specifically trained or charged with working with the children, and none of us were parents. The case manager considered the children her clients, along with their parents; she planned special children's activities and groups, but her primary responsibility was to the adult members of the families. The housing search worker also loved children and had a great deal of experience as a nanny, so she gave them a lot of extra attention. Her time was limited, however, as she had a stressful and busy job.

This program had the resources to provide each family with their own two-bedroom apartment, with full kitchens. There was also an apartment that housed both the staff offices and a common living space where children could play and families could hang out in the evenings.

Relatively speaking, the families in this shelter had a great deal of privacy. Mothers did not have to feed or discipline their children in view of other families, and they could choose whether to spend time in the common areas. Our policy was to maintain the authority of the parent. We had rules designed to protect everyone's safety, around children's supervision, discipline, and baby-sitting, but the policies were liberal and we often modified them based on residents' input.

Even in these relatively ideal circumstances, I often felt like an intruder, witnessing private interactions between parents and children that I had no right, or desire, to see. Yet if what I saw was particularly concerning, I had an obligation not only to the family but also to the state. As human service workers, shelter staff are obligated to report any abuse or neglect of children to protective services. And as shelter director, I not only had to be concerned about the welfare of a particular child, and the families in the shelter at that point in time, but I also had to worry about the agency's future liability in case a critical report was not filed.

The few times when I did file a report on a child resulted in huge ramifications. I never did so without many consultations with the parent and other staff and without countless sleepless nights. Nevertheless, in addition to the strain on the relationship with the particular family I was reporting, in most cases many of the program residents became wary of myself and the other staff, and all of the work that had gone into building strong relationships with these families was jeopardized.

Toward the end of my tenure at this agency, we were fortunate to receive a grant to fund a part-time child advocate position. It took a great deal of time for the families to feel comfortable with this staff member, due to parental concerns that, as child advocate, it was her job to spy on relationships between parent and child, report to DSS, and have their children taken away. The job was also overwhelming. By the time this position was created, the agency had grown and was sheltering twenty-nine families, with an average of some seventy children at a time. In a twenty-four-hour work week, the child advocate was charged with providing support for all of these youngsters and their parents. Despite all of these difficulties, this position was an incredible boon to the agency. Finally, there was one staff member with expertise in working with children and, more important, whose primary responsibility was to the children, the shelter's unacknowledged clients.

While having a child advocate on staff does not remove the tensions inherent in working with mothers who are attempting to parent their children in crisis-filled circumstances, this addition does acknowledge that kids are growing up in family shelters. They, along with their parents, are in crisis, and they need extra support to make sense of all of the changes occurring in their families. Some parents are able to provide this additional support to assist their children in dealing with the upheaval in their lives, but many are too disempowered, ashamed, and overwhelmed by their own circumstances to do so.

By offering assistance to both parent and child, and by providing each member of the family with a safe place to work through the many issues raised by communal living, it is to be hoped that we can bolster the parent-child relationship through this difficult time. We cannot help a child without respecting the parent's authority. If I intervene with the child, I hinder respect for his or her mother, during a time when both parent and child are already feeling out of control. They need each other's support in order to get through these trying circumstances. And if the child leaves the shelter without respect for her parent, where does that leave either of them in the long run?

Recently I conducted a focus group at a family shelter program. While I waited for the conclusion of a previous session, a volunteer supervising the children brought them to the group, so that a child who was upset could connect with his mother for a moment. As the children's group left the mothers' session, observing that the children were generally a bit upset, I offered the volunteer some snacks that I had on hand for the focus group. The volunteer responded by saying that she didn't know how the mothers would feel about offering the snacks to the children. Her appropriate and respectful response reminded me that sometimes, even in seemingly simple situations, it can be difficult to honor parental roles.

Shelters can be incredibly overwhelming. There are lots of families from varied backgrounds living together in cramped quarters. They are in shelter because they have no other options; most have already done everything and anything within their power to stay out of shelter, but they've hit rock bottom and have nowhere else to go. It takes a highly trained staff with access to many resources to recognize and support both the strengths and the needs of these incredible women and their children.

Massachusetts' family shelter system was designed to serve adults, not children. The state-funded system was planned to provide temporary housing, not services. This dispute continues today, as advocates argue for increased shelter budgets to offer necessary services and state officials maintain that all assistance not directly related to housing is unwarranted. It is time for the state to recognize that until the affordable housing crisis is solved, shelter stays will continue to be long enough to require provision of services for both parents and children.

Reflection: Family Life Advocate, Mary Lewis

Responding to parenting concerns is one of my most difficult tasks. Being a "good enough" parent is at the core of each parent and is a cherished piece of a parent's identity. Homeless parents living in a congregate setting are forced to parent children—some of whom are upset due to the upheaval of homelessness—in public. Most parents feel a constant sense of being judged rather than supported. The dilemma for me, as a shelter staff member, is how to support each parent's right to her own parenting style, while preserving the sanity of the shelter and assuring the safety of the children whenever that comes into question.

Our shelter has rules about bedtime, quiet time, mealtimes, and appropriate child discipline. All children under ten must be with their parent at all times. Guests may not baby-sit each other's children if the parent is off property. Child care is provided only during mandatory group meetings. These are our rules, not necessarily the parent's rules. The challenge is to find ways to reinforce the parent's authority in an environment where the rules may not be their own.

As a parent, each of us does more than discipline our children. We nurture and protect them. We teach them and learn from them. We teach flexibility and respect as well as reading and numbers. As parents, we must be creative in our efforts to teach our children our values within an ever-changing and sometimes nonsupportive and nonaccepting environment. This is what a parent does. Sarah Ruddick (1989) states that the tasks central to mothering are the preservation of her children's safety, the nurturing of their growth, and the fostering of their social acceptability. The goal of fostering our children's social acceptability is manifest in teaching our children how to respect the rules of the community in which we live while holding onto our own family values. This takes creative thought and exploration.

Although all families must deal with this task, homeless families must deal with it much more intimately. Whereas I must adjust to rules outside my "home," they must adjust to rules within their "home" as well as within the community. This job is more difficult and needs more energy and support to be accomplished successfully. As a family life advocate I see my role as the person with whom a parent can explore the values she wants to support while in shelter. How can she nurture or support her children in ways that are acceptable in this shelter? How can she define her own family rituals that others within this community do not practice? Most important, what are the goals that she is trying to reach by performing this action or ritual? How else can she reach the goal within the framework of the shelter?

Families who are homeless have gone through a great deal of loss, criticism, and shame, both internal and external. They feel battered and weakened by the events that have forced them into the shelter. During this time of upheaval, parents have given their children the best that they had to give. For many, the sense that they are "good enough" parents is the one thing that they have left. To tread, even lightly, on this sense feels like an intrusion. However, I am responsible for assuring that the shelter runs smoothly and that mothers care for their children appropriately. This means I must ensure that parents put children to bed at a fixed bedtime and that children wear appropriate clothes and eat healthy meals. I must make sure that parents provide needed educational or day care programs and appropriate health care. I am also mandated to ensure that parents treat children safely and respectfully.

The advice from the mothers with whom I work is very helpful when entering this area with a parent. When there is a concern, I *ask* rather than direct. I ask with an open mind and clear desire to hear and understand. I *listen* rather than assume. I listen for the goal that this mom is trying to reach. I *respect* rather than judge. I respect that she too, wants to be a "good" mother and is acting in ways that she feels are supporting her goals. As worker and parent, together we can begin to develop goal-oriented, alternative means or behaviors that are more acceptable within our shelter community

A good example of this came from an incident with a parent who constantly took food (cookies and milk) up to her room in the evenings. Health concerns about insects and rodents made it impossible to permit this. The mother knew the rule, had been spoken to about violating the rule, yet continued with the same practice. Following the theory of resistance (see chapter 1), I asked what the sharing of cookies and milk in the evening in the privacy of their own room meant to her and her family. It turned out that it was a way she and her children had to spend calm, nurturing time together. It was a routine that they used to regroup and care for each other. It was an important family practice. She was responding intuitively to the children's need for nurturance, and this responsiveness needed to be honored by me as the shelter worker. However, we could not allow it in the shelter. Through conversation, the mother and I began to explore issues within her family that she identified as needing her extra attention. I began to understand that this mom was concerned about her daughter's difficult adjustment to the new school, the shelter, and the new community. The mother felt responsible for her daughter's hurt and sadness and wanted to nurture her. We began to brainstorm ways that this mom had used to nurture her family and this particular daughter in the past. We also discussed new ways to nurture that were acceptable within the shelter community. After we developed a list of acceptable strategies, she was able to make choices that she felt best supported her family. As parents, we are constantly faced with this challenge of flexibility verses consistency in maintaining our goal of family support.

Parents have the right to discipline and care for their children. No parent can do it all alone. It is my responsibility to assure the smooth running of the shelter and to guarantee that there is a fairness (not always equal) in all families' adherence to shelter rules. It is also my responsibility to respect the parent's rights. The most effective way I have found is to work with the parent to discover their parenting goals by asking them directly and listening to their responses. Then I can help them develop a list of ways to respond to their children in a manner that is comfortable within the community where they live now. Their time in shelter is short when compared to their lifetime. It may be difficult but need not be degrading. The skill of helping our children with social acceptability is one that we all use and need to continue to develop as effective parents.

4

Shelter Rules

The ethical imperative: act always to increase the number of choices.

—Heinz Von Foerster, *The Invented Reality*

Families who live in the shelter have to follow certain rules that govern their daily routines. They have to be up, dressed, and fed by 9:30 A.M. Preschool children have to be in bed by 8:00 P.M. each night. Residents are not allowed to visit each other in their rooms. Cooperative babysitting arrangements among parents are allowable, with staff authorization. The evening curfew for all families is 7.30 P.M..

Unbalanced power dynamics are unavoidable once staff members introduce shelter rules to parents. If a rule is meaningful at all, it has to be enforced. As agents of the sheltering organization, staff members, whether they like it or not, are the enforcers. As enforcers, they have authority over parents and their children. These rules are part of the very first conversations that take place when a family is considering entry into a family shelter. Agreement to a shelter's rules is a required part of the contract parents make with program staff in exchange for moving into the shelter. All families arrive at the shelter door stressed, most are traumatized by their immediate homeless situation and all of the events that have led to their being without a home. Desperate for a roof over their heads, parents have little to no choice other than to agree with the conditions laid out by the program.

Rules have some obvious advantages. They have the potential to be helpful in taking the surprise and unpredictability out of regular interactions among parents and children. Rules reduce the numbers of ways parents and staff have to negotiate with each other to work out each party's role in these everyday interactions. Negotiation takes time, energy, and patience. Assuming that most parents' and staff members' patience runs thin at times in these communal settings, if some interactions are predictable and not up for grabs each minute, rules could function as stress relievers.

Undeniably, some rules are necessary for maintaining safety and order in communal settings in which large numbers of young children and their parents live together. However, staff members and directors have the power to establish rules that go far beyond this purpose. That is, they can create rules that reflect their opinions about how parents should live their lives, including how and what they eat, how they handle personal hygiene, how they spend their time, when they go to bed, when they rise, and whom they befriend. A distinct disadvantage of rules that go beyond maintenance of safety and order and aim, in a paternalistic manner, to modify parents' personal behavior is the contribution they make to increasing parents' sense of low self-worth by setting into motion a humiliating parent–child dynamic in the relationship.

How mothers and staff work out authority and power issues within the family shelter context is similar to the dynamics between families on public assistance and their local welfare workers. Paternalistic practices have been codified in federal and state welfare legislation and in government contracts with the nonprofit organizations that carry out government's work with families in need of public assistance and emergency assistance. Welfare reform stipulations in every state include behavioral and procedural requirements as a condition for receipt of cash assistance. Local welfare workers, like family shelter staff and managers, are caught in the middle as the implementers of policies they did not create. They may find ways to counteract the paternalistic stipulations in their contacts with families or fall prey to an insidious process of control and power that in the end serves to disempower both them and those they serve. The experiences of managers, staff, and mothers explored in this chapter are instructive for all stakeholders in the welfare debate.

This chapter examines the diverse ways shelter programs establish and monitor compliance with rules. These rules cover most aspects of families' daily lives, including the care of children, shared living spaces, daily schedules, alcohol or drug use, budgeting or saving money, and mandatory meetings. The stories of managers, staff, and mothers provide a glimpse into the impacts of these rules on the mothers and children who are subject to them, as well as on the managers and staff who enforce them. We have explored some of these areas of rule making in previous chapters, such as rules covering the care for children, meal times, protection of belongings, and household chores. This chapter provides detail on how rules work in other areas of shelter life and explores the cumulative impact of shelter rules on families and on relationships between families and staff.

When I first began this study, I had no idea that rule making would cover so many aspects of families' lives. Several key studies[1] had informed my intellectual, researcher-self about these issues. However, I found that by speaking with several articulate mothers who had lived in a family shelter with their children,[2] my mother-self became engaged. As these women told me the details of their experiences, I imagined what it would be like for me and my family to have been in their shoes. I am convinced that I would have had a very difficult time stomaching being told what to do by other adults, even if they found the nicest ways of giving me the messages. As I listened to the stories of managers, staff, and mothers, and observed them as they interacted with each other around some of the rules, I gained a sense of respect for all of the parties to these delicate negotiations. Imagining myself in the shoes of managers and frontline staff, I was at a loss at times in envisioning better ways of handling some of the difficult situations that they described to me. I also witnessed mothers putting aside their egos for the sake of their children and accepting direction from adults who in some instances were not parents, were younger, and did not share the same ethnic roots.

There are no simple ways of dealing with the complex and sensitive matters that come up hourly and daily in these settings. Programs that try to be responsive and respectful of families have a difficult balance to strike. That is, they have to determine the areas of life in which the safety risks are too great to allow deviation from the norm and the areas of life in which there is room for experimentation and diversity. The scope of issues and variety of decisions these managers, staff, and families must deal with related to shelter rules is very extensive. On average, programs had rules in thirteen of the sixteen dimensions of shelter life that I included in my questions. Almost universally, programs had rules regarding the supervision of children, household chores, alcohol or drug use, curfews, visitors, child discipline, overnight passes, child bedtimes, and phone use. However, programs differed considerably in the specific ways they formulated and enforced their policies.

The experience of shelter living may be quite different for families, depending upon which shelter they found themselves living in. In Massachusetts that is largely a matter of chance.[3] For example, parents in some shelters were required to rise at a certain time each morning, while those in other shelters were free to set their own rising time. Parents in some shelters were required to cook the evening meal on a rotating basis for the entire community, while those in other shelters cooked only for their own families. Some families lived in shelter programs in which visits between residents in their rooms were restricted, while others visited freely with each other throughout the shelter.

Based upon the stories managers and staff members told me, certain problems arose with families that seemed to drive program personnel to consider the creation of a rule. Sometimes programs created rules to avoid problematic experiences they had had with families who had lived in the shelter in the past. Those rules continued even though current resident families might not have had a propensity to deal with similar situations in problematic ways. For example, some programs would not allow parents to baby-sit for each other as a result of past abuses of the practice. While there are risks associated with allowing cooperative baby-sitting arrangements, the benefits have been documented.[4] As I have already mentioned, the majority of the state's congregate shelters have found that the benefits outweigh the risks and have decided to allow this practice.

Some programs created rules as a way of refraining from singling out particular parents who were having a problem. Ironically, such attempts could inadvertently result in every family feeling that it had been singled out. For example, a few staff members described their concerns about the personal hygiene of some parents and their children. One of these staff members told me that the solution she was planning for her shelter was to require that each family accept instructions about hygiene and a hygiene packet, containing washcloths, toothbrushes, and soap, during their intake interview. She said that she was going to do this as a way of avoiding having to single out any one family. My hair stood on end as I listened to her. I imagined how humiliating it would be as a parent to be lectured to about how to keep myself and my children clean. I would assume that this staff person believed that my family was homeless because I was a deficient parent, not only in providing a roof for my children but also in caring for them in other basic ways. I found myself doubting that this one lesson would eliminate all hygiene problems. If a family had trouble keeping clean, staff members would have to deal with that family in a very particular way to address the problem.

No mother I interviewed thought that shelters should do away with all rules. They believed that some rules were essential. Although shelter rules were difficult to deal with, mothers understood the need for rules that increased the predictability and safety for themselves and their children. Mothers' dissatisfactions tended to be related to the inordinate amount of power managers and staff members had in determining and enforcing the shelter rules, as compared with their own limited avenues for influencing shelter operations. While all of the mothers told me that house meetings were the one way in which parents could voice their dissatisfactions with shelter rules and try to change them, they said that the most basic rules, such as allowable smoking areas, curfews, or overnight passes, were not negotiable. Those rules that were open to negotiation were, for the most part, less consequential.

On the positive side, mothers in all programs told me that staff did their best to make the changes that parents recommended. Their negative assessments were very specific. Some mothers told me that at times staff needed to be tougher rule enforcers with other parents. Many complained that staff did not ask for their input about house meeting agendas, that rules became harsher if parents raised objections, and that, without notice or consultation with parents, managers and staff devised new rules as they wished. Mothers I interviewed from programs using a "family support" approach were considerably more satisfied with program rules on the whole than were mothers in programs using a paternalistic approach—67 percent compared to 42 percent. Considerably higher percentages of mothers in the family support programs were satisfied with program rules in nine of the sixteen rule-making areas, with some differences being quite large. The detail on these matters follows.

Shelter Rules

Other chapters cover shelter rules related to mealtime routines, household chores, locking bedroom doors (chapter 2), child bedtimes, supervision of children, and child discipline (chapter 3), and mandatory meetings (chapter 5). In the following section I explore additional areas of shelter life commonly addressed in shelter program policies in Massachusetts.

Bathroom Use

The overwhelming majority of programs had no rules governing shared use of bathroom spaces. For the most part, families sorted this out among themselves. Those few programs with a rule about bathroom use focused on the responsibility of parents to supervise their young children in the bathroom, clean the bathroom after use, and remove their belongings immediately after use. One manager described a more extreme, and apparently ineffective, policy related to personal hygiene:"Everyone is expected to shower daily and keep the bathroom area neat and clean up after their family's use. This is all ideal circumstances.You realize none of this happens," she said.

None of the programs I spent time in had rules governing bathroom use. The staff members I interviewed were satisfied with this approach but were concerned about the ways in which families maintained the cleanliness of the bathrooms and worked out sharing time among themselves for use of the bathrooms. For the most part the mothers I interviewed were fairly satisfied with the ways programs enabled families to work out shared bathroom use among themselves; this included over half of those in "family support" programs and nearly three-quarters of those in programs with a "get tough" orientation.[5] Those who were dissatisfied worried about the cleanliness of bathrooms and told me that negotiating "time-sharing" with other parents was difficult.

Accommodating Visitors

Another aspect of communal living involves accommodating visitors—that is, friends and family of parents and children living in the shelter. Only two shelters had no rules regarding visitors. About one out of ten banned all visitors. These program managers told me that the prohibition was the result of either limited space or concerns for the safety of family residents. "We don't allow visitors. . . . That's become more important as we've gotten members of gangs in the shelter. In this town, gang members shoot each other. So we want to avoid any of that happening in and around the shelter," one manager said. He made exceptions for family members who visited from out of town.

The vast majority of programs had developed rules governing who could visit, for how long, and in what areas of the shelter. A few shelters banned all male visitors. A few others prohibited abusive husbands from visiting. One manager put it this way: "If there's a restraining order against that person by a resident, they can't visit. . . . That situation has happened three or four times in the past six months." Several directors described polices in which staff either have to approve all visitors or have to be notified of any prospective visitors. A few programs set limits on the numbers of visitors any one family could have during a visit.

The timing of visits was highly varied among those programs that allowed visitors. Some had no designated visiting hours but asked that visitors leave before the evening curfew. Others designated certain hours of certain days as visiting hours. One manager tied her program's restrictive hours to the shelter's limited space: "Generally we ask clients to let us know when they expect visitors, as a matter of confidentiality. No visitors during meals or after curfew. We're very small, one big common area. We encourage moms to do something with visitors [outside the shelter], rather than sit in there with everyone else. The whole set-up is tight." A majority of programs limited visitors to the common areas within the shelters. An uncommon and highly restrictive rule described by three managers was a prohibition against residents visiting with each other in their bedrooms or living units.

Other approaches for incorporating visitors were more receptive than those described above. For example, a handful of programs welcomed visitors to join in the communal meal or to stay overnight. One manager described her reasoning this way: "[Visitors] are encouraged and they are welcome for meals as long as guests sign them in. . . . Kids visiting may be here overnight, like nieces or friends of kids." Another manager said, "We permit visitors to come at any time as long as they are not destructive to the program, and they can stay overnight as long as seven days." Several other managers encouraged the active involvement of fathers, who were not living with their families in the shelter, in helping with child-rearing tasks (e.g., preparing children for sleep at night).

All five shelters I spent time in had visitation rules. A few staff members told me how hard it was to strike a balance in making the shelter a comfortable place for families to bring visitors, while protecting the privacy of other families. About half of the mothers I interviewed were satisfied with program rules regarding visitors, 52 percent for those in the family support programs and 50 percent for those in the paternalistic programs. Those who were satisfied told me that the visitation rules, though difficult, were necessary to protect the safety and privacy of families. Several mothers considered time and space restrictions on visits unreasonable. Other mothers told me that they were most upset with the ways in which staff members unfairly enforced visitation rules.

Staff members in the program that had a "no adult male visitors" policy told me that the rule was established because so many of the women living there had suffered physical abuse at the hands of their partners. They wanted the place to be calm and safe for all. They had had trouble in the past with male visitors. Mothers in this program were upset with the rule. "[The rules about visitors] are not good because you can only get female visitors, and this is not a battered women's shelter. This is a regular shelter, and my boyfriend cannot come here to visit me. He is not a bad person, either," Rosa told me. I asked her if she had brought the issue up with staff. She responded,

"They said my son's father can come visit him, but it would have to be at a certain time and . . . and I don't like it."

A staff member in the program that restricted mothers from visiting with each other in their bedrooms told me that the rule was established to cut down on the development of cliques and factions among families. Several mothers from that program were very upset by this rule. "I didn't like it that you couldn't really be in each other's room . . . unless the child was there, too. If my child was playing with someone else's child, but at night like we couldn't be in each other's room," Lydia told me. In response to my question about her understanding of the reason for the rule, she said, "I don't know. I just didn't think it was right. . . . We brought it up at a meeting. Their [the staff] thing on it was there were enough other places for you to sit and talk with someone . . . maybe they were [afraid of] drug use or something. . . . Their claim was it was a community setting . . . but like I said, I had a friend in there who I had known for five years, and I couldn't go and sit and chat with her in her room."

TV Use

Programs also differed widely in the ways they handled TV use by families in the common areas of the shelters. Two out of five programs across the state had no rules about TV use at all. They left it to families to work it out among themselves. Those programs with rules prescribed when the TV could be turned on and what programs children and/or adults were allowed to watch. These rules were devised for a range of reasons, primarily reflecting the values of staff rather than the need for safety and order. Directors' justifications for TV rules included assisting families to negotiate with each other, preventing children from being exposed to violent or adult material, encouraging children's programming, and discouraging mothers from spending a lot of their daytime hours watching TV. A few programs prohibited families from having a TV in their bedroom. Many others allowed this option.

One manager, whose program did not have a rule regarding TV use, used the physical setup to discourage TV watching. "The mothers are not using the TV as much as they used to in the previous site, where it was very tempting to turn it on. There were comfortable chairs," he said. "Here it is in a spot where it's not that comfortable to sit back and watch TV. The kids watch cartoons. We have it set up physically in a not too comfortable place in the dining room. That has done the job. The mothers sit in the living room [at night] and do handicrafts."

A few managers struggled with how to create a fair use of the TV for families whose primary languages were diverse. One described the use of a policy approach, saying, "When families' first language is not English, [the policy] is to take turns on English and the other language channels." Another used a more informal approach: "We from time to time mediate and help residents to resolve disputes, like English and Spanish channels. There's not an ironclad policy. We use it as an opportunity to help people to develop conflict resolution skills rather than have a rule about it."

Two of the programs I spent time in had no TV use rules. The three others restricted TV use to certain times of the day or allowed only certain types of programs to be viewed. Mothers and staff members in the programs with no restrictions were satisfied with this program approach but told me that working out disagreements among families about which programs to watch was difficult, especially between English- and Spanish-speaking families. Sixty-one percent of mothers in the family support programs and less than a third of mothers in paternalistic programs were satisfied with program rules governing TV use. Dissatisfied mothers in programs with TV restrictions told me that they felt humiliated by the ways staff used their authority. Sheila's story provides a vivid example of such treatment: "Humiliating. I can only go from my own personal experience. I found a job and I was excited about working and was supposed to start school. I was ready to go, but that got cut off and changed. So basically, first you go into a mode of depression, a deep depression. And you have to realize that life goes on and you still have to raise your child, and you have to be positive for him. I used to stay in my room and totally seclude myself from everybody. I started coming out and just flipped on the television, just like a normal person. I don't even watch TV, but just to hear it going makes it kind of normal because other things are going on, instead of just dead silence out there. So I flip on the TV and go into the kitchen and start making something and my son would be running around playing, and she (a staff member) would come down, 'What are you watching? You aren't supposed to be watching that, only channel 2. You can get a warning for that. Turn it off or change it.' It was just the way they said things to you. It made such a difference you know. . . . Just little things that drive you up the wall. You can't even watch TV. You lose everything else. The TV is just one more thing on that little notch to drive you crazy." Staff members in these programs told me that parents should be working on their goals or spending quality time with their children during the day, rather than watching TV. They all approved of program rules restricting TV use.

Phone Use

Nine out of ten programs in the state had rules related to time limits for phone use or payment for phone calls. Over half of the programs spelled out how long family members could be on the phone; the others left phone-sharing arrangements up to families to work out among themselves. A vast majority of programs had both pay phones and business phones available for families' use. Generally, the pay phones were used for personal calls, while the office phones were used for business calls such as calling potential landlords, talking with children's teachers, arranging medical appointments, and so forth.

A few managers told me about the privacy protections that they built into their rules governing phone use. The following comments typify these policies: "Staff and residents all share one office phone. We take a message if it's for the resident. They return the call on the pay phone. We say, 'We can't tell you if that person is here, but if she is, we'll give her the message.' The welfare, social services, school, day care, and doctors can call and talk with the resident privately on the office phone."

All of the case study sites I visited had rules governing phone use. Seventy-four percent of mothers in family support programs and 38 percent of mothers in paternalistic programs were satisfied with the ways programs handled families' phone use. Typically they were satisfied with the number of phones available and with staff flexibility in enabling them to reach their friends, family, or business contacts. However, many mothers told me that negotiating phone use with other parents was hard at times. Mothers in one of the five case study sites were particularly vociferous about their dissatisfactions with the ways that staff abused their power when it came to phone use. Staff members limited the hours the office phone could be used by families, they told me, and listened to their private conversations, which in that shelter took place in a staff office shared by four to five employees. Limited privacy was a concern several staff members voiced to me, including one of the staff members in this program. She said that she advised parents to position their bodies in certain ways in order to gain some privacy.

Rising Times and Adult Bedtimes

Managers of over two-thirds of the state's programs told me that they had rules governing when parents must be up in the morning. One manager told me that this policy was in place to address depression and the needs of children: "This helps to deal with women's depression and they all have children. Children are awake," she said. Another manager of a program without a rising time reported that problems with depression were handled individually: "No policy [about rising times]. But if someone was coming down very late, we would explore it with her, like if there's a depression." Some programs went so far as to prescribe the morning tasks—breakfast and chores—that had to be accomplished by a certain hour. Others took responsibility for giving families a wake-up call. One did this using an intercom system. Other programs left this in the hands of families. Managers of three programs told me that, in addition to having rules governing adult rising times, they also dictated when parents were to be in bed.

Three of the five case study sites, the programs with a family support orientation, had no rule dictating when parents and children had to be up. Staff members in these programs were satisfied with this approach, as were 78 percent of the mothers I interviewed from these programs. If an individual mother had trouble getting up in the morning to go to school or to be with their children, staff handled this on an individual basis. A staff member in one of these programs had misgivings about the practice typical in one of these programs in which a staff member knocked on families' bedroom doors at a given time each morning. He was worried that this practice would inadvertently create a parental dependency on staff for something that parents should be in charge of for themselves. Several mothers in this program found the practice objectionable, as well as unnecessary and ineffective.

Staff members in the two paternalistic case study sites that did legislate a rising time approved of these rising time rules. Only 44 percent of mothers I interviewed from these programs were satisfied with rules in this area. Staff members were aware that parents didn't like to have scheduled lives, but they did not understand why parents had such trouble with the rule. In my conversation with Jane, one of these staff members, she began to talk about her own experience as a single parent with four children. "I am a firm believer and I will tell you why. . . . It relates to my own experience. I was a single parent and raised four children, worked full time, and went to school nights. When I came here, there were mothers who wouldn't get out of bed to send the kids to school. I didn't like that at all. I would physically go upstairs and make them get up. . . . Mothers who just skip the mornings, the child will suffer. I believe that mothers should be up with their children, most definitely and get them off to a good start, and also teach them responsibilities about getting to school on time and dressed properly and having the time to dress them and groom them, which a lot of mothers didn't do." Mothers I spoke with in this program told me that they found the heavy staff monitoring of their wake-up times very upsetting.

Weekend or Overnight Passes

Although nearly all programs had rules governing when parents could be away from the shelter overnight, their approaches for issuing passes were very diverse. In two out of five programs across the state, parents earned the right to be away overnight. Several programs limited the number of overnights per family per month. One manager described the rule this way: "If a person has no warnings for the week, has been following their service plan, and their housing search program, they may request a weekend pass to be approved by the family life advocate. That means they can leave on Friday if they have a safe place to go and need to return on Sunday at 6:00 P.M." In a few programs, families lost overnight privileges if they violated shelter rules. For two out of five programs, overnight passes were issued at parent request for a limited number of nights per month. Two programs provided these passes at parent request without any conditions.

Managers of a handful of programs described liberal overnight pass policies for children. The following description typifies these approaches: "Yes [we have policies regarding overnight passes], but not for children who can have them anytime their parents want them to have them." Several of these managers encouraged parents and children to get away, especially for the holidays. "It's good for kids to be with other family members," one manager told me. Another manager expressed concern for family members' safety when they are away from the shelter overnight: "If for some reason, where they go, it becomes unsafe or for whatever reason, they can come back. They just call the staff and come back. They can always come back. Don't stay in an unsafe situation," she said.

Each case study site had restrictions on the number of overnights parents and children could be away from the shelter. Some of these restrictions reflected programs' understanding of state policy rather than program policy per se. Nearly three-quarters of the mothers I spoke with associated with programs having a family support orientation were satisfied with the ways that programs handled parents' requests to be away overnight or for a weekend. Most families spent these overnights with family or friends who were able to open their homes for one or two nights periodically but could not provide them with a permanent home. Many told me that they needed to get away from the shelter to relieve the stress they felt from shelter life and to renew ties with family or friends. Those few mothers who were dissatisfied told me that staff should not have power over parents regarding these decisions. Others told me it was difficult being stuck in the shelter on weekends with so few other families around.

Staff members in these family support programs had mixed feelings about families using overnight or weekend passes. They felt that families do need a break from living in the shelter. One staff member expressed concerns about the amount of money families have to spend when they are staying with family or friends. He also observed that, while the overnight might be positive and important for the parents, children tend to want to stay in the shelter. When they were staying with relatives or friends, they sometimes had to sleep on the floor or in other uncomfortable and unfamiliar places.

Staff members in programs operating from a paternalistic orientation told me that they were skeptical about whether people were really homeless if they could stay with family or friends on weekend nights. One of these staff members also told me that she monitors the places mothers take their children for an overnight, with the knowledge that some of the mothers have problematic relationships with relatives or partners. She only grants overnights to parents who are in full compliance with the rules. Only 13 percent of the mothers I talked with from these programs were satisfied with the program's approach to granting overnight passes. Once again, mothers were dissatisfied with the inordinate amount of power staff had in granting or rejecting their requests.

Evening Curfews

Nearly universally, programs across the state mandated when parents and children must be in the shelter at night. For a small number of programs, the curfew was 7:30 P.M.; for twenty programs, it was between 7:30 and 8:30 P.M.; for thirty programs, it was 9:00 P.M. or later. Most programs extended these hours during the summer months and on weekends.

Every case study site had defined curfew hours. Three-quarters of mothers from the family support programs and over 40 percent of mothers from the paternalistic programs were satisfied with rules governing curfews. Those who were satisfied didn't necessarily like having a curfew, but they agreed with staff that the consistency was important, especially for children. However, several mothers thought that the curfew for weekend nights should be later. Another viewed the curfew as a form of punishment. Many of the women in the paternalistic programs complained about staff members' use of favoritism in enforcing the curfew and reprimands that caused them to feel like children and to feel like they were in prison. Staff members in all programs agreed that curfews were especially important for creating consistency in children's schedules. However, several of these staff described how difficult negotiations with mothers were when it came to curfews. One mentioned that curfews were often the "battle-

ground" for conflicts between staff and parents. Another described her
discomfort with "telling adults when to come in, especially on weekends."

Alcohol and Drug Use

Nearly three-quarters of programs across the state would not allow
parents with an active substance abuse problem to move with their
children into their shelters. Every program had a rule governing alcohol or drug use for parents who were residents. This was the one area
in which managers were resolute about the program rules. Nearly a
third of managers told me that they asked families to leave the shelter
if parents were caught possessing drugs or being inebriated or high.
The remaining managers based consequences of drug use on an
assessed level of safety risk posed by the parent's inebriated state and
on the parent's willingness to address her difficulties, including use of
alcohol treatment services. For the most part, managers had developed
avenues for parents to be connected with treatment services should
the situation arise. One manager described the way her program supported both parents and children while the parent was in treatment:
"No alcohol or drugs are allowed," she said. "If we suspect drug or
alcohol use, if not out of control or violent, we'll go by the individual
circumstance. It depends on the assessment by staff. Staff may take care
of kids while the parent goes to bed. We don't ask the family to leave
at night. We try to offer help and devise a program for them. We have
sent the parent to detox and kept their children here." "The only time
people can come in through here with an alcohol or drug problem
more than once is if they go into detox," another manager said. "We'll
allow them to come back. We'll help them notify relatives and arrange
for children during that time." A few programs conduct random urine
screens with any parent whom they suspect may be abusing sub-
stances.

A manager told me about her program's approach with parents in
recovery. "Upon entry, if in recovery, if a relapse [happened], we
would work with them to get more appropriate shelter. If someone
who isn't an identified substance abuser, comes in drunk, we first talk
to them. They would receive a written warning and the second time

they'd be talked to again, an option again to follow the rules. The third time, they'd be offered treatment but would have to leave the shelter. Detox may not be appropriate, they may need longer-term treatment. But they could come back later into the shelter when they are in recovery. . . . They are not banned, the criteria is being homeless." Another manager told me that a parent with a known substance abuse problem would have to be sober for six months to become eligible for entry into her shelter.

A program in which the shelter was a primary residence for some of the staff served alcohol at certain times. "If occasionally for parties, alcohol may be served here, like beer or wine," the manager said. "They [parents] are not allowed to bring it in for their own use, and those in recovery are not allowed to have it any time. If high or inebriated, we would try to get them to bed and address it in the morning."

Every case study site prohibited the use of alcohol and drugs. Nearly every mother and every staff member I interviewed applauded this policy. Mothers told me that the rule gave them a feeling of safety and that this safety was important for them and their children. Those mothers in recovery said that being in an alcohol- and drug-free environment was essential for their recovery process. The one area in which staff and mothers at one case study site were at odds with each other in this area had to do with the practice of locking up all medications in the staff office and requiring parents to dispense medications to themselves and their children with staff watching. Mothers were very upset with this practice. Staff expressed satisfaction with it.

Budgeting and Saving Money

Parents' responsibility to save and budget their money while they were living in the shelter was another area of rule making that I asked managers to describe. In April 1995 state policies were enacted that changed the cash benefit levels for families receiving AFDC while living in a shelter. That is, $150.00 per month was irrevocably subtracted from each of these families' public assistance checks while they were living in a publicly funded shelter. Shelter providers and advocates vociferously opposed this policy change, fearing that this loss of funds would make it harder for families to pay their debts and save money toward renting an apartment—that is, for a security deposit, first month's rent, furniture, and so on. The policy change may have led shelter programs to reconsider their budgeting and savings requirements. The following analysis is based on descriptions of rules provided by managers, staff, and mothers prior to the enactment of the new state policy.

One-third of programs across the state had no rules requiring parents to save money but offered them support and advice regarding budgeting, paying off debts, and so forth. The remaining programs asked families to save a percentage of their income each month. Several managers told me that they no longer required families to save a set amount of their income, because they had learned it was illegal to do so. "No, there is no policy. When I first came here, it was mandatory that they had to put 50 percent of their money in savings. A family brought this to legal services. We were told we couldn't do it [require savings]." A few managers told me how frustrated they were with not being able to mandate savings, particularly when they saw parents spending their money rather than saving it for a future move. Another manager described an incentive system in which weekend passes were given as a reward to parents for saving 30 percent of their income. Some staff monitored parents' behaviors in saving money. Although the managers may say that they are not requiring savings, the following comment, typifying what I heard from several managers, indicates that the programs were in actuality using their positions of power to enforce mandatory savings: "Well . . . we can't require [parents to save a set amount of their income], so I like the word 'encourage,' " one manager told me. "They save in a savings account. Their passbooks are made available for staff review upon request of the family's case manager." Another manager told me about a dilemma families had to face if they tried to save large percentages of their incomes while living in a shelter: "If they save too much," she said, "they may inadvertently become ineligible for public assistance."

Three of the five case study sites had rules governing parents' saving and budgeting their money. Two were the paternalistic programs; another was one of the family support programs. Staff members in the family support programs described difficult dilemmas associated with assisting parents to budget and save money. They told me that cultural-educational norms and past victimization experiences affected parents' habits in this area of their lives. Jenine told me that she did not like this part of her role as a family's case manager: "I feel like I'm chasing an adolescent and trying to teach them." Staff members in the paternalistic programs, on the other hand, expressed considerable comfort with their ways of working with parents on this issue. In fact all of the staff members I talked with from these two programs wanted to institute more stringent savings requirements. Tina, one of these case managers, told me that she required parents to show her their bankbooks and that she called the bank for families' savings balances. She wished that the program had a wall safe in which bankbooks would have to be locked up.

Surprisingly, many mothers were very pleased that the staff were helping them to save money (65 percent of those from the family support and 44 percent of those from the paternalistic programs). Many said that budgeting and saving money was a new experience for them. Lily's comments reflect these mothers' perspectives: "[Staff help on budgeting and saving money] was great. Well, I was working a lot. I was cleaning on my own and I was able to save a lot of money, which helped. [They required] 30 percent. That is what my case manager [required]. . . . He went to the point where he even gave me some budget sheets, some papers, to keep track of everything and to see where it was going. . . . I had no problems. I trusted these people and my money was there for me, too. . . . I trusted my case manager. I trusted everyone, you know, the staff people." Those who were dissatisfied considered requirements for saving money violations of parents' rights. On the other hand, some thought the requirements should be more stringent. Others simply said that staff assistance with budgeting and saving money was just not helpful.

Parental Roles in Making and Changing the Rules

Systemwide, parents had little say about these matters. Program practices designed to give parents a formal role in deciding shelter rules were present in some programs and limited or nonexistent in others. However, a foundation existed for shelter programs in the state to further engage families who were living or had lived in shelter programs as partners at this level. I asked managers about the role parents—current and former residents—had in advising shelter programs about their policies and the design of their services or in contributing to the program's operations in other ways. The two most typical roles for current residents were to provide support to other parents and to provide periodic feedback to the program. Two out of five programs across the state engaged current residents as peer mentors for other parents. A handful of programs involved current residents as trainers of their staff or as members of their agency advisory boards. No program involved current residents as members of a parent advisory board.

Former residents were involved to a greater degree in policy-making and supportive roles in shelters than were current residents. For example, four out of five shelters had hired former residents as staff members. Two-thirds had developed formal avenues for receiving feedback on program operations from former residents. Nearly half engaged these parents as peer mentors or as members of their agency advisory boards. Fewer enlisted these parents as trainers of their staff or as members of their parent advisory boards.

No one I interviewed from the five case study sites could describe a formal decision-making avenue in which the manager, staff, and parents collaboratively and regularly assessed the effectiveness of program rules and made changes based upon this joint evaluation. While program personnel may have had good reasons for blocking this kind of joint decision making, the lack of input into the most important decisions affecting families' daily lives was a sore point with nearly all of the mothers I interviewed.

Rule Enforcement

The conversations I had with managers, staff, and mothers regarding rule enforcement were full of emotion and mixed feelings. Many managers described having a progressive warning system, in which parents were confronted once, twice, and three times. Upon receipt of a third warning, families were be terminated from the program or "exited," to use a term coined by many staff and managers. The state funding agency became involved if the situation had escalated to that point. Universally, program personnel described these terminations as last-resort measures, ones they did not like to have to use. To avoid these circumstances, many programs used less formal avenues for dealing with rule infractions, such as one-on-one confrontations or problem-solving sessions or the development of individualized contracts for change. Some created ways for parents to experience negative consequences for breaking rules, such as the humiliating "job jar" punishment described in an earlier chapter or losing overnight privileges. Many managers told me that they viewed some rule infractions as more serious than others. For example, the use of drugs or alcohol and violent behavior were unacceptable in many shelter settings and resulted in terminations. For the most part managers wrestled with how to be fair and flexible while ensuring safety for all families as they went about enforcing the rules of their programs. Some stood firm: a rule is a rule. Others valued flexibility as the norm and problem solved rule infractions with parents on an individual basis. Others gave warnings but only if the staff as a team had given the go-ahead.

The strongly held views of one program manager are instructive. "When you're running a shelter, it's much easier to be institutional. There is always a tension between the law-and-order staff people and those staff who aren't. There is always a tension between the law-and-order guests and those guests who aren't," she told me. "We think that's okay. In general people have to keep their word. If they give their word, we believe them. We expect them to negotiate. We listen in good faith. We try to keep it human. This is their home for whatever time they are here. We try to keep it a healthy home, not by rules but by expectations of normal daily life. In fact, if you choose to get into a power struggle with your guests, staff will always lose. The only hope is relationship, being respectful. If they feel respected, then they'll respect you back. If you spend 90 percent of your time enforcing, they'll spend 90 percent of their time trying to go around the rules."

Staff members struggled with rule enforcement as well. A few told me that they were working on becoming more relaxed and flexible about rules, recognizing that many situations are not very clear-cut. Phyllis reflected that when she first joined the shelter staff, she was

very rigid about enforcing rules and realized later that this had
harmed her relationships with several mothers. One of those mothers,
whom I interviewed in her new apartment agreed with Phyllis's
assessment: "[Phyllis] was right behind you, letting you know that you
didn't follow the rule." Joanne, a staff member in the same program,
kept a perspective on enforcing rules in the shelter by drawing upon
what she had learned with with her own family. Her words reflect
ideas several other staff members expressed to me: "I think I learned
from my adoptive son, you don't set up battles you don't want to
fight. So you have to pick them . . . and be careful how you phrase
your ultimatums or else you may be sorry and you might have to do
what you don't want to do. . . . There are some things you can get people to do out of charm, with a smile, a hug, and a nudge. I am willing
to do that as opposed to, 'Here is another warning.' Because there are
times when you will have to do that. There are times you have to be
that way. Then you end up being an angry kind of person who is like
that all of the time. I kind of decided that I save that in my back
pocket until I have to do it, and then it is like . . . We have talked a lot
and that is that."

Mothers in the programs that operated from a family support orientation were for the most part comfortable with the mix of flexibility and consistency with which staff enforced rules. Some told me
that staff had the right to take control for the sake of everyone living
in the shelter. Many were clear that some rules were more important
than others—such as the use of alcohol or drugs, curfews, disciplining
children—and should be handled with more seriousness. Some were
vociferous in their complaints about staff favoritism with parents who
were more compliant, "who kissed up" and were willing to disclose
their private family secrets with staff. Others described inconsistencies
among staff in the ways they used their authority, as reflected in Elizabeth's remarks: "You basically have to kiss up big time or else you get
the brunt of [Angela's] authority. . . . They had the option to do room
searches whenever they want. I had this thing where I was addicted to
candy and I had it in my room, and you're not allowed food in your
room because of the cockroaches. So I got bagged for it so many
times. . . . [Angela] would not even knock, just come in and start paw-
ing through my drawers right in my face. Now this is very hard to

watch somebody just do whatever they want, right in your face, and looking through your personal things. . . . There is a difference. Linda [another staff member] would knock and say, 'Do you mind if I look around?' Just that little asking, which she doesn't have to do. She has the authority to walk in and do whatever the heck she wants. Just the asking makes it like, 'Sure.' "

Mothers from the programs operating with a paternalistic orientation were, with the exception of one mother, very vehement in their displeasure with the ways staff enforced the rules. They provided examples of what they considered to be favoritism, unfair treatment, arbitrary rule creation, excessive use of written warnings, conflicts between management and staff, and inconsistencies among staff. Several told me that the battles with staff over shelter rules were extremely stressful. Cindy, whom I interviewed in her new apartment two weeks after she and her son had left the shelter, told me that she was still "de-shelterizing" herself, waking up to the fact that she was in charge of her own schedule and life again. This young mother had become homeless as a consequence of a fire that destroyed all of her furniture and belongings. In response to my questions about how rules were enforced, she asked me rhetorically, "Know how it feels like you're crazy and everyone else is normal?"

Dilemmas with Enforcement of Rules

I asked managers and staff members what, if any, dilemmas they experienced related to enforcing rules with parents. I heard an earful. Managers described walking on a tightrope as they attempted to strike a balance in both respecting the uniqueness of each family and creating a safe and predictable environment for all families. Some worried that while they wanted to maintain a homeyness in their shelters, rules created an "institutional" feeling. Having so many rules, while necessary, undermined their program values related to the empowerment of and a partnership with families. They struggled with determining how flexible to be, in recognition of families' diverse needs and cultural backgrounds. Some said that at times parents actually wanted them to be more rigid in enforcing rules than they as managers wanted to be. Managers were also troubled by having to deal with parents' reactions to rules. That is, parents became angry, resistant, overwhelmed, or too dependent upon staff. Managers did not like having to put energy into monitoring parents' behaviors or having to ask families to leave the shelter. Rules exacerbated the power differences between staff and parents, which some managers told me they regretted. Other managers expressed their frustration with being unable to make a good connection with some parents whose goals were different from those staff had for them. They told me that one family in trouble with others in the shelter could have a major impact on the whole group. They sometimes felt powerless to help these families change and adjust. The final area of frustration many managers told me about had to do with working with their staff on enforcing rules. They told me that developing consistency among staff members, settling disagreements among staff, and training new staff members was difficult work for them as managers.

Nine of the ten staff members I interviewed spoke with one voice on the dilemmas associated with rule enforcement. Only one staff member told me that she experienced no difficulty in enforcing rules. The most common struggle voiced by the others was finding ways to enforce rules while protecting the dignity of the parents as adults. Their feelings matched what I had heard from mothers. Enforcing rules created a parent–child dynamic in the relationships between staff members and mothers that was hard to deal with and nearly impossible to eliminate. Some staff recognized how overwhelming the program demands were on parents and thought that the program itself was being unreasonable. Several staff said that they at times disagreed with the opinions of their program managers regarding how to handle rule infractions. Having to carry out confrontations that they did not believe in and dealing with the consequences of those confrontations was very hard. Many staff were adamant about how hard it was for them to confront parents. Joanne described the impact on both herself and a mother in one such situation. "If I have to talk to them again . . . then I will say if you don't do this, I will have to give you a warning for breaking the rules," she explained. "Some (other staff) are just more cut and dry with that kind of stuff. . . . When I knew a guest was here and (she hadn't signed up for the sixth time) and she knows the rules, and I am not going to go after her. . . . It is not my responsibility to check this out, it is hers, especially if I had said the last time something like I'm not going to ask any more, and it will be embarrassing for me and it will be embarrassing for the person [when I confront her] . . . I find that really hard."

Parents' and Children's Responses to Rules and Enforcement

Staff members and mothers had similar observations regarding parents' and children's responses to shelter rules. Several told me that parents' responses vary from person to person. While parents don't like them, the majority follow them. Both mothers and staff told me about stages that parents go through in coming to terms with the imposition of rules. One mother said that when she first came to the shelter, she was thrilled. She thought it was wonderful. She couldn't understand why another mother who had been there for a few months had such a bad attitude. Then, when she had lived in the shelter for the same amount of time, she also found herself yearning to get her freedom back and adopting a bad attitude. Staff members described this cycle in some detail. Alice labeled the stages in the following way, reminiscent of Elizabeth Kubler-Ross's stages of coming to terms with dying.[6] She told me that parents are first in a honeymoon phase, receiving shelter while they are "reeling from the shock of being homeless." Then, they go into stages of denial, anger, rebellion, and, finally, acceptance. Joanne elaborated upon this cycle. "The general pattern is one of relief when they come here . . . a good feeling of acceptance and love and a kind of nurturing which I think people settle into like a comfortable chair. They are scared," she said, "but it feels good, and after a week or ten days they can really get into that chair and they like it. . . . Then after a while it starts eating on them, and it is boring, you know, because things are too predictable . . . there is some boredom in not having a constant crisis and living on the edge of the pit all the time. That boredom is kind of angry . . . they need something. It's like an irritation. They get into a period of irritation and they are not happy going to groups. They are irritated about having to fill out forms for housing. They are irritated about having to put savings away. . . . So, they are always looking to bend the rules a bit. That usually seems to get worked out after a period of time and they end up finding activities they can get involved in. Then you go through a real nice smooth period for a while. Occasionally they get irritated with the rules, living in the community, the lack of privacy, the lack of space. . . . They are delighted to be out of here."

What staff and mothers told me about children's reactions to rules ran the full gamut from extreme dislike to extreme satisfaction. Several staff members and a few mothers told me that, while the rules and structure are hard for parents, children thrive in the environment and benefit from all the attention. Staff members expressed divergent opinions regarding at what age children have the easiest and hardest time. Lydia thought that shelter life was harder for preschool and elementary school children but not as hard for babies and teenagers, while Michael had observed that shelter life was hardest on teenagers. Many mothers and staff thought that children's reactions were very dependent upon their mothers' adaptations to shelter life. Some mothers told me that their children took advantage of the situation and respected their authority less. Some staff members worried about this dynamic as well. A few staff members expressed irritation with parents who relinquished their authority as parents and allowed their children to become angry with staff over some of the shelter's rules.

A family's shelter experience is greatly affected by the ways in which the program deals with rules, their creation, and their enforcement. Although every program has a screening process—presumably for both parties to assess their mutual compatibility—by definition, families are in a desperate position at the moment of intake. "Most of the time they are broken," one manager told me. "Devastated, distraught, stressed, not even having the ability to think straight. Everything in your life has been turned upside down. The effects are severe." These are the circumstances under which managers and staff must find ways to establish a contract with parents regarding norms for living that will be beneficial to each family in the shelter.

All the managers, staff, and mothers I spoke with agreed that, given the constraints of the physical environment, rules are a necessity for maintaining safety, order, and predictability for children and parents living in family shelters. In this regard, nearly all programs in the state had devised norms for the use of alcohol and drugs, supervision of children, child discipline, child bedtimes, evening curfews, weekend or overnight passes, and household chores. The negative effects of rules can be offset by the size of shelter settings. Shelters that house small numbers of families can afford to be less rigid in their rule making and more flexible in their rule enforcement. Safety and order is easier to manage with smaller numbers of children. Under the best of circumstances, families can put up with shelter rules for short periods of time, but these constraints can take on a very large life if families stay in shelters for months.

The mothers I interviewed realized that some rules were inescapable and recognized the complexities of the circumstances staff faced in enforcing program policies. Mothers rejected laissez-faire policy approaches. However, these women were very sensitized to the ways in which staff could use their power as rule enforcers to humiliate and stigmatize shelter residents. The chance for humiliation is high in this dimension of shelter life and can easily set a parent-child dynamic into motion between mothers and staff. In some programs, rule making went beyond safety and order and attempted to mold parents' personal behavior. These rules were offensive to all the mothers I interviewed. Facing mothers, at intake and throughout their shelter stays, with value-laden, paternalistic regulations is like putting up a mirror in which the faces mothers see are those of flawed women who, staff assume, make poor judgments regarding their relationships, their hygiene, the care of their children, the use of their time, and so forth. These systems stigmatize and humiliate mothers for simply being homeless. They reify unsubstantiated differences between homeless mothers and other people. Such interactions undermine the building of an egalitarian partnership between a mother and a staff member, clearly putting the mother in a one-down position. They contribute to mothers' sense of low self-worth and become another difficult obstacle to overcome. Mothers have to work actively to resist these negative messages in order to connect with their inner strengths and move forward.

Establishing and enforcing rules in a shelter is very difficult for staff and managers. For the most part, they detest having to enforce rules as much as mothers hate to be the object of such enforcement. At times staff members have no choice. They must make a judgment and step into the shoes of a rule enforcer. Some rules have to be hard and fast. Some mothers may understand, while others may chafe. The challenge for staff and managers is to develop the skills of making a judgment without being judgmental, rejecting the behavior without rejecting the person. Many situations that arise in shelters fall into a gray area when it comes to rule enforcement. Effective practice involves development of a facility in deciding what to ignore and what take a stand upon. Becoming a supersleuth rule enforcer as a staff member can have consequences for staff members themselves. In the words of a staff member I interviewed: "You end up being an angry kind of person who is like that all of the time."

Substantive family involvement in rule making, a core dimension of the family support model, is a crucial and largely untapped resource. Parents and children are highly knowledgeable regarding practices that demonstrate a respect for their strengths and for the rights of all families to be treated with dignity. Mothers I interviewed stood ready to share their views with staff and managers on ways of handling the complex and sensitive situations that arise regularly in shelter settings. Many implied that they would need concrete reassurance that they would not receive retribution for sharing their opinions. Satisfying, egalitarian relationships between staff and families are more likely with policy approaches that emphasize safety, order, and predictability for all and are the product of ongoing family input. Under those conditions, rules may work to build a sense of community among families and staff. Rules can facilitate family control over their actions and daily routines and enable the community to make room for change based upon the personalities and preferences of the families who happen to be living there at a given time.

The reflections of Rosa Clark, a mother and shelter staff member, and Margaret Leonard, director of an agency that operates a family shelter, follow this chapter. Together, they represent over twenty years of experience in supporting highly stressed families who have lost their housing and are living in a family shelter.

Reflections on Chapter 4

Reflection: Mother and Staff Member, Rosa Clark

Rules were not something that really bothered me. I came in not knowing a lot about the system and rules. The staff explained some of the rules and gave me a copy of them. I don't know if I said yes because of the position I was in needing to have shelter, but to me it was not an issue. Safety was an issue and I did feel safe. I would say that the rules are made to keep the children, to keep staff, and to keep the families safe because there's a lot of movement in and out of the shelter. Different people are in them for different reasons. People come from various backgrounds, from different situations. There needs to be some type of a structure, some type of a saneness throughout the day. In my particular case the rules were good, I knew what they were and I followed them and I knew that by following them that it would lead to me not getting kicked out of a shelter. But I wasn't interested in challenging rules at that point in time. I was glad to be safe. As far as the frontline staff were concerned, there was realness in them. If they were saying something to me about a rule, then I had to give them some credit because they were the ones on the front line and had the experiences. So I valued that and I wanted them to let me know something up front instead of letting me kind of stumble into a problem. So if I asked a question about a rule, I got an answer.

As far as safety was concerned at the shelter, I remember that the

night before I got into the shelter I had to be placed in another shelter with my nine-month-old son. The worker had done some investi-
gation and found out that there was another shelter with one room,
and so I would have to stay there for the night. I think that the shelter
I ended up in for that night was a shelter for battered women. I was
not battered physically although I would say there was some verbal
abuse, but I was not in physical danger. I was placed in that shelter for
the night because I had nowhere else to go. When I walked in that
door, I felt afraid. I did not feel comfortable. No one greeted us at the
door. People were hardly around. No one knew what was going on.
They took me up to my room. I was scared the entire night. I didn't
sleep. There was no one to say, "Well, if you want to fix your child a
bottle, here's the kitchen or the bathroom." Things were just not organized, so that night I didn't sleep. I put my bed behind the door. I was
scared. I heard a lot of noise downstairs. At one point I went downstairs and there were people around who obviously were under the
influence of either drugs or alcohol and it made me scared. It was
dreadful.

So, early that next morning, I called the worker and I said to her,
"Please, please get me out of here. I don't feel safe." She did some leg-
work and found out that there was an opening at Project Hope. She
came over, and because she knew me so well she advocated strongly for
me. She even brought the coordinator at that time. I'll never forget her.
My worker told her what a wonderful person I was. She said she would
put herself out there for me, so please take me. They would not regret it
and they did. So that was how I ended up at Project Hope and so that's
why I could tell the difference between shelters, by how safe I felt.

So now, since living at Project Hope and after that becoming the
coordinator of Project Hope and having to be the one on the inside,
I understand so clearly the work that is done in shelters and how difficult it is. When I think back to my stay, I realize how difficult it must
have been for the frontline staff at times to deal with the unpredictability of certain families who are very challenging.

For me, one of my goals in running the shelter was to try to maintain the balance of respecting the families but at the same time trying
to explain the need for rules, the need for safety. Whatever the families wanted to ask about the rules, we would have answers for them.

When they challenged them, we gave them answers that were based upon our past experiences. These were not rules that we suddenly thought up one day. I remember clearly at one point we reviewed all of our rules and we had all of our rules reviewed by a committee of women who used to live in the shelter. It was incredible because when we did that review process with families who lived and were affected by these rules, they all unanimously said that these rules needed to stay the way they were.

So for me trying to maintain that balance has been such a incredible journey, from the day that I walked into the shelter living here with my child to the days when I ran it. I just felt so proud and I tried my best to treat everyone with dignity and respect. I tried to answer every question that was asked of me, remembering at times what it was like, even though my experience was different. I was not one to be too challenging. But that experience of running the shelter for seven years was an incredible journey into the lives of so many families and children. I see how each one of them is so unique in its own special way. During the challenging times you have to resist shutting them out but let them be heard. For me at times some of the difficulty was trying to get the frontline staff to understand some of that. At times, due to confidentiality, they did not have all of the information about why a family was behaving a certain way or why this one gets to do something when the other one doesn't. Trying to be consistent with all of them at times is a difficult thing because every family's needs are different. I think that at times it's hard to get the frontline staff to understand that. But one of the things that I tried to focus on and tried to talk about was how important it was for frontline staff to get good training, good training in conflict resolution, good training in the sensibilities of not taking things personal.

I have been cursed out, I have been called every name in the book. At times I have wanted to just throw in the towel and just say forget this, this is ridiculous. And then at that moment someone or something would happen that reminded me why I was doing the work that I was doing. It wasn't only to give back because people gave to me when I was in need. I became so committed to wanting to work with families who are in such a struggle with the system, with families, with friends, with authority. That's been my goal to reach out to fam-

ilies, to let them know that we're not here to demean them. I want to
help them to get to that other side. It can be such a struggle. At times
I have been able to reach the families and at times I have not. At times
the issues were so great for that family that they just couldn't see
beyond their situation. I know that my life was changed and I would
say that their life was changed by our interaction.

At times I had to make decisions for the safety of everyone and yet
still there were people who disagreed with that decision. They
thought we should give that person an extra chance, even though I
know that I had already given them just about as many chances as I
could. I continue to do this work and try to meet the needs of families, with their assistance. I know that I'm not Superwoman, and that
I'm not going to be able to do it all, and that there are going to be
people who are not going to be ready for rules.

Reflection: Executive Director, Margaret A. Leonard

This chapter on shelter rules conjures up in my mind all types of
images that convey a messy quagmire where the most difficult and
painful negotiations of shelter life get played out. It is the place where
we seek to delineate boundaries between individual rights of families,
of families collectively, and of the community of families and staff. It is
the place where the test of being a family support model is truly tried.
It is the arena where the learning community of families and staff
embark on an uncharted course.

How *do* we live these moments of formulating shelter rules at Project Hope? As executive director of Project Hope, I, and my colleagues
in mission, raise a question critical to ensuring that our collective
journey, while filled with uncertainty about routes, pitfalls, human
conflicts, is also accompanied by mountains climbed, community
experienced, and growth shared. The most important questions that
confront us are these: How do we prepare for the journey, and what
are the resources we bring with us?

I will attempt to respond to the substance of this chapter and these
questions by raising and responding to two additional questions. What
does it mean to be seeped in mission? And what does it mean to be
committed to an inclusive process?

Seeped in Mission

The mission of Project Hope embraces the family support model as defined by Donna Friedman in this book. Exploring the meaning of family support with the help of my old friend Webster provides a lens into the wider mission of Project Hope.

support: "to sustain, to carry, to hold up, to bear the weight or stress of, to uphold by aid or countenance, and to act with, as a community."

family: "a group of closely related individuals and groups," persons who are kin to one another.

So when we talk about a commitment to a family support mission, we are simply saying that we wish to relate as an extended family, a community, "kin" who seek to create an atmosphere that sustains, supports, upholds, and acts with one another not for or over one another. Roles within such a family, be they house manager, housing advocate, family life advocate, resident family, etc., are not defined exclusively by functions or tasks although this is a core part of any role. What we are primarily talking about are relational roles such as sister, aunt, grandmother, friend, mentor. And these relational roles become the context in which tasks and functions are lived out, as together we seek to create an atmosphere, a spirit, a family support spirituality that nurtures and sustains the growth and development of all members of the extended family, staff and families alike.

In sharing this with you, I am conscious that there are many who would challenge crossing the sometimes sterile boundaries between professional and relational roles, or using the language of spirit and spirituality. It is our collective experience that moves us to cross these boundaries. For among all of us who are first of all human beings there is a search for meaning, a human cry for connecting, bonding, the experience of community. We see its resonance all around us, particularly in the not-for-profit and corporate sectors who now speak openly of mission, retreats, and, less frequently but increasingly, of spirituality.

A family support mission is one that we are committed to create. Over the years it has been tried and been found true. Many former residents of Project Hope's family shelter still refer to themselves as part of the extended family and community.

Commitment to an Inclusive Process

Shelter Rules: How are they defined by those who embrace a family
support model? Webster gives us a clue among the multiple ways in
which he defines rules. One of these is a "guide for conduct, action."
Who creates the guide? Who embraces it? Who monitors it? Who
evaluates its effectiveness? These are questions that demand our reflection. Rather than focus upon the substance of these rules, it is first
important to discuss the process of rule making.

If rules are a "guide for conduct and action" among an extended
family or community, all of the family members must be engaged in
their formulation, staff and families alike. We are therefore committed
to the implementation of a four-phased process for developing such a
guide to action.

1. Sharing the guide already in place with new families when
   they enter our family shelter. We share equally with them
   the spirit in which the guide was formulated and chosen,
   with an emphasis upon creating a safe, secure, nurturing, and
   just atmosphere for all families, and assure them that their
   voice will be heard in the ongoing critique and evaluation
   of these rules.
2. Engaging families with staff to review the guide for action on
   a regular basis to discuss its effectiveness in achieving the purpose for which it was created and to make modifications as
   decided upon together.
3. Holding weekly meetings of staff and families with appropriate facilitation, to work out tensions and conflicts and to share
   ways for all of us to create a safe, nurturing environment.
4. Facilitating retreats with staff and families to develop, critique, and evaluate the guide and to develop diverse programs
   created to provide families with resources on their journey to
   permanent housing and interdependence.

Many of the house managers are former residents of Project
Hope's family shelter, and frequently we ask former residents involved
in other programs to share in these encounters. They bring a lived

experience that is extremely valuable to this process, to which we as a staff are committed. The hectic activities that surround us sometimes impede our desire to implement it fully and accurately. Books such as this one are a wake up call to be more faithful.

A Learning Community

Our collective experience is filled with stories that speak to the effectiveness of this model. Perhaps the most positive stories are those of formerly homeless women who are now staff at Project Hope. Formerly homeless women are engaged in several of our programs and are willing to be mentors to others who are currently homeless and interpret for them the benefits of regulations that sometimes make residents chafe at the bit. We can also recount many stories that reflect our negotiations to make these rules just and compassionate for all. One that is uppermost in my mind is a story in which a mother had broken all the rules and her final days at Project Hope were numbered. The families came together and encouraged the group to give this woman and her family one final chance. The response was affirmative. They nurtured her back into community. Another story was the communal grieving that we shared together when we had to take action to have children who were neglected taken from their parent.

Our stories of failure also are vivid and alive among us. Steps we shouldn't have taken, our process not followed, actions that should have waited, fill our memories and our discussions. This is a difficult quagmire, an uncharted course in which we are a community of learners. Perhaps this is one of the most important lessons. We do not have the answers! Answers need to be discerned and discovered together, and we have much to learn from our personal and collective mistakes.

In concluding this brief reflection, I am conscious that I was asked to reflect upon this chapter from the position of being an executive director. What are the supports that are needed to implement such a challenging mission? Briefly, I would like to identify a few essentials:

- That the mission be identified, owned, and articulated by staff and that each person understands that the mission informs the atmosphere, the spirit in which actions are taken, decisions are made.
- That staff being hired understand and make a commitment to the mission that shapes and forms Project Hope, and that the interview process include a values screen.
- That ongoing support, supervision, and resources are readily available to families and staff as we chart together these sometimes murky waters.
- That ongoing in-service training addresses not only tasks but also spirit and mission, as well as ways of embodying them in all our actions.
- That oversight and evaluation is a regular and ongoing process.

5

Individualized and Standardized Services

No gardener ever made a rose.
When its needs are met a rosebush will make roses.
Gardeners collaborate and provide conditions which favor this outcome.
And as anyone who has ever pruned a rosebush knows,
life flows through every rosebush in a slightly different way.

—Rachel Naomi Remen, *Kitchen Table Wisdom: Stories That Heal*

Phyllis and her twelve-month-old son became homeless when her apartment building burned down. After a stressful bureaucratic tussle with two welfare offices, she was able to move to a motel for a week until an emergency family shelter had an opening. In exchange for shelter, she had to sign the program's standard contract—that is, agreement to attend eight hours of mandatory meetings each week, including classes on parenting, budgeting, nutrition, and housing search, in addition to individual meetings with a family life advocate, a housing search worker, and a child specialist. She also had to volunteer to provide child care two hours per week. Phyllis, whom I interviewed in her new apartment a month after she left this shelter, told me how bitter she was about being treated like a child and being treated as someone who was flawed. She reported struggling with self-doubt about her parenting abilities resulting from this treatment.

A family support framework emphasizes mutual accountability between helpers and families, leading to adult-to-adult interactions and shared responsibility for reaching desired goals. Using this model, helpers build on family strengths and provide parents and children with individualized support. Empirical evidence from the fields of child development and maternal and child health strongly suggests that a family support approach to service produces favorable outcomes, including parents having higher levels of perceived control over resources,[1] more positive assessments of relationships between themselves and their helpers,[2] and a heightened sense of their own competencies.[3]

An alternative one-size-fits-all, prescriptive approach is more prevalent in welfare reform policies and is based upon an assumption that poverty is the result of bad habits, immoral behavior, and the lack of healthy values.[4] For example, welfare reform experiments across the country typically include stipulations mandating that, in exchange for cash benefits, parents must engage in a set number of hours of work or unpaid community service. These stipulations are congruent with a belief that poor people have bad work habits and need to be taught how to keep a job and contribute to the community.[5]

Can help be harmful? Receiving help with no expectation of having to do anything in return, sometimes referred to as a "handout," is a key indicator of problematic help.[6] Helpers can step in and do too much for parents, taking over their lives and shouldering families' problems as if they were their own. These practices have detrimental effects. Parents experience a lack of control and indebtedness, internalize a sense of self-doubt regarding their competencies, and become more dependent upon the helpers for resolving future family issues.[7] Helpers begin to feel resentful of parents for not being more grateful for the help they have been given.[8] A negative, nonconducive dynamic begins to contaminate the relationship between helpers and parents.

These issues are complex and hard to resolve. The ways that program managers, frontline staff, and mothers negotiate these situations within family shelters provide a microcosm for exploring these issues and thus are instructive for the broader welfare reform discussions currently taking place in the United States.

This chapter explores the ways that shelter staff deal with situations when they think a parent needs help with a problem that may or may not be on a parent's list of priorities. Family support criteria provide a lens for examining the help-giving scenarios included in the rest of this chapter. Do programs' helping practices hold both parents and helpers mutually accountable for solving problems that arise? Is teamwork encouraged? Is there a match between the services families are offered and families' own goals? Are helpers respectful and honest in their communications with families? When families reach their goals, do parents view themselves as the agents of their own change and thus capable of resolving future issues that will arise in their lives?

Service Approaches in Family Shelters

Shelters across the country provide a range of services to families above and beyond beds and food. Most provide assistance with obtaining housing and public benefits, education or job training, and medical or other treatment.[9] The majority of these shelters require that families meet with a caseworker, send their children to school, and seek housing. Most offer other services, including support groups and skills in basic living, on a voluntary basis.[10]

Family shelters in Massachusetts also attempt to assist families with many needs beyond temporary shelter and access to housing. In Massachusetts, family shelters are required, as part of their service contract with the state, to offer an array of service supports for each family that directly address the needs of children, teenagers, and parents and are documented in the family's individual family life advocacy plan. Almost universally, directors who participated in this study described services and supports for children and families in their programs that addressed these contract requirements.

Programs either offered these services on site to family members or referred families to the service networks in their neighborhoods or communities. Programs varied in the ways they formulated each family's individual family life advocacy plan. Some used an individualized approach to service delivery. That is, services were voluntary and individually tailored to each family's circumstances or needs. Others used a standardized approach in which services were mandatory. Some mixed a core set of mandatory services with other individually tai-

lored voluntary services. Specifically, nearly one quarter tailored services to the needs of individual families and had no service requirements. About the same number of programs required every family to
participate in six or more mandatory services. The rest utilized a mix
of individualized and standardized services.

On average, parents attended four mandatory meetings each
week. These usually included group meetings, such as house meetings, housing search meetings, or parenting group meetings, as well
as individual meetings with the family life advocate or other staff
members. Families in three programs participated in as many as
eighteen mandated services, requiring parental attendance in as
many as thirteen class hours each week. Several mothers involved
with programs that required attendance at a large number of weekly
meetings reported to me that they had to quit their jobs to attend
the mandatory meetings.

Other national studies of family shelter services have identified an
association between the size of programs and mandatory services.
Larger shelters had more mandatory requirements for family participation in family support programming.[11] I found no such association
with the programs in this study, a difference that may be related to the
smaller size of family shelters in Massachusetts (serving from four to
twenty-two families) compared to the programs surveyed by other
researchers[12] (serving from two to two hundred families).

Types and Focus of Services

I asked directors a number of questions related to the services they
offer that seek to support parental competency and the development
of very young children. I wanted to know how programs learn about
a family's need or desire to participate in these support services, the
kinds of services they provide or refer families to, a family's "typical"
involvement with these services, the services families seem to prefer,
and the extent to which services were directed toward family members not living in the shelter.[13]

Almost universally, directors reported that they provided services
focused on the needs of children and parents. Most programs carried
out an individual family assessment at intake as part of the process for

determining a family's interest in parent- and child-oriented services. However, programs varied considerably in the approaches they used to develop a family service plan. For example, some programs tapped families' own hopes and aspirations. One director put it this way: "Living in a shelter puts the families under a microscope which is both distressing and which creates an opportunity for them to be able to holistically look at their life, figure out what they want, what the obstacles are, and have a wide range of assistance to get beyond them. Each family's service plan begins with them. What do they want, where do they want to be in five years, what are their dreams for their family? From there we work back to what steps they can begin now to work towards those goals. . . . We strongly believe that social dynamics, racism, sexism, poverty throw up huge roadblocks for our families, and that in the face of that, with all of the resources we and they can muster, together we can find ways for them to realize these dreams."

Other programs required every family to participate in a set array of services during their stay: "Each family must participate in parenting, as well as other educational programs." Some used information about the family—such as screening for child problems, using reference checks, and so forth—rather than a parent's self-assessment to help them determine which services would be mandatory for an individual family. "During the first week of stay, we assess parenting skills to determine if they are in need of services," a director told me. Still others periodically developed service contracts mandating participation for those parents who have exhibited parenting inadequacies. For example, one director wrote: "If a parent is seriously lacking in skills where the child is suffering, we will adapt an inservice making a parenting class mandatory."

The directors' survey included a listing of twenty-four parent, child, and family support services programs might provide for children, for parents, and for parents and children together. On average, programs reported that they provided fifteen of these services on-site. However, directors responses' indicated that tremendous variability existed across the participating programs. That is, programs provided from a low of three to a high of twenty-one of these services. Detail on shelter services for children and parents follows.

Services for Children

Nearly three-fourths of programs regularly referred families to licensed child care programs. Indeed, one program offered licensed child care on-site. Over a third of programs encouraged families to utilize a child care program operated specifically for preschool children living in family shelters. These shelters had a contract with a day care agency for a certain number of slots reserved for children in their shelters. About a quarter of programs did nothing to assist families with their child care needs.

Supervised child play was the one service for children most shelters provided on-site. Other services that shelters provided were: on-site tutors; linkages with early intervention, Headstart, and parent-child centers; structured child development curricula; and on-site early intervention or preschool groups operated by community groups. Several directors reported that they included children in the shelter's house meeting or scheduled a separate house meeting just for children. An innovative idea one director told me about was her shelter's practice of recording minutes from the children's meeting and sharing them with the parents at their house meeting, usually prompting actions by adults to address the concerns the children had raised.

Two-fifths of the programs required a child health screening, and nearly half required primary health care for all children living in their shelters. Concerns about contagion in the congregate settings were the basis for this requirement. A few programs offered this service on-site. Most assisted families in making connections with outside agencies for obtaining this medical service. According to directors, families used early childhood programs more than any other child-focused service. Nearly two-thirds of directors described parents' high usage of either community-based early intervention, Headstart, parent-child centers, day care agencies, or their on-site infant/toddler or preschool programs. Supervised child play was the second service mentioned most often by directors as highly popular with families, with the child health services following as the third most popular.

Services for Parents

I asked directors about services focused on supporting parents in their roles as parents. The services most commonly available to parents were: skills in using community resources, child behavior management information, child nutrition information, advocacy skills, and training for solving family issues. In contrast with studies carried out in other parts of the United States,[14] a higher percentage of Massachusetts programs directly offered a parent-to-parent support component, which was usually voluntary. Between one-quarter and a half of programs required parent participation in services focused on child nutrition, child behavior management, child development, training for solving family issues, and skills in using community resources.

According to directors, parents highly valued activities that stimulated the growth and development of their children, such as health care, early intervention and preschool programs, and structured playtimes. Parents also appreciated services that increased their competencies, self-esteem, and social supports. Child care was reported to be a service that supported the development of children as well as freeing parents to more easily carry out their search for housing and their other responsibilities. Families especially enjoyed activities that allowed parents and children to have fun together. Directors were clear about the positive impact of services that allowed parents to get some respite from child care, distracted family members from their homeless situation, enabled children and parents to have fun, and facilitated the building of friendships.

The keys to success, many directors told me, were having effective workshop presenters, using nonthreatening, nonstigmatizing and nonjudgmental teaching approaches, answering parents' questions, and providing accessible and flexible services. Almost universally, families were involved in these program components throughout their shelter stays. Nearly one-fifth of programs offered their parenting and child development services to fathers who were not living in the shelter.

In summary, the majority of participating congregate family shelters had developed an array of supports for children, parents, and family units, in addition to those they offered for individual adult parents. These shelter programs operated in many ways as multiservice centers, providing families with a wide array of services beyond temporary shelter. Programs and families utilized several key community services for children—in particular, primary health care, health screenings, and early childhood programs. Most programs had mandatory service requirements, although nearly one-quarter enabled families to participate in all of their services on a voluntary basis. Services specifically focused on child health, safety, development, and behavior were the most likely to be required for all children and parents. These results appear to reflect the priority programs gave to making sure that children's basic needs were met and that parents were equipped with strategies for guiding the behavior and promoting the growth of their children. For the most part, concerns for child health and safety were the basis for some service requirements, reflecting the need programs may feel to limit individual autonomy in the interests of protecting the physical well-being of all children in the shelter.

Individualized Support

This chapter began by identifying criteria of expectant help-giving, using a family support framework. To re-encapsulate, these criteria are: helpers and parents hold each other accountable for their work together; the specific help people seek and the help they are offered matches; communication from the helper is respectful and honest; and parents view themselves as the agents of their own change, capable of resolving future challenges. This section provides illustrations of help-giving scenarios, considered successful by both the mothers and shelter staff I interviewed, that I believe met these criteria.

Teamwork to publish the family's story.   I came upon an example of very individualized support during a visit in one of the shelters. Wilma told me her story over a cup of tea one afternoon as we sat at the kitchen table. She had immigrated to the United States, with her twelve-year-old son and five-year-old daughter, to be with an American man who had promised love and commitment to them. She and her children had experienced horrific treatment at this man's hands once they reached the United States. Wilma showed me an eighteen-to-twenty-page document. She had dictated her story in her native language to someone who translated it into English for her. She told me that she was trying to get it published, and she offered me a copy of her story, which I gratefully accepted. Mimi, who was on duty that morning at the shelter was helping Wilma contact magazines with Polish readership, as a vehicle for publishing her story. Mimi told me that she thought this could be very empowering for Wilma. I wondered how other shelters might treat this. As a crazy idea? Not worth helping Wilma with? They might decide ahead of time that the idea was a dead end. Mimi was treating Wilma's desire to publish her story with seriousness.

Wilma told me that she and her children had been turned away from a number of shelters in the area because of her son's age. This shelter had not turned the family away. I thought to myself how traumatic it would be for them to be separated from each other, especially after their horrifying experiences. Wilma uttered these thoughts aloud. She talked about the director's kindness. The director gave Wilma a hug as she passed through the kitchen, and then said to me, "These women's stories should be told."

Teamwork to save money.   Janice told me a story that illustrated teamwork and mutual accountability between herself and Yolanda, a young mother living in the shelter with her infant and preschooler. This story centered on Yolanda's struggle to save money. Janice said that this is a common struggle for people she knows who are poor. "One of the ways that folks get into trouble at this level of poverty is to spend all of the money at once, paying back everybody they borrowed from since the last time they had a check, and then ending up without money again." Janice and Yolanda had been talking for some time about how Yolanda could get control of her money. Janice had been "bugging her" to open a bank account. "[Yolanda] wanted to do it, and she talked with her aunt, who is a great support to her. She said, 'Okay, I'm going to open a bank account.' . . . I asked her if she wanted me to go with her. She said yeah. So, we set up a date, and she blew that date off, and in fact, she stayed out all night. We gave her a warning letter." In planning for the next time Yolanda received her public assistance check and expected to open a bank account, Janice said to her, "Yolanda, the stakes are very, very high . . . what if I give you a letter of concern [rather than an official warning]. She said, 'Good, if I don't go open a bank account, you give me a letter of concern.' Well, the next check came, and she blew me off, but she called me at the time that we were supposed to meet and said that she was out with her aunt, and they were opening an account, and told me the amount for which she had opened the account, and showed it to me the next day." In response to my asking how Janice felt about this situation, she said that she felt good. "[Yolanda] used me to get what she wanted. She used a figure of authority to get what she wanted."

Teamwork to complete applications for housing.   Every mother in a shelter has to get onto as many waiting lists for subsidized housing as possible. In Massachusetts, each of the 250 housing authorities has a different application form. Lily, a mother of two young children, described a situation in which Phyllis worked with her to complete these applications. "Phyllis helped me fill out applications because I didn't know how at first. Now I can do them on my own. I felt great about her support," she said. "It makes me feel like I am a person again, because someone was willing to sit down with me and help me. I never got that until I came here."

Teamwork to obtain housing.   Janice, one of the staff members I interviewed, described a situation in which she and Lydia, a mother who had been fighting to rid her life of drugs, worked as a successful team. Lydia was afraid to move out of the shelter. "Having her own apartment," Janice reflected, "meant using drugs again. That is what she had done every [other] time she left a shelter and got her own place. That was a trigger for her." Using straightforward and frank communication, Janice worked with Lydia to determine her readiness to leave the shelter. When Lydia said she was ready, she and Janice set up a schedule ahead of time, giving Lydia two weeks of preparation before they began to look for apartments. Janice knew that the timing was right, because Lydia kept to the schedule. When I asked how it felt to work with Lydia, Janice said, "Really empowered. Lydia and I worked together very easily. Her success was like . . . the energy was shared [between us]. . . . It was an easy and wonderful relationship."

Teamwork to fight a bureaucratic battle.   Joanne told me a story about a time in which she and Betty worked together to appeal the welfare department's decision to cut off public assistance for Betty and her children. "Betty was kicked off AFDC," Joanne said. "I felt there was reason for appeal, so she had to get a lawyer. . . . So my making phone calls to find out who she could talk to, and then her picking up the pieces of doing it, and her calling me because she needed to fax information to her lawyer. She didn't have an answering machine and she had a block on her phone [in the shelter apartment]. I was often used as a conduit for the communication. So, I felt like we were in this together, but I couldn't have made this work without her, but I'm not sure she could have without me either." Joanne followed this story with a self-reflection on her way of giving help: "The question I always ask myself in a relationship is making sure that I am not doing too much. That somebody else can be doing for themselves, and just always weighing that to make sure that, even though it is easier to do it yourself, then to get them to do it . . . always weigh that and make sure that . . . the next time she would know who to call and how to do it."

Teamwork to obtain access to college. I interviewed Sylvia in her home, located in the same town as the shelter she and her two children had lived in for eight months. I asked Sylvia if a situation came to mind in which she and Sheila, a shelter staff member, had successfully worked together as a team to get a resource she needed. She responded within seconds: "When I first came to the shelter, Sheila asked me what my goals were. I said I really wanted to get my GED [Graduate Equivalency Diploma] and go on to school. She told me when the lady came to help parents work on their GED." Sylvia took part in those classes. "Then came the time for assessments for college. Sheila said to me, 'Why don't you go and take them so you can see . . . ?' I said I wasn't ready for college. She told me I could really do this. She pushed me. It wasn't like she said I had to go. So I went and took [the college assessments]." Subsequently, Sylvia applied for and was successfully admitted to a local community college. Sheila also helped Sylvia to overcome child care and transportation obstacles that might have prevented her from attending classes regularly. Sylvia's face was full of emotion as she described the impact of Sheila's help: "It makes me feel good . . . that somebody believes in me. For a long time, I didn't believe in me. Then, once I started to do all this stuff, I can't stop believing in myself . . . that I can really do it." At the time I interviewed Sylvia, she was a full-time student working toward an associates degree in the same college she attended while living in the shelter.

Mandatory Group Meetings: Up Close

Almost universally, congregate family shelter programs in Massachusetts required parents to participate in a weekly house meeting. Almost universally, the parents, directors, and staff members I interviewed thought this meeting was essential as a vehicle for resolving issues that came up in the course of their daily lives together in the shelter. I participated in three mandatory group meetings. Two were house meetings, one was a parenting class. What follows is a detailed portrayal of the dynamics between staff and parents at two of these meetings, a parenting group and a house meeting focused on child discipline.[15]

A Parenting Group

While I was waiting for the evening parenting group to begin, Hilda suggested that I sit in the staff office. Belinda, a night staff member, was sitting in the office. I had heard from many parents that Belinda was great, "very human." She sat down at the desk near a window, opened the window next to the front parking spaces, and said that staff suspected some drug activity, for which she was keeping her ear out tonight. After hearing a little about my study, Belinda told me how she felt about working in the program. She had been on the staff for eight months. She emphasized how hard it was for her to bridge her way of working with the program policies and approaches other staff used. She had to squelch her gut instincts in order to keep within the flow and rules of the program. She ran into trouble with management because she was not as stringent about enforcing the rules as were other staff members. She said that she really liked her contacts with the families. I could understand why the parents held Belinda in such high regard. She referred to them in very human terms and did not place herself above them.

Around 8:00 P.M., I went into the living room where the parenting group was to be held. The group was scheduled for Monday night when the parents usually liked to watch a certain TV show. Needless to say, they didn't like the schedule. The sounds of children filled the halls as I passed through. Four parents, Martha, Diana, Jane, and Laura, who came dressed in her pajamas, were already present. Martha, Diana, and Laura began talking with Jane about staying away from diet soda during her pregnancy. Laura, a forty-year-old woman, had two school-age children. She had tattoos on every uncovered part of her arms and legs. She was full of humor and had the whole group laughing. Diana was frazzled. She had left her groceries in her friend's car trunk and was waiting for her to return. Another couple entered the room, the only African American family I had seen that evening. Hilda, the group leader, was late for the meeting by about half an hour. Two fathers and a another pregnant woman joined the group. The parents talked and laughed among themselves about what happens to them when they're late, pointing out the double standard for Hilda's lateness.

When Hilda arrived, she apologized for being late without offering an explanation. She passed around an attendance sheet and asked if everyone knew me. Several said that they didn't. She asked me to tell them why I was there. I told them that I was a student, learning about what it was like for parents to care for their children in congregate family shelters. I thanked them for letting me be present. I told them that I was visiting four other programs in the state and really appreciated their openness to my being there. After they introduced themselves, Hilda summarized what they had done in previous meetings. She laid out some ground rules: no discussing specific problems. They needed to use individual sessions with her for that. She wasn't going to give advice, because she wanted them to use the time to get parenting ideas from each other.

She asked them to share their experiences with the homework, spending some quality time with their children. One father, the African American man, said he had helped his son make a book and that he had waited on his teenage son for dinner one night. Diana tried twice to say that she had given two birthday parties, but no one seemed to hear her. She gave up. She was having a good time holding and playing with Jim's three-month-old baby. Preschoolers came in and out during the meeting. A lot of babies were crying. I wondered how children who were trying to sleep could stay asleep with all the noise.

At one point Diana and Susanna began talking about how stressful it was for them to care for their children in the shelter. Hilda immediately cut off that line of discussion. I asked her later that night in our interview about her decision to do this. My presence was one of two factors she identified. "They had their chance to tell you what they thought in your individual interviews," she said. Second, she thought they were diverting attention away from having to deal with their own parenting troubles by blaming their stress over their kids on the shelter. Hilda asked the parents to leave their guilt at the door. She also shared her own parenting story. She had been a "yeller" when her children were young. Her preschool son gave her feedback about her yelling, which, Hilda indicated, led her to change this habit. The parents were glued to Hilda's words as she spoke. I was impressed that she had shared this story with them. However, I was disturbed by her reactions to parents' stories. She gave them advice about doing a better parenting job. She was not directing them back to each other, as planned. I felt uncomfortable about her messages, because she knew so much about each parent and they were fully exposed in front of her. I was amazed that they were willing to share their parenting inadequacies under these circumstances. I admired the courage of these women and men.

At about 9:00 P.M., Hilda called for a five minute break and urged everyone to return promptly. After five minutes the parents gathered together again. Hilda failed to return for another fifteen minutes. They grumbled once again among themselves about her lateness and the double standard at work, and expressed anger about not being able to discuss the difficulties of caring for their children in the shelter. Jane said that her outside counselor couldn't believe they weren't allowed to discuss the stresses of shelter living at meetings and said she was planning to volunteer to lead such a group. Jane asked how the others would feel about having a chance to get stuff off their chests, to vent. No one responded enthusiastically. Emily, another parent, brought some fresh-baked cookies in for the group. She and Laura had arranged for their children, who periodically wandered into the living room, to watch a movie in one of the family's rooms while the parenting group was taking place.

When Hilda returned, the discussion shifted to the topic of making changes as a parent and finding yourself sounding exactly like your own mother when you had vowed to never let that happen. A number of parents could relate to that line of thinking and told the others their stories. Martha and Laura took the lead in the storytelling, both interjecting considerable humor. Laura used some very funny, vulgar, and graphic language that broke up the whole room. Hilda ended the meeting by reading a story written by a father, a story about his change from a yelling to a nonyelling parent. Tears were running down Martha's cheeks as she listened. Hilda reread the last paragraph, with an emphasis on taking nonyelling one meal at a time. It was 10:00 P.M. at this point. Diana told Hilda, "Your time is up." The meeting needed to end.

Later, after Hilda and I finished our individual interview, Jim was in the foyer completing his chore. He was singing and kibitzing with Belinda, who was kidding him about being off-tune. Another father, also completing his chore, joined in. I enjoyed watching their spirited banter. This was the only time I witnessed relaxed and fun communication between a staff member and parents during all my visits to this shelter. Most of the interactions were formal. This stood out as an exception. Pondering this idea, I left the shelter and headed home, exhausted. It was 10:45 P.M..

A House Meeting

I arrived early for the 10:00 A.M. house meeting. Rosalita, the house manager, was there first. I felt unsure about where to sit in this room and looked for a seat that would allow me to fade into the woodwork, to no avail. The room was small, and every seat was in the middle of the action. I picked a spot on the floor, next to the couch. The Spanish interpreter arrived. She sat next to the one mother in the house who spoke Spanish exclusively. Juanita, the leader of the day's discussion, entered the room. She worked in a local agency that provided training and consultation for a group of family shelters in the community. She put a newsprint sheet up on the bathroom door located at the front of the room. This sheet had four questions on it, all related to child discipline, the topic of today's meeting. Gradually, the room filled up. Janice, the family life advocate, came into the room announcing that one of the mothers was not feeling well but that she had asked her to come anyway. "If she's not feeling good, why did you ask her to be here?" another mother countered. Janice ignored her question.

Janice and I were the only Caucasian women present. Rosalita sat on her desk next to Janice who started the meeting by having each of us introduce ourselves. She then announced some change in the ways that children would be supervised when volunteers came later in the day. This change seemed to be related to the exit of a family that the staff had found problematic. In our conversation a day earlier, Rosalita and Janice had referred to the mother in this family as the "brat of the house." Juanita started the discussion by using what Janice had said and suggesting that they work together and all use the same approaches, that the consistency would be better for the children in the shelter. A few mothers expressed how hard it was to get their children to behave in the shelter. Through the interpreter, one mother said that she couldn't get her child to do homework because he wanted to be with the other children. Juanita emphasized the mother's ability to control what happened inside her room, saying she could choose to let her son play after he finished his homework. The mother disputed her power to make this happen.

Juanita wanted to know what each of them thought child discipline was. Rosa challenged Juanita to tell the mothers what she thought first, which Juanita did. I got distracted by some mothers talking on the side, saying, "If you are open, Janice will be watching you." A few minutes later, Rosa addressed her fellow mothers: "You people are all lying. You know what you do to discipline your kids." Immediately, a loud discussion broke out, focused on hitting and spanking kids. Juanita said something about the reason the mothers were present was to have more options for parenting. A chorus of voices broke out: "No, you've got that wrong." This meeting was mandatory, and the mothers did not have a choice about the topic.

Against all odds of being listened to, Juanita received permission from the group to role-play how it feels to be on the receiving end of a parent's yelling. She talked about her father's mistreatment when she was a child. She had watched the different ways her mother and father disciplined her and followed in her mother's not her father's footsteps with her own children. Her mother had used talking not hitting to change the children's behavior. Rosalita played the role of a stubborn child not wanting to do homework. Juanita yelled in her face. Rosalita really got into the role. She described for the group how she had developed into a young angry kid as a result of her mother's mistreatment. She graphically and humorously played out how she tried to communicate with her daughter in a different way, how she lost her cool sometimes, and how her four-year-old son imitated her swearing behavior. The mothers in the group were spellbound. One of them made a joke about how talking things out makes you sound wimpy. Rosalita chimed in that, in spite of having those same feelings at times, she got good results by talking with her kids. Another mother said that spanking worked but talking didn't.

Janice jumped in about her upbringing, what she and her sister would do to get attention, mostly negative attention, from her parents. She admitted that she doesn't have children. The Spanish-speaking mother, Delia, became very vocal. For a while she and Juanita carried on a conversation in Spanish. Gradually, most of the other mothers left the room. Janice called out, exhorting them to return. The mother who had said she was sick left the room, grumbling that she was sick and that others who were not sick had left the room. The meeting did not get pulled back together again. Delia continued to talk with Juanita and Rosalita, while Janice tried unsuccessfully to draw the other mothers back into the room.

I stayed for a debriefing with Juanita, Rosalita, and Janice. Janice praised Juanita for riding the "bucking bronco" so well throughout the meeting, indicating that they had made a dent with Delia. I learned later that some of the staff's concerns about this child discipline issue were the result of an incident that had taken place between Delia and her son the previous day. These three women asked my opinion about what I had witnessed. I observed that they allowed mothers to air the difficulties they had with parenting their children in this setting and had noticed that the cross-cultural issues seemed pretty significant. All three jumped in to assure me that the mothers were hiding behind cultural differences because they did not want to look at their parenting. I was not convinced. The staff goal for this session, getting mothers to use talking rather than spanking to discipline their children, did not appear to be the mothers' goal. These women had not wanted to be present, and they had not picked the topic. The staff might have been right in thinking that certain mothers needed to change their parenting behaviors. However, I doubted that staff efforts to feed them new child discipline ideas would be fruitful, unless the mothers were invested in this learning. On the other hand, the mothers may have been listening and soaking up the information staff were providing, while acting uninterested as a means of saving face with each other and with staff. If this was in fact the case, the disconnect between parents' outer and inner worlds would be problematic because it might make it difficult for parents to be open with staff about their parenting concerns and struggles.

Perspectives on Mandatory Services

The five case study sites varied in several different ways, including the number of mandatory meetings parents were required to attend. The two shelters that operated from a prescriptive, deficit orientation had a significantly higher number of mandatory service requirements than did the three shelters that operated from a family support orientation—eight vs. an average of two meetings per week, respectively. What follows is a glimpse into the ways that the directors, frontline staff, and mothers thought about programs' service approaches.

Prescriptive Orientation

The directors of the two programs that operated from a prescriptive, deficit-oriented belief system shared similar opinions about their service approaches. Both felt satisfied with the large number of meetings parents were required to attend. Their frustrations had to do with parents' negative response to these requirements. One said, "Parents don't like to be told what to do." The other articulated an even more despairing viewpoint, "Sometimes, parents don't care. They don't have the basic skills and they don't want the service."

The four frontline staff I interviewed from these programs expressed mixed feelings about service requirements. On the one hand, they all considered the mandatory meetings very valuable. They had witnessed mutual growth among parents as a result of the group meetings. Those who had the skills enriched the learning of others. One staff member articulated her worry that if meetings were not mandatory, residents would never show up. Another said that at times one person's problem can be dealt with in a group setting rather than by singling her out individually. Also, even though parents complained about the meetings, at times, once they were in session, parents did not want them to end.

On the other hand, several of these staff were concerned about families' important outside commitments. The number of mandatory meetings each week created difficult dilemmas for these families as they tried to balance all the demands they were juggling. One staff member voiced another concern about the inappropriate parent-child dynamic that these service requirements set up in the relationships staff have with parents. "The requirements are hard to enforce," she said, "while protecting the dignity of adults."

Mothers I interviewed from these programs had definite opinions regarding the number and types of meetings they were required to attend. A few parents were negative about all the meetings and felt that the program's approach had made their families' shelter experiences harder. Some liked the individual meetings with a staff member more than the group meetings. Some expressed deep frustration with having to juggle so many demands on their time, particularly between the shelter meetings and their outside commitments. One person expressed the distinction between helpful and not-so-helpful meetings: "Some weren't worth it to be honest with you. Some were. Like the house meeting. Nine times out of ten, I was giving the information to everyone else. If there was something good coming out, then fine. Call a mandatory meeting. If not, then why make us stay there just to sit there listening to nothing." Another mother was very positive about some meetings and negative about others: "The best meeting is the house meeting, because everybody gets to discuss their problems with other residents or staff members or whatever. That's really good because we need to get those things out in the open. The child advocate meeting is a joke. The housing meeting is a joke. The visiting nurse is good. She is really helpful. She listens to you and helps with questions, and is really nice." Only two of the sixteen mothers I interviewed from these shelters were neutral about or satisfied with the mandatory procedures.

Family Support Orientation

Directors of the three programs that operated from a family support belief system expressed satisfaction with the few mandatory meetings they required families to attend. One director emphasized how important the house meeting was as a part of their program's group empowerment philosophy. This program strived to have significant resident input into the program's policies and procedures.

Another director also saw house meetings as a vehicle for parents to provide input to the program. However, each of them expressed dilemmas they struggled with related to their program approach. One director said that scheduling was hard, given the number of outside commitments parents have each week. Another voiced how difficult it was to balance the group needs for order and security with individuals' needs for autonomy. The third director said that she tried for a balance of structure and flexibility, and that she and her staff often worked out individual contracts with parents, focused on that parent's unique needs and desires.

The six frontline staff members I interviewed from these shelters reflected similar viewpoints to the directors of their programs. However, they provided more detail about their struggles in implementing and enforcing the limited mandatory service requirements. Each thought that the house meeting was very important as a vehicle for receiving input from parents. One staff member reflected upon how hard the process of receiving input really is: "It takes a lot of work and thought to listen to families," she said. Two staff members reflected upon the ways that mandatory meetings become a battleground between parents and staff. Figuring out when and how to confront a parent was something that both women struggled with. They used conversation or "charm, a smile, a hug, as a nudge." "Angry confrontation is a last resort," said Joanne. "Don't set up battles you don't want to fight."

Mothers I interviewed from these programs were mostly positive about their experiences in attending mandatory meetings. The few expressions of disgruntlement I heard had to do with schedule conflicts or the occasional ineffective meeting. Uniformly, these mothers indicated that the house meetings were very important. "We needed that house meeting. We had it just for the guests living there to air their differences." Several mothers expressed frustration that parent input did not make enough of an impact. One mother put it this way: "Parents didn't speak up enough. Half the problem was us, but half the problem was the staff." A mother who viewed herself as shy reported that the group meetings helped her. "It helped me talk about things that I had buried so far down inside myself," she said. "That is probably why I got so angry, because I had no one to ever talk to. I am finally opening up. It wasn't comfortable at first, but after a while you hear everybody talking." One of these programs offered a parent nurturing program on a voluntary basis for parents and children. These group meetings included a community supper, some talking time for parents, some talking time for children, and fun parent-child activities. All of the mothers I interviewed who took part in this service talked about the experience very positively.

One mother said she asked for help from the staff that resulted in a contract requiring her to attend five meetings a week. She had just left a half-way house and was in recovery from an alcohol addiction. She wanted structure. "They asked me what I wanted, and I said, 'five meetings.' I enjoyed going to the meetings and it didn't affect my AA meetings. I always had plenty of time to get to my meeting. If I didn't have time for lunch before I went to my meeting, they would make sure to save me lunch. That was good." She added, "The meetings were all interesting and helpful. I learned a lot, especially about housing and mainly parenting. They did some work on self-esteem and some recovery work. I found it very helpful." Fourteen of the twenty-three mothers I interviewed from these three shelters were satisfied with the mandatory meeting requirements. Nine expressed some dissatisfaction.

The evidence presented in this chapter runs counter to prevailing negative beliefs about "getting tough" with people using public assistance. Rather, it demonstrates that helpers can hold parents accountable for their actions and commitments without using a punitive, one-size-fits-all framework. Mutuality in the relationship is the key. Helpers and parents hold each other accountable. It is possible for parents to move toward their goals and to learn new skills when they are active partners in developing their own service plan. Parents' aspirations and hopes, however deeply buried, can be tapped. It is also possible for parents to learn, if they can trust that their helpers will withhold judgment when their flaws and vulnerabilities are exposed. Mutual accountability that recognizes and builds upon the strengths and expertise parents and staff bring to their work together produces very powerful results. "I can't stop believing in myself" and "Now, I do it on my own" are two very striking expressions of the efficacy of such help giving.

Helpers need considerable organizational support to enable them to assist parents without taking over, to set limits without anger or judgment, and to tailor services to each parent's unique learning style. Organizational permission and opportunities for skill development are essential for helpers to engage with parents as adults, with a sense of mutuality in the relationship. Organizations can engage parents as allies in evaluating program effectiveness, using the family support criteria as a standard. The evidence in this chapter illustrates that parents are discriminating evaluators. They are hungry for good help. The stakes for parents and children are high. Help that injures the spirit is harmful. When parents feel broken and flawed as a result of their interactions with helpers, their children suffer. When parents feel centered, strong, and hopeful as a result of their interactions with helpers, their children have reason to be hopeful as well.

The reflections of Elisabeth Ward, a mother and staff member, Mary Lewis a frontline staff member, and Nancy Schwoyer, director of a family shelter, follow this chapter. They offer diverse but complementary views on the issues covered here, based upon their work at Wellspring House in Gloucester, Massachusetts.

Reflections on Chapter 5

Reflection: Mother and Staff Member, Elisabeth Ward
My personal experience of homelessness was nearly ten years ago, and the political climate regarding affordable housing was different than it is today. Access to family shelters was not problematic since shelter stays averaged six to eight weeks and state and federal government housing subsidies were available to homeless families. My shelter experience was brief, about seven weeks. Although I was required to attend two meetings a week, I did not feel that the shelter staff were invasive or that my life was overly scrutinized. Last year I had the experience of working in the same shelter where I had been a guest years ago, and life in a congregate family shelter has clearly changed.

In the years since I was homeless, affordable housing resources have dwindled and the poor, especially poor women with children, have been portrayed in the media and by politicians as fundamentally dysfunctional. Shelter access is controlled by the Department of Transitional Assistance (formerly the welfare department), and many families are locked out of shelter due to extremely rigid definitions of what constitutes homelessness. The shelters have had to adapt practices to comply with the requirements of the state government. For example, shelter guests must do twenty hours a week of housing search work and are now asked to report their daily schedules, along with phone numbers where they can be reached, to shelter staff. The guests' sense of autonomy is now severely compromised, and it is not surprising that many homeless women feel they have very little control over their lives while living in a congregate shelter.

As I have already mentioned before, my shelter stay was only seven weeks long. I did not feel it necessary to share every detail of my life with the staff, since I was intensely aware that the fundamental issue was to find affordable housing for me and my son. I shared the circumstances of my homelessness with the intake worker and the director of the program. If the other shelter workers knew intimate details about my life, I was not aware of it. I believe that my privacy was respected.

Although my life was in crisis and I was under an enormous amount of stress, I understood the move into shelter to be a means to an end. I needed affordable housing and this was how I would accomplish that formidable task. My almost singular vision was to obtain a subsidy and find an apartment. Other aspects of my life were under control, as far as I was concerned, and the shelter staff took my word that this was true. I did have a couple of minor conflicts with one of the staff. When my son, who was a busy two-year-old, dashed out of my sight, I was told that I "needed to keep him with me." I told her that I could always spot a human service worker by their incessant use of the word "need." Later, when I became a human service worker myself, I was always careful about the use of the word. I remembered how it felt to be told what I "needed" and how it felt to have my parenting skills unfairly criticized.

The environment at this particular shelter was, and still is, supportive and nurturing. The difference between now and ten years ago is the amount of time the staff spends to "manage" the lives of shelter guests. There are multiple reasons for this change, the most obvious being the length of time the families now live in shelter before obtaining affordable housing. As a shelter worker, I often felt we knew more about each guest than was necessary and that the staff was at risk of becoming enmeshed in the lives of the guests. Boundaries were sometimes unclear, and privacy was almost nonexistent for the shelter guests. Each guest is obliged to follow an individualized "program"; they may be required to attend domestic violence groups, to go to individual or family therapy sessions, or to attend twelve-step meetings. This is in addition to the other mandatory groups of the shelter, as well as performing twenty hours of housing search. Although there is some flexibility in the "programs," it seems to me that the expectations placed upon the guests are much more demanding now than they were ten years ago.

Shelters interested in having high standards of practice would be well advised to hire staff who are sensitive to issues surrounding the experience of homelessness. It is important that staff feel free to question and address concerns regarding the practice standards of the shelter without fear of reprisal. Also, it is vital for staff to remember that the primary focus for each family is to obtain safe, affordable housing.

Reflection: Family Life Advocate, Mary Lewis

As a frontline worker who believes in and works at a shelter that supports the "family support" model of help giving, I am struck by how difficult today's contractual expectations make it to work through this framework. I agree with Donna Friedman's contention that contract requirements are firmly based on society's popular assumptions that poverty and homeless are the result of bad habits, immoral behavior, and the lack of healthy values. These assumptions are expressed in contracts through requirements for parents' mandatory participation in certain programs. The apparent belief is that once made to learn more responsible behavior, parents will achieve a more productive life style and thus develop a happier existence. Although this line of thinking may be well meaning, and may even share a few elements with the "family support" model of help giving, the problems with this framework have been well documented in chapter 5. I would like to take this time to reflect upon what I see as needed supports for those in help-giving positions who practice from the family support model.

Like Belinda in chapter 4, I worry about the time that I will not be able to follow through on the enforcement of a "mandatory" requirement. Will I be asked to leave my job or, worse yet, will I cause the shelter to suffer? Even if neither of those things happen, Belinda and I are still at risk for burnout or cooptation unless we find support for ourselves while working within a system that has expectations that we find contrary to our practice. These supports include, but are not limited to:

- A clear but always growing framework of practice;
- Team input and support that can also be called a "community of resistance"; and
- Time to allow and encourage the growth of the practice framework and safety to ask for support and correction from colleagues.

First, the development of a clear and flexible framework of practice is a constant job of reevaluation and clarification. Shelter staff need to be allowed, encouraged, and paid to take courses, attend workshops, and have access to adequate supervision and consultation. From many studies, it is clear that frontline shelter staff are underpaid and often lack an adequate educational background and job experience as well as on-the-job training and support.[1] Without these supports it is impossible to develop the kind of practice framework that allows for both clear boundaries and mutual, supportive help giving.

Second, to work within the family support model we as shelter workers are called upon to resist concepts and demeaning opinions of poor and homeless families. The question of how to do this is answered, I believe, in the creation of what Welch (1985) calls "communities of resistance." These communities or groups help to clarify the forces that we resist in order to maintain our vision of practice. The community of resistance provides support and definition to its members and allows the creation of a safe place to discuss common concerns. It has been my experience that any time a help giver's framework differs from the mainstream, it is essential to find support. No one of us has the resources to resist alone, but together we can build a common shelter.

Finally, time is important. Staff need time to process the stresses, successes, and failures of their work. They need to learn and grow from their experiences. The creation of a shelter team that can evaluate, support, and call its members to task when necessary is critical. This must be done in a safe and respectful manner, which takes time and the willingness to work through the process.

The supports that I as a shelter staff person need are very similar to those that the shelter family needs. All of us need support to develop clarity in our direction, encouragement to follow through on our practice and decisions, and safety to fail as we learn and grow. Workers cannot be expected for long to give that which they do not have themselves. As the call for more and more mandatory services increases, we must be aware of the basic beliefs from which they arise. We need to evaluate whether these beliefs are in accordance with our own, and if they are not, to create ways to join with others of like minds to resist them. We do this not only for ourselves but also so we may be role models for those with whom we work. We all must learn together.

Reflection: Executive Director, Nancy Schwoyer

We can safely assume that when families are homeless and in shelter they want one thing and that is to have their own homes again as soon as possible. I also think that the majority of shelter workers want to help families achieve that goal. So, it seems to me that we can evaluate the appropriateness of support functions in shelters by asking the question, "Does this program piece help families to get housing?" At least that is a question we have asked at Wellspring House for more than fifteen years. Now, with welfare reform, we ask a second question: "What can we do to support families while they are in shelter to prepare for the reality of time limits and the transition from public benefits to work that provides a sustainable income?"

I believe these are the first questions to be asked by shelter program developers, not whether programs will be voluntary or mandatory. My experience tells me that only if programs are meeting the real needs of homeless families will those families participate in them. As an educator I believe that homeless adults must be treated as adult learners and that they should be able to expect well-prepared and effectively presented groups and other services. However, if program components in shelters are primarily a way to structure shelter life, then mandatory programs may provide some control but will most probably not lead to mutual respect and mutual accountability between staff and residents. Without these, shelters can be desperate places in which to live and work.

The landscape for homeless families and shelters has changed dramatically in the eighteen years that I have been living and working with homeless families, and that has necessitated constant evaluation of the services offered. Between 1982 and 1989 we had resources in

Massachusetts provided by state legislation known as Chapter 450: An Act To Prevent Homelessness. It provided appropriations not only to shelter homeless families but also to prevent homelessness and assist families to move from shelter to housing. There was money not only for back rent to keep families in their homes but also for unpaid utility bills, storage of furniture for three months, and moving costs. Another piece of legislation, Chapter 707, funded a housing subsidy program so that between 1983 and 1989, six thousand homeless families were able to leave shelter and move into housing that was affordable.

The landscape of the '80s in Massachusetts was bleak because of the reality of homelessness, but it was not without hope. Public policy ensured resources both for prevention of homelessness and for solutions to it. Many of us believed that with such help we could end the nightmare of homelessness. I remember those years vividly. There was always movement in Wellspring's shelter—families moving in as others moved out with a good-bye party and hugs and promises to keep in touch. Length of stay was a matter of weeks—perhaps six to eight weeks—seldom more than three months.

At Wellspring we had a framework of groups and individual services to support families during their shelter stay and after they moved into their new homes. The framework was appropriate to the situation of fast movement; it was also flexible and supported guests who were working or going to school to continue to do so during their shelter stay. There were three weekly groups for guests whose schedules permitted them to attend. A weekly house meeting was a forum to sort out the difficulties of group living and to share information and a time to say good-bye to a guest who would be leaving that week. A weekly housing workshop, facilitated by the housing advocate, helped guests to navigate housing authorities and the other bureaucratic systems that regulate access to housing. Recently, I met a woman who had been at Wellspring twelve years ago, and she told me that, in addition to getting her own home, the most valuable thing she got from her Wellspring experience was learning the "ins and outs" of the 707 and Section 8 programs. "Learning how the system worked gave me real power and a sense of confidence in myself," she told me.

The third group was facilitated by the family life advocate and involved the guests in making a social analysis of their homelessness. (I have explained in my response to chapter 1 why we at Wellspring think that learning about the systemic causes of poverty and homelessness is so important.) The other topic that the women wanted to study was "the cycle of violence." The experience of violence was one many of them shared, and they wanted to end it for themselves and their children. The family life advocate was a skilled facilitator and adult educator; she understood the process of mutual learning, as well as the balance between the value of group members sharing experience and herself, as teacher, giving information needed by the group.

In addition to the support of these three groups, each family worked with a staff person on issues particular to the family, and as the time came to move, she helped the family to establish connections in the community to which they were moving. The housing advocate also met several times a week with each family to address particular housing-related issues, e.g., applications, references, moving plans, etc.

In general I can say that this program framework was a successful structure. It supported families in achieving their goal of getting their own homes, and it supported the structure of the shelter. In their evaluations done when they left Wellspring most, though not all families said that support from staff and the groups had been helpful to them. Years later, in research we did in 1991, the respondents who were former shelter guests said so again, though they also expressed that the time in shelter had been stressful and difficult not only because of the trauma of being homeless but also because of the irritation and stress of rules, group living, loss of privacy, and parenting in public.

In the past decade of the '90s the landscape for homeless families and those who work to end homelessness has become more barren, cold, and raw. Our public policy is inhospitable to poor people. In Massachusetts the policy makers have taken actions that have resulted not only in tighter restrictions concerning eligibility for shelter and for public housing; but they have also defunded prevention resources and other resources necessary to end homelessness, including the 707 program and affordable housing development programs. The cost of rental housing in the Commonwealth is among the highest in the country, most especially in the eastern part of the state, and there has been very little increase in the stock of rental housing in the last ten years. As we who work to end homelessness say, "The front door to shelter is hard to open and the back door is blocked, if not locked." Imagine a farmer trying to grow food without land. We are trying to do our work without the essential resource of HOUSING.

With the loss of resources for affordable housing, the length of stay in shelters has consequently increased dramatically. Between 1990 and 1994 we saw the average length of stay creep up to six months; between 1994 and the present, the majority of families have stayed at Wellspring longer than six months, a few for a year or longer. In addition to the loss of homelessness prevention and solution resources, homeless families now lose a portion of their income from TANF while they are in shelter, thus limiting a family's ability to pay old utility bills and to save money for the first month's rent and security deposit.

In addition to all that, the requirements of welfare reform, in particular the twenty-four-month time limit, place additional stress on homeless families and also on shelter workers. This is the richest country in the world, but it is also one that tolerates homelessness and blames poor people for its budgetary ills and legislates them to work, even though the figures show that there are not enough jobs to employ them. At the same time our system denies them the education to prepare for jobs that pay a sustainable wage, pretending there is adequate child care, affordable housing, and health care available. What kind of supports do homeless families need in this inhospitable culture? This is the complex question we must ask the families and each other as providers again and again as we design shelter programs suitable to these desperate times.

At Wellspring we are adapting to the reality of welfare time limits in the context of longer shelter stays and the Department of Transitional Assistance (DTA) requirement that families in shelter do twenty hours of housing search a week. We still have the same program framework because it works for the families—a combination of group and individualized services, although the groups have changed somewhat. A house meeting and housing group are still in place. We have added a group called New Beginnings, a series of workshops for women in transition and a support group. In 1998 we joined with the other North Shore family shelters in a collaborative called Transition To Work, a program funded by the U.S. Department of Housing and

Urban Development (HUD), in which we help homeless families move successfully from welfare to work.

Wellspring's framework of family support to help families get housing and jobs is very flexible because it is designed to meet the particular needs of each family. Flexibility in services requires a skilled, adaptable, dedicated staff who work together as a team. Staff have to adapt their one-to-one meetings with families to accommodate their school and work schedules. They have to facilitate groups that change in membership, both in numbers and people. Staff also have to be resourceful in helping families to locate local transportation and quality child care. Wellspring is very fortunate to have such a staff. On the whole there is mutual respect among staff and between staff and homeless families, whom we call guests. There is also mutual accountability. Staff expect guests to follow through on achieving family goals and guests expect quality services from staff. Staff also have to be accountable to each other and be responsible for their piece of the family work. Mutual respect and accountability not only characterize the support services at Wellspring. They are also the foundation of the structure of Wellspring's shelter. For us, the issue of mandatory or voluntary services is not the structural question!

6

The Paradox of Self-Sufficiency: Building Community and Interdependence

The welfare rhetoric is that people should depend on themselves only.
We help them learn to give and get help from each other,
to support each other, use each other . . .
The benefit to group living is that they learn it is not a deficiency to
ask for help from staff
as well as other residents.

—Manager of a congregate family shelter, Summer 1994

The day before a family leaves the shelter, the whole community has a celebration meal together. The meal follows a group meeting in which the children and parents who are leaving get to hear from staff and other family members what it was like to live with them, what they have given to the community.

Self-sufficiency is an impossible goal to attain. While notions of self-reliance and independence have deep roots in the American psyche,[1] no one has or ever will realize this mythical state of being. All families have to find ways to nurture and provide economic support for their members. None can do it well in isolation. Many struggling with poverty survive through elaborate and deeply important friendship and kin network exchanges.[2] The need for real community and interdependence cuts across income lines.

In previous decades, when fewer middle- and upper-class American women participated in the paid labor force, their husbands relied upon them to take care of internal family affairs, including raising the children. Indeed, families with ample incomes and a male breadwinner often relied upon the labor of very poor women to care for their children, to clean their houses, and to farm their land.[3] Although cultural shifts in male-female nurturing roles are taking place in America, the work of women on the home front continues to be vital in enabling men to function in the paid labor force.[4] Further, mothers and fathers could not function well in their work lives today, without the help of those poorly paid child care workers, primarily women, who care for their children while they work. Community and interdependence are essential for physical, social, and psychological well-being for all men, women and children. They always have been and they always will be.

What does the community owe its members, and what do members owe the community?

The current welfare reform policies and regulations seek to promote self-sufficiency, meaning poor people should permanently end their reliance upon the government for income support. One stated objective of the most current federal and state welfare reforms is to eliminate recipients' negative dependence upon the government,[5] reflecting misguided beliefs that welfare recipients do not work and do not contribute to community life. In fact, the vast majority of women and men using welfare do work. They rely upon public assistance during predictable periods of hardship associated with dealing with the vicissitudes of the low-wage labor market and with meeting the needs of children.[6]

With the passage into federal law of lifetime limits on receipt of public assistance, the stakes for the nation's most vulnerable children and families have been raised. Establishing time limits is a clear example of the level of risk we are willing to take to dilute our commitment to some members within our national community: these policies and their state variations will result in some children and parents having no source of predictable income. An entire group of children and their parents are being banished, because they appear to have failed as community contributors. Parents and children who rely upon this form of public assistance for even short periods of time are stigmatized and experience isolation from rather than connection with their higher-income brothers and sisters in the nation.

A healthy national, state, or local community is one that recognizes our common human bonds. It is a safe holding place, a physical and emotional space in which members are accepted for both their flaws and strengths. In such a community, the strengths of members are the foundation of reciprocity among members. Each member gives and takes, according to her means and capabilities. Supportive communities are places in which members supply safety, nourishment, and hope for each other. In such communities, members are provided with the safety to be vulnerable. They are open to the humanness of themselves and of others. They are assured that they will not be violated or humiliated if their flaws are exposed. Members are honored, first and foremost, for their capacities and contributions to the good of the whole; flaws are deemphasized. In a healthy community, when members need a helping hand, they are supported and are not cast off as damaged goods.

Community Building in Congregate Family Shelters

A congregate family shelter setting is a microcosm for exploring interdependency among a subset of community members who, as a consequence of losing their hold on housing, have been isolated from mainstream society. Within the enclosed shelter environment, they can either join together in solidarity or maintain isolation as family units. I learned in my research that managers, frontline staff, and mothers held strong views regarding whether connection and mutuality among families with common problems was a good thing to nurture. They had views regarding these obvious questions: Since families in shelters have similar problems, wouldn't mutual support simply add to their troubles? How can parents help each other if they are so stressed themselves? Wouldn't they just bring each other down? Isn't it better for parents to learn that they have only themselves to rely upon?

The stories I heard from mothers, managers, and staff lead me to think that as a whole shelter programs have not adopted the "self-sufficiency" framework as a guiding principle. As difficult as community building is to nurture and create in family shelter settings, most managers and staff spend considerable time, energy, and resources with this objective in mind.

Positive support networks are essential for all families.[7] Parents need positive connections with friends and family to carry out their parental nurturing functions. Program managers, staff, and mothers I spoke with were nearly unanimous in echoing this viewpoint. I had the sense that for the most part relationship building was the heart and substance of a considerable amount of time parents and staff spent with each other. Building community for some program managers was a pragmatic as well as philosophical matter. That is, if parents developed new skills in managing conflict and building support networks, new worlds might open up to them when they moved to their own home. One manager put it this way: "We see young women without a support network. Congregate living gives them a chance to expand it. If you don't have it, you have to create it."

The challenge of obtaining and keeping housing that families with very low incomes could afford in many parts of Massachusetts is formidable. Parents need to have confidence in their negotiation and conflict resolution skills if they are to consider housing options such as sharing an apartment with another family or if they are to effectively settle differences with future landlords and other tenants. "Congregate living exposes people to the possibility of living closely with others," one manager told me with eloquence and passion. "Maybe it's not something they would choose. [Once they leave here] they could opt to share some space with another mother and kids. Like there's another way of living other than in an apartment all by myself. The friendships they form with each other . . . when their kids are in bed, they're together. They are playing cards or watching TV. It becomes their network. They haven't had many women friendships. They also learn the whole sense of living cooperatively, sharing some child care. They continue to do that when they leave. They share transportation. The kids have extended family with each other, too. Suddenly another woman in the shelter is like an aunt. Listening to the kids greeting each other in the morning is adorable, especially the two- and three-year-olds. But I'm biased. There's too much *isolation* [speaker's emphasis] in the country."

Some managers talked about the ways in which mutuality in the relationships among staff and families aided the healing and growth process. The usual pathway for families who have lost their housing involves moving in with a series of relatives and friends.[8] These periods of unwanted and unplanned shared housing exhaust the financial and emotional resources of everyone. Others are escaping a violent partner.[9] These situations would strain the strongest relationships. "Often when they move in here initially they are very cut off from what they define as their family," a program manager told me. "Usually even if there is cut-off, often during the stay we've reconnected them to some degree. They have a stable place from which to reconnect without depending upon their extended family for housing. Often reconnection happens and the sense of family both broadens and narrows. Many come to feel like the friends they make here are their family, or they begin to define themselves and their children as family."

Another manager talked with conviction about the positive impact on families that results from life in a healthy community—that is, one in which support among members is mutual, reciprocal. A give-and-take exists. "The positive effect is that once they've been here a while, they develop strong bonds with other guests and staff," she told me. "They become a tight unit. It is the re-creation of a healthy community system, not with negative dependence. It's the first time that someone isn't casting them off. We're never willing to cast them off here. We give unconditional support. 'No matter what you're doing, I care about you.' Former guests are our volunteers. No negative effects on self-esteem or the parental role. Ties remain with each other. It's common to see two women who had trouble with each other while they lived here walking down the street together, keeping their friendship."

The loss of control over children and the disruption of family routines were extremely frustrating aspects of congregate living for many mothers. However, many managers told me about the benefits children receive from the close connection with other children and the close contact with staff members. "The children really thrive here. Over the years, I've seen kids in such crises. After they're here for a couple of days, they love it. They have constant playmates," one manager told me. "There's always a staff person paying me attention and treating me special. They like and respond to the structure and care.

It's like a big party constantly. This is frustrating to the parents, but children thrive."

A few managers, staff members, and mothers that I interviewed expressed a clear minority view: they actively discouraged community building. They pointed out some of the problems with how this works in a congregate shelter setting. First, in their view, each family has its own stresses and challenges it must overcome. Taking on those of other families will take away from what should be their own primary goal: to find housing and leave.

One manager with this viewpoint directed a program located in a rural part of the state, whose mission statement reflected her opinion: "To empower individuals and families to lead independent and productive lives." She told me, "The parents who really love their kids isolate themselves from other families as their kids learn negative behaviors. Lots of parents report not liking their kids any more after they live here a while. Four or five cases in the last two years I've been here have wanted to give their kids away. Living here just puts some kids and their parents over the edge." She also told me that social isolation, along with its concomitant social problems, seriously debilitates the surrounding community. This manager clearly viewed isolation as a negative circumstance for families in the community outside the shelter but did not see herself or her program as having a role in building connections among families, even temporarily, during the time that they resided in her shelter.

Staff in only one of the programs I spent time in were vociferous with me about the threats posed by friendships among parents and by my research. In this shelter, which operated from a paternalistic helping orientation, parents were prohibited from visiting each other in their bedrooms. The two staff members I interviewed expressed their worries early on in the interviewing process regarding the trouble I was causing by asking mothers what they think about the shelter's rules and about the working relationships between themselves and mothers. They told me that they did not want the research to undermine their authority with families in their shelter. They expressed fear that parents would compare their responses to my questions with each other and subsequently coalesce as a group to protest shelter operations.

A mother and staff member in this program told me about several hazards in making connections in these settings. Being thrown together by difficult circumstances leads to a sense that parents are friends when they actually aren't. Parents may come to regret having disclosed very personal thoughts and information with people who were actually strangers. Susan, a staff member I interviewed, went into detail on this subject as she told me about a situation in which one family's money had been stolen by someone else in the shelter. "Yes, you want everyone to be your friend, but you are basically living in a house with strangers," she said. "Take the time to get to know them if you like, but remember you are all going your own way. Some of these people you are never going to see again. Some of these people you may become good friends with. I can't dictate that either way. But I know that your main concern here is to take care of you and your family first. After that, you can become friendly."

One mother in this program felt betrayed by other mothers when they joined with a staff member in confronting her about her suspected drug use. She moved out of the shelter before she obtained permanent housing as a result of this "intervention." "You got all of these families acting like your friend and yet they are not," she said. "You are living with these people because you have to, not because you want to. So one thing I can say to people who have to go into shelters, 'Don't trust anybody. . . . Don't think they are your best friend because they are not going to be. Unless you move out and move into the same building, you are probably never going to see them again once you move out of the shelter.' "

According to a few directors and staff members, the connections between parents end up leaving children out. "One real difficulty in a congregate situation, the parents tend to ignore the children and socialize with each other," one manager told me. "It may be like this in their own home, but they would be pushed to take care of their child, but here there's backup. Socialization is more important than the child." A few others told me that some families are more vulnerable to the negatives of community living. That is, they are just more shy or quiet or private than others. Or they come into the shelter with lower self-esteem than others and are more vulnerable to the criticism that naturally arises at times in a group setting.

Based on what I heard from quite a few mothers and staff, a positive experience of community is somewhat dependent upon the particular mix of families present at any time. Families who are more troubled than others or who don't fit in are often ostracized by other families. Incidents of violence, terminations of parents and children, or children being removed from their parents' care send waves of fear, sadness, and distress through the entire community. One staff member provided considerable detail on this type of event. "You haven't asked any questions about how volatile the environment [can be]," she said to me. "[A violent episode] sometimes takes weeks to get over. . . . Violent [episodes] and of course [being thrown out and having] their children taken away, these are the two most upsetting things in the shelter. . . . It's sad for the whole community. The community reaction, a mixture of sadness and fear. Immediately I know they are thinking, 'This could happen to me.' A lot of sadness. . . . There have been a couple of times when I have cried with them, although I try not to do that."

When parents and children get close to each other living in the shelter, they have trouble leaving. Leaving creates sadness and worry. Being in a new home without your friends puts families in the position of knowing what they are missing. "We emphasize community, helping each other out," one program manager told me. "Their children make friends, like a woman who gave birth to her second and third children while she was here. The environment is what they became used to. They and we got worried about what it would be like without this many people around them." The woman she was referring to was in recovery from a serious drug problem that had previously resulted in her children being removed from her care.

Community Life

Despite the perceived hazards, most managers and staff in the Massachusetts network put a considerable amount of time and energy into community building. Managers used colorful similes to describe community life in their shelters. "We're like a small town," one manager told me. Another likened the experience to a close family. "The whole group becomes like a unit. They [the children] become like little brothers and sisters," he said. "A family of two or three becomes a family of fifteen, very close. The mothers themselves start getting the same feelings. Former residents, their best friends are the ones they became friends with here. They form a bond."

Connection at Entry

A few of the programs I spent time in and others I learned about from interviews with program managers set the stage for community life by easing the way for new families just entering the shelter. Many asked "veteran" mothers to become buddies to new family members, to introduce them to other parents and children, and to give them the inside scoop on how the community routines worked. Mothers I talked with who had been asked to take this role with other families expressed satisfaction with helping out in that way. Many program directors took time when a family first entered to prepare them for the fact that they would probably connect well with some families and not with others.

Handling Gossip

I heard from both staff members and mothers about issues having to do with violation of personal boundaries and privacy protections in these settings, the downside of being like a "small town." Everyone knows everyone else's business. In some instances, gossip among parents has hurtful consequences for those parents who become the targets of collective criticism and scrutiny. A mother was thankful for a staff member's direct intervention to stop gossip among mothers. "There was a girl that came in here. She was pregnant, and real shy and real timid. She came in on the weekend and I am a very outspoken, outgoing, and I consider myself a friendly person," Lonita told me. "Stella [the staff person] was like, 'Can you show her around?' But there was a time when I thought she may have done something to hurt my daughter. Like I left her alone in the room, and my daughter was crying, and I made the mistake of telling everyone else. Stella heard us. She was in the middle office and she heard us. We were basically gossiping and she came in and said, 'Stop. . . . This girl just got here and you don't know if that happened and you need to lighten up and give her a chance.' And I did, and we are good friends today."

Staff do not always have such a positive influence on mothers' social lives. In some cases they participate in the gossip. I witnessed or heard about staff-initiated privacy violations in every shelter I visited. In some cases a staff member spoke with mothers in negative terms about other mothers. While the staff person's intent might have been legitimate, for example to intervene in conflicts between mothers, the action was nonetheless a violation of the trust that each family should be able to expect from any help giver. Janice, a staff member, provided me with some detail on such an incident. "I basically listened to her [complaint about another mother] and I always encouraged her to talk to the woman she had a problem with," Janice said. "I also acknowledged to her, which may have been unprofessional, that it was difficult talking to this woman . . . and that I could understand her dilemma because I found it hard to talk to this woman around parenting issues."

On other occasions staff members disclosed negative personal information to me about certain mothers that clearly fell outside the agreed-upon parameters of my research.[10] In my conversations with mothers, many told me that they had been burned by sharing very personal information with staff members only to find out later that the information had been divulged to other staff members. They had learned it was best to keep as much of their personal business hidden from staff as they could.

It is clear to me that violations of privacy are a definite danger in shelter settings, especially in those that use a team approach to service. A norm can easily be established under which providers come to believe that they have a right to know everything about a family's comings and goings and internal workings. This norm violates the privacy protection regulations for human service settings that are written into state law.[11] That is, the laws require service providers to determine who needs to know what, for what purpose, and to err on the side of disclosing as little as possible.

Handling Conflicts

Nearly universally, house meetings were a pivotal avenue for building support and addressing conflictual situations among families, including those related to resolving cultural or racial differences. The following comment from a program manager typifies what many others told me. "The whole group will work together to help people get along, if two people are having trouble with each other," she said. "It's about building community in a congregate setting." Another strategy managers and staff used for handling conflicts among or between families was one-on-one communication, with staff mediation. Many mothers told me stories similar to Linda's, in which staff members were instrumental in helping them to settle differences with other parents. In Linda's situation, the staff member facilitated but was not directly involved in mediating between herself and another mother. "There was this girl . . . she acted like she didn't like me because she thought I didn't like her," Linda said. "So, Dina was the one I went to and I was talking to her about it. So she arranged to have us brought together and we talked about it and found out what was wrong and why she felt that way. Dina wasn't at the meeting, but she arranged it." When I asked what she thought about Dina's way of helping in that situation, Linda said, "Dina is a good listener. . . . She is a good person to go to. She is a listener."

Sandra, another mother, told me of an incident in which she went to Glenda, a staff person, to help her with a conflict that Sandra was afraid might get violent. Glenda's way of helping was to remind Sandra that she was older than the other mother, that she was a "good woman," and that she had confidence Sandra would find a way of dealing with the situation. When I asked how that way of helping felt to her, Sandra said, "It was fine to me . . . [the message she gave me was] that it was okay for me to make decisions on my own."

Bridging Class and Racial Boundaries

Class and racial differences between staff and mothers.   I asked managers to describe the educational[12] and ethnic profiles of their staff and the families they were serving, the similarities or dissimilarities between these two groups, and their ways of bridging the cultural divides that might have existed among and between staff and families. Directors of forty programs (73 percent) provided partial or full profiles of 167 staff members involved in parenting and child development services. On the whole, staff members were more highly educated that the mothers they were serving. Only 18 percent of staff members were listed as having a high school degree or less, in contrast to 80 percent of mothers. A higher percentage of shelter staff were white, and a lower percentage were black, Latina, and Asian American than were the mothers served by these programs (i.e., white staff, 76 percent/white mothers, 40 percent; black staff, 15 percent/black mothers, 30 percent; Latina staff, 9 percent/Latina mothers 25 percent; no Asian American staff and Asian American mothers, 1 percent). On the positive side, 56 percent of programs did have a staff constellation that was similar to the ethnicities of the mothers they served. However, for 44 percent of programs the ethnicities of staff and mothers were dissimilar.

My white, middle-class worldview.   I am acutely aware of the limited worldview I brought to the task of understanding the experiences of mothers who had no option but to seek public assistance for family shelter. First, I speak one language: English. This drawback eliminated the possibility of my interviewing mothers whose spoken language was other than English. Second, I was able to work full-time carrying out my research because of receiving financial support from my spouse and from the private university in which I was enrolled. Obviously I was not living in poverty. Third, I am white and have mixed ethnic roots: Italian, Scotch, and English. I have many close friends and workmates whose incomes, educational experiences, and ethnic roots are very different from mine. However, mostly white households populate the neighborhood in which I live.

I brought an experiential connection to this research. That is, I grew up in a family that moved from one neighborhood to another nearly every year during my childhood and early adolescence. My sisters, brother, and I overheard many heated arguments between our parents having to do with moving to the "poorhouse." We had no idea what kind of house that was, but we knew that moving there would be bad news. The constant uprooting was extremely painful. Just as we began to feel connected with friends and classmates, my sisters, brother, and I would find ourselves packing our bags again for another neighborhood, just far enough away to require a change in schools and friends. As I met with each mother during the course of this research, I felt the distress and made educated guesses regarding how the family's struggles and frequent moves had affected the children. I believe that my childhood experiences, less severe than they would have been if we had actually become homeless, sensitized me to many of these families' struggles. However, I had no experiential base for understanding the ways in which families' racial and ethnic characteristics exacerbated their stresses.

Managers I spoke with were, almost without exception, very aware of the class and ethnic differences that existed between themselves and the families they served. "We question where our beliefs are coming from. Is it justified that we set down rules about this [child discipline]? Is it cultural differences?" a program manager said to me. Another manager was mindful of the need for cultural self-reflection before taking actions when staff are questioning the behaviors of parents. "If something happens that is questionable, we have to take cultural differences into consideration," she said. "We would privately meet with the parent so that she would understand our concern. . . . We do seek the parent out and discuss . . . what some solutions are. If you listen to the parent . . . it may be cultural. What you think may be because of your set of values and norms. Something is unacceptable if someone comes from a different set [of norms], but if it's not harmful to the child, you have to look at that."

Another manager reflected upon differences she observed in the ways that staff and families viewed parents' attention to their children, intimating a strong connection between poverty and child abuse and neglect. "We realize we're looking at this through a middle-class lifestyle, not through poverty, neglect, or abuse, which would certainly color your perception of how you're going to do something," she said. The staff working in this program were all white and mostly college-educated, while the mothers they served were 50 percent black and 50 percent white. I wondered if the staff perceptions would be less judgmental if the staff constellation was more similar to that of the mothers.

Addressing cultural barriers and racial prejudices.   I asked managers two open-ended questions regarding strategies they used to overcome language and cultural barriers with families. The two most frequently mentioned approaches were to hire bilingual or bicultural staff who understood and spoke the languages of the families they served (twenty-three programs) and to arrange for staff to receive training related to cross-cultural issues (twenty-five programs). Many directors turned to community resources for these trainings. A few managers provided financial support for staff to increase their cultural competency skills. "We sponsor an annual 'Undoing Racism' institute in conjunction with a [college]," one manager said. "Staff are paid to attend a twenty-two-hour weekend training. . . . We provide ongoing reading materials on racism throughout the year." A handful of managers told me that they used bilingual materials and translators or interpreters.

One manager described a comprehensive approach to addressing cross-cultural barriers: "We hire bilingual/bicultural staff at every opportunity we can. We have books, audiotapes, and videotapes in both languages. We provide translators (staff or volunteers) at all groups and educational programs." A few managers described the ways families or staff taught other staff about their cultures, "[We] ask families from other than the American Caucasian experience to talk about their culture, to cook their food, to teach staff their language." And, "We use our staff, residents, and former residents as resources." Managers told me that they try to avoid putting children in the position of translating for their parents, although this sometimes happened in a crisis. Only a handful of managers told me that they provide no staff training on these issues, primarily as a result of budget constraints. A few programs refused entry to families without basic proficiency in conversational English. Two managers voiced the opinion that they had no reason to concern themselves with these issues. One of these managers directed a program in which the ethnicities of mothers and staff were dissimilar.

With emotion in his voice, one manager described the class and ethnic prejudices he has witnessed among families. He emphasized the ways in which some families (who are newly poor) view themselves as superior to others. "There are forty people living here. Not optimal, but better than a hotel. There is an undercurrent of racism, xenophobia, class distinctions. . . . They think they know better than staff. . . . Dare I say this? I'm extremely objective," he said. "We have to hold our personal opinions and feelings back. . . . [There are attitudes about] deserving and undeserving among the guests themselves. A woman feels as though there should be air-conditioning in the shelter. She pulls up in a Buick Park Avenue. Her attitude is that she shouldn't be here. 'I'm not like the rest of these people. I wasn't brought up like this.' Now she's with black people, Vietnamese, Hispanic."

In another shelter an Hispanic male was scapegoated by other families as a result of racial prejudices. "We recently had some things stolen in the household," the program manager told me. "People pointed their fingers at an Hispanic male . . . in the house meeting and in individual meetings. It could have been anybody. We had to reiterate that people are innocent until proven [guilty]. The young man got teed off from others [including a staff member] staring at him and accusing him. He had a bad experience as a child with being accused. So this incident brought up a lot of issues for him. We do express to families that living in the shelter is not easy. Everyone has different problems and stuff going on. . . . It's not easy at all."

A manager told me the following story in which she and her staff helped a Native American woman who was seriously depressed. "This Native American mom was depressed . . . mental health couldn't help. A good friend was called. The shelter helped the mom to get a Native American healing process," she said. "It's the norm of the individual and that's what she needed."

Issues related to the care of children are central to cultural differences between staff and families. Several managers told me specific stories on this issue, one of which was particularly cogent. "[Our town] has a very high Hispanic and Haitian population, with a very different philosophy than ours. Building community in these settings offers an opportunity for breaking down racial and class stereotypes and prejudices. Their values and norms are really turned around when they're living in the shelter. Those are not valued behaviors in our culture. . . . An Haitian value, by hitting a child, you're showing that you really care for them. In our culture it's not seen that way. With infants, Hispanics and Haitians, not a lot of physical contact. They believe that spoils the child. Like around three years, when a child is hurt, to attend to the child makes the child weak. That's their first concern; injury or harm to the child is second. We see a lot of that." This particular program had no staff member whose ethnicity matched that of the Hispanic and

Haitian families living in the shelter. The staff were all white and mostly college-educated. I was not surprised to hear from the manager that the cultural differences were so difficult to handle.

Another manager told me about the permanent damage caused by a new staff member's insensitivity to cultural issues as they played out in a mother's care of her children. In this program over two-thirds of mothers were black or Latina. The staff was made up of one Latina and three white women. Three of these four women spoke Spanish. "Hispanic mothers believe that healthy babies are fat babies," the director told me. "They feed their babies enormous amounts of food. The right thing for staff . . . as a staff, how much control should we take? A new staff member chastised this mother's way of feeding her child. You shouldn't do that. The relationship was ruined. Our job is to give information not control their lives."

Another director told me about the complexities of counteracting parents' deep sense of internalized shame associated with their ethnic identities. "Being supportive to the family unit. Really, support is usually what they benefit by. One half may be Hispanic. They feel what they are doing is wrong," she said. "We [staff] remind them of their ethnicity and there's nothing wrong with their way of doing things. . . . It's a very stressful situation in a shelter. . . . It makes them feel inadequate, like 'bad mothers,' or failures because the norms are . . . or the books say. . . . or this person says . . . even defeats their self-esteem. Even if they have something good there, it gets thrown out the window."

At times a staff member can be on the receiving end of prejudicial attitudes. A mother I interviewed told me about a time in which one of the other mothers spread the word throughout the shelter that a certain staff member was gay. "He [the staff member] brought it up in a house meeting, and just kind of said that it wasn't the right thing to do," she told me. She expressed a sense of respect for the direct and straightforward way this staff member handled the situation.

Bonding Rituals and Events

Families and staff developed strong connections with each other through having fun together, celebrating events together, relaxing together, and weathering difficult experiences as a unit.

Planned family activities.   Many program managers emphasized the community-wide benefits they observed from families being able to have fun together outside the shelter. Many planned occasional family trips off-site to parks, roller skating rinks, and other places. Getting some relief from the emotional stresses, having a way of relaxing with others, and seeing their children having fun had restorative benefits for those who took part.

One program incorporated playfulness into a voluntary service that focused on enhancing parenting competency by combining fun activities with reflective time for both parents and children. "It's a three-hour-a-week, intensive, fifteen-week program where parents come and they have kids in age appropriate groups and they all talk in their own way about the same topic of nurturing," the director told me. "Then they have dinner together. We provide dinner, and then they have a family playtime where they play games and sing songs, and then they end with a family hug. Then everyone goes back into the group for a summary, and then they go home." Both mothers and staff in this shelter talked positively about this service.

Meals, holidays, and other celebratory occasions.   Community meals were for many programs an avenue for building community. Some managers told me about the monthly fiestas in which the whole community had the opportunity to feast on foods native to the ethnically diverse families who lived in the shelter. Others described the ways in which the community celebrated holidays and birthdays. "We really try to encourage people to do the holidays the way they do the holidays," one program manager told me. "Support them to do that, like for Christmas and for birthdays. If in a family, the birthday child gets to choose the menu and the mom bakes the cake, the whole house gets into that. Or if they stay home from school on their birthday or camp out, we don't interfere with that." The warmth of these occasions can also trigger sadness for some families, an awareness of what was missing with their own families. "Eating with other people was difficult for Judith," a staff member told me. "I remember her talking about how sad it made her feel because it was such a warm feeling and she never had that."

Reading to children as a community-building ritual.   One manager told me about the powerful actions a mother took that both enhanced life for the children and bonded all the mothers together. "A Hispanic parent, model homemaker, she set the standard in the shelter. Other mothers would get involved. It's contagious," the program manager said. "We had four 'Sally Homemakers' in the shelter. Maria started a story reading in the play room before bedtime each night. Then all four mothers went into the rotation and one of them would do it one night, the other would do it another night. They got to be very good friends."

End-of-day and weekend kaffeeklatsches.   I heard from many managers, staff, and mothers about the importance of evening and weekend "downtime" as an avenue for mothers to build connections with each other and with staff. A typical scenario for the end-of-the-day time together was that children would be asleep and mothers would gather in shelter living rooms or kitchens. They would watch TV together, do handicrafts, play cards, or just chat. "Congregate living is very difficult," one manager told me. "Self-esteem is so important. Peer support is really important. On any night of the week, there is a kaffeeklatsche in the kitchen." One of the mothers I interviewed in her new apartment was nostalgic about her family's time in the shelter. She missed having other parents to share cooking, household, and child care tasks with, and to socialize with each evening.

Weekends were also times when mothers and staff members could be more relaxed with each other. One staff member, a weekend house manager, told me how she used this time to solidify her relationships with mothers. "I try to develop a rapport with them," she said. "On the weekend, I think that is a lot different. . . . We just sit and have coffee and have time. . . . [It's] easier on the weekend because during the week they have meetings and stuff."

Support through crises.   At times the whole household within the shelter has to mobilize to support each other. A young mother whom I interviewed in her new apartment told me of a poignant incident that took place when she and her two children were living in the shelter. She remembered the event with tremendous gratitude. "I had an incident there with my husband," she said. "I had to get a restraining order, and everybody was, it was unbelievable how they helped me. He had entered the house and just forced his way in and I was holding [my three-year-old], and someone else was watching the baby. And [the girls that lived there and the staff members] took my three-year-old upstairs. . . . [My husband] wanted to take him. And there were a lot of phone calls afterwards from him and the staff and girls were really great about everything. They just supported me."

Community After Shelter

Moving Out

Many managers told me that if families have limited support to look forward to in their new community, it is very hard for them to leave the shelter because of the attachments they have made. Janice really worried about some families who left the shelter in which she works. Community and interdependence are core values for this shelter. However, some families leave the program without many friends in their new neighborhoods. "We are not really a facility that helps [mothers] develop friendships outside of here. . . . there's difficulty with that for some families when they leave," Janice told me.

"It is very, very hard if the family is in the shelter too long," one manager said. "The first few months they want to get out into their apartment. If eight or nine months goes by, they get very attached. I'm sorry, that has a very negative effect on the family, very negative on their self-reliance, lower independence than when they came in. They say, 'I'm lonely. I don't know what to do.' They are getting accustomed to the communal way of living. For some families it can have a devastating effect when they get ready to leave us because they don't have that support there."

Another program manager noted that the age of parents greatly affects their feelings when it is time for them to leave the shelter. "Most tend to get worn down when they're here," she said. "They struggle to fit into our structure here. When six or seven months have passed, it gets old. Those over twenty-one years who've lived independently say, 'I'm too old to be living like this.' The dynamics among people get to be too much to take over time. An analogy is like a teenager leaving home. The younger families who are leaving to move into their first apartment are afraid to leave. Some will even undermine their leaving because of fears about being on their own. The older families really need to leave."

Other managers observed that children and parents have different reactions to leaving. "Children do better [living in the shelter], find it easier than the parents," a manager told me. "It's a hard time, but after a while, it's like you have your friends here, more activities, wonderful play space. When it's time to move out they (children) say, 'Do we have to go?' Different than the parents who are dealing with a different reality."

Another manager described the bittersweet experience many families go through when they prepare to leave the supportive shelter community: "While there's great rejoicing when they get their Section 8 [housing subsidy], there's also tears, fearing isolation and being alone." "Before they leave, the last house meeting is totally devoted to telling that person what it's been like to share life with them."

The Reasons Families Leave Shelters

I asked managers a number of questions regarding families' exits from their shelters: how many had left within the past twelve months; what had been their average length of stay; and what were the circumstances under which those families had left.[13] Over one thousand families had exited from the forty-one programs that provided responses to these questions. The length of stay for these families varied from two to nine months, five months on average.[14] The percentages of families who left shelter programs to move into permanent housing was highly variable, from a low of 8 percent to a high of 100 percent, the average being 60 percent. An average of 7 percent of families left to move into transitional shelter programs.[15] The remaining 33 percent of families exited programs without permanent housing or transitional shelter: 15 percent left involuntarily, due to rule violations; 2 percent left due to expressed dissatisfaction with the shelter programs; another 13 percent left programs voluntarily before securing

permanent housing; and the remaining 3 percent left for other reasons, including loss of custody of their children.

It appears that for a rather large number of families served by shelter
programs, their transciency continues after they leave the shelter. What
motivates families to leave before moving into permanent housing?
Where do they go? How long will they continue to be on the move?
What impact will this have on the well-being of children and the relationships between children and their parents? Are there certain aspects
of congregate living or of programs' helping approaches that contribute
to families' decisions about leaving prior to obtaining permanent housing? These outcome data, as yet unavailable in Massachusetts, are critically important as a basis for evaluating the impact of shelter programs
on assisting parents and their children to obtain and keep housing they
can afford and to put an end to homelessness in their lives.

That 60 percent of families on average left the shelter to go into
permanent housing may be a positive outcome. That is, it may be that
considerably fewer percentages of families who are homeless but do
not have access to publicly funded shelter, were able to obtain permanent housing. In other words, the emergency shelter system may be
the primary avenue for homeless families in the state to access permanent housing.[16] A portion of families who found permanent housing
left the shelter system to move into private, market-rate rental apartments, without a housing subsidy. These families are at higher risk for
becoming homeless again. It is now well documented that a housing
subsidy operates as a deterrent to repeated occurrences of homelessness and as a protective buffer in preventing homelessness for low-
income families.[17]

I analyzed information provided by managers to determine whether
or not program orientations toward help giving were related to the reasons families left their programs. That is, do more families leave shelters
to move into permanent or transitional housing from programs whose
managers espouse prescriptive, get tough or family support ways of
helping? I found no significant differences on this measure between the
prescriptive and family support programs. However, significantly more
families left shelters for positive reasons and significantly fewer families
left for negative reasons from programs whose managers espoused prescriptive helping practices as compared with those whose directors

espoused no clear helping orientation.[18] It may be that programs with a prescriptive orientation consider access to housing the most important outcome for all families and therefore work with families in a focused way to reach this primary goal. A tendency was evident for more positive results with programs that operated from a clear helping orientation, be it prescriptive or family support. Those with a less clearly defined orientation may be more likely to deviate from a focused goal, leading to more mixed results with respect to the reasons families leave shelters. I had no way of finding out through this research study how families from these programs fared with respect to maintaining their hold on housing over the long term.

Community for Some in New Home; Isolation for Others

Over a cup of coffee in her new apartment, Celina told me about her family's new life. She referred back to the philosophy of the shelter she had lived in and her efforts to continue that commitment to community in her new neighborhood with her children. "The whole [shelter] community changed things. . . . To work with people and reach out because you've got to reach out to people," she said. "They are not going to come to you, and even when doors seem to be shutting, I just kept going . . . helping people out when you can, the whole community thing . . . and caring." She described a range of community activities she was engaged in with her children. She was clearly building a new support network for herself and her family.

Celina stands out in my mind as someone whom I felt would do okay in the future. She had completed applications for enrolling in a college program that would lead to a teaching degree. She had a clear plan for her future and that of her children. However, I found myself worrying about many other mothers whom I interviewed in their new homes. Five of the nineteen mothers were enrolled in school; six others were working full- or part-time jobs. The mothers I was most concerned about were those who had left the shelters without a housing subsidy, and those who continued to associate with an abusive current or ex-partner. Those families without a housing subsidy lived in apartments that were run-down, extremely crowded, or located in isolated, unsafe neighborhoods. One of the two women I interviewed in their new apartments, whose homelessness had been the consequence of domestic violence, had begun to have regular contact with her abusive ex-husband. The other woman's apartment was completely closed off from the outside world. Blinds covered all the windows. She was extremely cautious in answering the door when I knocked. She seemed afraid. Her isolation was palpable.

As hard as community life in shelters was for so many families, I could not help but feel that the social connections they made with each other in these settings were central to their recovery from the devastation of homelessness. Granted, they also had to deal with the difficult aspects of living so closely with others. However, these congregate environments provided children with easily accessible playmates. Parents had ready access to other adults for sharing a laugh, lending a helping hand, and providing companionship.

For the most part program managers and staff recognized that parents and their children in these settings were persons with strengths who had something to offer each other and themselves as human service workers. Some programs worked hard at creating opportunities for supportive exchanges among and between families. They recognized that the development of friendships in the shelter setting laid the groundwork for parents and children to build friendships and to become active in their home communities when they moved into their own apartments.

We have moved as a nation in the direction of weakening our commitments to the most economically vulnerable members of the community. Establishing time limits on the receipt of public assistance is a clear example of the level of risk we are willing to take to dilute this commitment. This sea change in our nation's welfare policy was facilitated through accentuation of the differences between welfare recipients and the working poor, the least powerful members of the community. Crossing racial, ethnic, and class boundaries by building community in shelters, in other human service settings, and in neighborhoods creates solidarity. Poor people in America have little political influence. Solidarity is an avenue to political power.[19] Community and interdependence are vital.

Reflections on Chapter 6

Reflection: Mother and Staff Member, Elisabeth Ward
When I accepted the assignment to write a response for this chapter, I thought it would be very easy for me to respond, that I certainly had plenty to say about these issues. It turned out to be not as easy as I imagined it would be. I have experienced shelter life from two points of view, as a guest and as a staff person. I must admit that shelter life is extremely complex, and my thoughts and feelings about shelter life are equally complex. When I was a guest, I did not appreciate or adapt easily to the community lifestyle of the shelter. But as a staff person, I enjoyed the communal aspects of shelter life. The main difference was that I had a home to go to when my weekend shift was over.

Every family that comes to shelter has its own unique composition and history. Each family arrives at the point of homelessness through their own tragic circumstances. I can say with confidence that no one ever plans on becoming homeless. Getting to the point of needing shelter is almost always a devastating chain of events.

Some families adjust to shelter life better than others. Some families are ready to grow and change, some do not need to change. Some families need many services and supports. Some simply need affordable housing and financial supports such as day care. There is the occasional family that needs more help than a shelter can provide, but that is a rare occurrence. Sometimes the families encourage one another while living in the shelter, other times there is tension and volatile behavior. I have seen some families form supports for one another after leaving the shelter, but many do not. Some maintain a relationship with shelter staff, as I did. The point is, every family is different and deserves to be recognized as such. A one-size-fits-all approach to shelter life is simply not helpful or useful for anyone involved.

Donna discusses class and cultural differences in this chapter, and I would like to add some of my thoughts to the discussion. Race and cultural differences were not as much an issue in my experience, mostly because the shelter is in an area that is predominately white, and cultural differences were not as apparent as class differences. Access to education, good jobs, financial institutions, the arts, and even health care such as alternative medicine, was profoundly different for the guests at the shelter than it was for the staff. Most of the staff had college degrees, even graduate degrees, while many, if not most, of the guests had never attended college at all. Education is highly valued at this shelter, since they know that education is the key to accessing a better standard of living. Those who have not finished high school are encouraged to do so while in shelter.

Most people involved in human service work are kind, giving, compassionate people. They would never dream of insulting the folks they work with. But it happens, and usually with only a few very telling words. I have heard phrases such as "women like you," and once someone told me, "Now you are one of us." The dynamic of us/them is a common one, even though no one likes it or wants to admit to it. Class boundaries are invisible, but everyone knows they are real.

Classism is very insidious and difficult to explain. It is a subject that makes people very uncomfortable because we, as a society, like to believe that everyone can have access to anything this society has to offer. This is simply a myth. No one gets through life without help, without some kind of break. When one does not have access to the institutions of the middle class, it is almost impossible to escape poverty. When politicians who make decisions blatantly deny access for poor people to get education and training, they are assuring another generation of poverty and despair. They are creating a permanent underclass, which is most assuredly not part of the American dream.

As I have mentioned, I much preferred communal life at the shelter as a staff person. I chose to be there every other weekend. I was not desperate and frightened, which was the case during my seven-week stay as a shelter guest. I looked forward to being there as a staff member, even though it was very hard work and often extremely emotional for me to be there. Memories of my homeless ordeal, without a doubt the worst time of my life, were often evoked by the guests' experiences. I was conscious of the difference in power between the staff and the guest. I had to examine my own assumptions and biases about class and about what class means in this culture.

I don't presume to know the answers to ending classism, but I can say that shelter directors and staff would be well advised to discuss and analyze the issue, rather than pretend that it is not a factor in homelessness.

Reflection: Executive Director, Margaret A. Leonard

Self-Sufficiency! Our preoccupations with it! Our proclamations and overuse of this concept and so-called American value being applied to the most vulnerable citizens in our nation—poor and low-income families—is a lens through which we see the dis-ease within our nation and culture! Who among us in the human community is self-sufficient? Who can attribute their human, economic, social, and spiritual growth to being sufficient unto oneself? A century ago Alexis de Tocqueville warned us that trouble was brewing in a promising land if we did not rein in our infatuation with individualism and opt instead to continue to develop our unique forms of local, grass-roots civic community and collaborations. In retrospect it seems that we have not heeded this warning and have allowed the communal structures in our nation to erode.

Perhaps the most prophetic task that our nation faces today is the discovery again and anew that we are essentially human beings in relationship to one another, family, community, neighborhood, nation, world, environment, and planet.

One of the most poignant cries that resonates throughout our nation today is the cry for belonging, for community. And we are neophytes, novices, learning the vital and life-giving lessons of community making. Our national survival and that of our environment and planet depends upon our positive learning.

Our Mission at Project Hope

The Mission of Project Hope and the values and beliefs that are integral to it are inspired by this prophetic cry, and embodied in this mission statement:

> Project Hope is dedicated to ending family homelessness; to building community that promotes dignity, self-reliance, and interdependence; to being compassionate by creating new structures which support families; to being unyielding in challenging systems that threaten basic human rights. We know this stance to be one of struggle and joy.

Our mission espouses a relational view of our world and raises up a highly prized and foundational value. This value is called mutuality. It is grounded in the belief that we are relational beings and that all growth is a shared process. Mutuality lived is the key to transforming a power-over to that of a power-with dynamic. A simple poem written years ago conveys its meaning:

> The power of growth
> is in RELATIONSHIP
> Even when life seems frail,
> when there is darkness and pain,
> confusion and complexity,
> the loving and caring of another person,
> can bring one
> sunlight and warmth
> and power to grow.
>
> Helping another
> creates meaning and hope
> in both.
> Being sunlight and warmth to another's life

nurtures growth in both.
To this growth we are pledged.

How does the value of mutuality embodied and lived have an impact on the day-to-day interactions at Project Hope? I will briefly respond to this question by focusing my lens on three areas: staff relationships, relationships between families and staff, and how resident voices shape program development.

Staff Relationships

A fundamental principle of communication is this: if we change our perceptions, we can change our feelings and ultimately our behavior. So how do staff at Project Hope perceive resident families at the shelter? This question brings up another that must first be answered: How do staff perceive themselves, their roles, and their functions at Project Hope? Herein lies the key to the implementation of this important value!

Staff are challenged to identify themselves not exclusively by what they do—by their roles and tasks—but to go deeper and understand their primary identity, the spirit from which behaviors flow. Our roles and functions do not define who we are! We are first of all human beings who on life's journey have developed significant assets, capacities, gifts, while still having multiple needs that yearn for fulfillment. This experience has a leveling effect upon all of us. At the core of each of us there is a common sameness. A primary identification at this level of sameness is essential to invest in a process of mutuality, a process of shared growth.

We are a community who share a common sameness—capacities and gifts as well as human needs. Within this community we have distinct and specific roles within teams that become organized around programs: shelter, adult learning, child care, neighborhood development. There are many differences among us: race, ethnicity, culture, class, education. Yet within the fray of the human community that we are becoming, we are conscious of sharing a common mission and of being givers and receivers to one another. We are all part of a learning community, and all of us work at creating a positive climate of communication among us.

Our aspirations are indeed lofty! Our experiences sometimes fall short! Recently, after a facilitated evaluation lasting two months, we formulated staff agreements that reflect our belief in the values of a relational view of the world and of mutuality. At a staff retreat we ritualized our ownership of and commitment to the implementation of these values. I quote briefly from a document entitled "Staff Agreements":

> We will make Project Hope a place where every one is treated with dignity, respect, and honor. We will create an environment here at Project Hope where we feel we can be ourselves, feel supported and understood; where all perceive that we are a family.

Relationships Between Families and Staff

There is an integrity here between how the staff relate among themselves and how they relate with the families. Stated briefly: "We wish to be what we want to create—a family, a community." We are a community of human beings who bring to any encounter our unique lived experience with our unique capacities and needs. In every encounter we are both givers and receivers. We seek to form relationships not from a role but out of our commonality, our humanity.

The way we see families in our family shelter is not as clients, homeless people, people with deficiencies and needs but as individuals who have a unique set of lived experiences and human capacities and needs. These perceptions level us and ground us in the human experience of being both givers and receivers in human interactions. Mutuality is the spirit in which we live our roles. The following anecdote provides a poignant example. When working on our video on welfare reform with a group of women who had experienced homelessness and had been on welfare, one women shared this thought: "When a woman comes to the door of a homeless shelter, we should look at her and say: this is a Woman of Strength because she has survived." We entitled the video *Women of Strength*.

Mutuality: Resident Voices Shaping Program Development

Commitment to a relational view of our world and the principle of mutuality has had significant impacts on how Project Hope has evolved as a community-based, resident-driven human service agency. These values need to be translated into policies, practices, and structures that transform power-over to power-with paradigms. The following are some examples of the richness of the resident voices influencing our development:

- Participation by former residents at a strategic planning retreat with board staff, former residents, and neighbors gave birth to our adult learning center, which five years later defines itself as a "Community of Learners," and defined its purpose thus: "We believe that empowerment occurs when people 'change their ideas about the causes of their power-lessness, when they recognize the systemic forces that oppress them, and when they act to change the conditions of their lives.' We believe that educating for empowerment and build-ing a sense of community can lead to collaborative efforts to bring about change in low-income neighborhoods."
- When encouraged by the State to develop additional shelter space, resident voices encouraged us to opt instead for the building of affordable housing. The Magnolia Cooperatives were created, a limited-equity, self-managed, home owner-ship cooperative that indeed built housing but, equally important, built families and community.
- When additional child care became a critical community need we were encouraged to expand our center-based pro-gram. Resident and neighborhood voices influenced our decision to opt instead for the development of twenty-five micro-enterprise family child care businesses in the commu-nity to open channels for women to own their own business and to share economic power.

Communal celebrations are nurturing events for most families. Thanksgiving Day celebrated the week before stands out in my mind.

Resident families and staff joined together to prepare a banquet;they then invited staff members and their significant others, as well as resident families and their friends and relatives to share a meal, fun, and thanksgiving together.

It was moving to see children being embraced by diverse open arms, moving from lap to lap. Conversations were alive, filled with laughter and real sharing. One would find it difficult to distinguish who was staff, resident families, extended family. A good time was had by all, and new bonds began to be forged.

In this era of privatization, managed care where bigger is better and more efficient, the voices of men, women, and children who are part of our extended family remind us continually of our commitment to a relational view of our world. These voices fortify our commitment to be a family support model that:

- addresses the holistic needs of families for shelter, affordable housing, jobs that pay a family wage, and affordable child and health care provided in the context of community within neighborhoods;
- reinforces our efforts in the political and funding community to maintain small-scale, community-based shelters whose focus is upon building relationships, accessing resources, and assisting families in their move to interdependence and community in new neighborhoods;
- strengthens our collaborative efforts to advocate for informed public policy that will provide the resources worthy of and essential for the growth and development of men, women, and children who make up low-income families today;
- And lastly, in all these different arenas, demonstrates mutuality by the concrete presence and actions of the men, women, and children with whom we share our life and mission.

Reflection: Nancy Schwoyer, Executive Director

This chapter points out that there are different goals directing staff efforts in the Massachusetts family shelter system: self-sufficiency for families or growth in community for families. These two goals cannot be achieved in the same setting—they are, I believe, mutually exclusive. This essay is an attempt to explain that claim.

The term "self-sufficient" is defined by the dictionary as "able to support or maintain oneself without aid or cooperation from others." That definition made it clear to me why the recent welfare legislation is called The Family Self-Sufficiency Act—as Friedman says, one stated objective of the legislation is to correct the dependence of poor families with dependent children on government aid. We all know, however, that no one of us is or can be self-sufficient. By our nature we are interdependent—with the air we breathe, the water we drink, the food we eat, with other people. Yet in spite of this scientific fact, there is a prevailing belief in the United States that there is virtue in going against our human nature, virtue in being independent, a rugged individual, self reliant, self-sufficient.

Therefore, it is not surprising that in our powerful country the idea of community is often a countercultural one or at least dismissed as a romantic notion. In fact, community is the appropriate way for human beings to live. The tiniest atomic particles of which we and all of reality are made are in relationship with each other. The scientific theories of quantum physics and chaos theory show that particles previously thought to be separate entities are in relationship because of unseen connections between them. All of reality lives in community. It is no wonder that human beings have a deep longing for relationships and love. It makes sense to me that our vision, values, and culture are meant to be consistent with our fundamental nature and, further, that the structures that organize us in family, neighborhood, places of education, work, and social services should be appropriate to support our communitarian reality and indeed express it—"the medium is the message." I believe that the experience of community in congregate shelters should not simply be a fortunate but accidental outcome; I believe we need to be intentional about creating the environment that facilitates community.

This reflection has been difficult for me to write because I am summarizing a very complex theory for the sake of argument in this piece. I am aware that it may sound simplistic, but I offer it here so that readers can glimpse the worldview from which I try to live and do my work at Wellspring House. I do not write about the Wellspring family shelter because I hold it up as a model; I write out of the Well-spring experience because it is the place of my experience. A particular place has significance if we believe that community, not self-sufficiency, is the hope and goal of our work with homeless families. Place, after all, is where it happens. On the other hand, if self-sufficiency is the goal, place is not important. In recent years advocates for homeless families have had to fight to reverse the placement policy of the Department of Transitional Assistance, which allowed families to be placed in shelters anywhere in the state. Now, once again, families are not to be placed further than twenty miles away from their communities of origin. That policy is important because we know that familiarity with one's community and local community supports are essential touchstones for families who have lost so much. Isolation and loneliness are destructive to families and individuals; they do not build "strong self-sufficient" families. Rosemary Haughton, associate director of Wellspring House, writes, "Place is the human connection to land and community, including sustenance and memories, history and skills."

I believe that we shelter providers need to think not only about the place that is the shelter but also the place of the neighborhood, town, city where the shelter is located. What does the shelter look like to the neighborhood? Does it look more like a factory than a human habitat? Do staff and homeless families participate together in caring for the shelter space? Is it an attractive place to come into? How does the shelter as an organization interact with the neighborhood where it is located? What can we do to help facilitate connections between the families while they are homeless and living in the community shelter and the local community? Finding answers to this last question may help to change the isolation experienced by some families when they move to their own housing that Donna Friedman has described in this chapter. It is also to recognize that community is not simply a fortunate consequence of families experiencing congregate living. Community is the way we're meant to live, so it is what families should be moving into, not just out of.

Before leaving the notion of place and its centrality to the reality of community I want to make a plea to shelter providers, advocates of the homeless, and policy makers to think about how the lack of affordable housing has contributed to the breakdown of community in our society. I believe there is a growing acceptance of the fact that homeless families from Massachusetts must move to communities and states where housing is more affordable, just as there is acceptance of a mobile work force moving (often repeatedly) to where the work is. Are we asking questions about the long-term effect of relocation and/or dislocation on families and on society in general? If homeless families are relocating for good reasons—for instance, because they want some distance to begin again or because in the present economic climate they have no other choice—then what can we as shelter providers do to help them build a support system in the new community? It is important to add at this point that helping families to build support systems cannot substitute for the work that is required to redress the severe lack of affordable housing and its effects on the fabric of community life in Massachusetts. It will take the commitment and collaboration of government, business, private investors, nonprofits, and other stakeholders for this essential work to be done. I propose it will also be necessary to shed the myth of self-sufficiency and to reclaim the fact of community, the importance of home and place, and the practice of hospitality.

At Wellspring we believe that hospitality is essential to community and is threatening to an ideal of self-sufficiency. Hospitality is the essential principle underlying all our work at Wellspring. Hospitality is about our openness to each other—homeless families with each other, staff with families, staff with each other, volunteers (including donors) with families. Hospitality welcomes diversity of class, race, gender, religion. The openness of hospitality does not negate the need for boundaries that keep us safe from abusive behavior and violence. Hospitality is not the lawless confusion of anarchy.

Commitment to living community and hospitality in our shelters requires hard work. It is not enough to want to live out of some romantic notion about community. At Wellspring, staff agree to operate from "bottom lines," agreed professional standards that guide our relationships. They include mutual respect, participating in conflict resolution and problem solving, giving direct feedback to each other, building solidarity with each other, supporting the values and mission of Wellspring, participating in supervision, and working in a way that is empowering to each other and to the shelter guests. A guiding question for staff is, "What power is the guest gaining by the way I am handling this situation?" Empowerment of guests, not self-sufficiency, is our goal. Empowerment leads to participation, and it is our hope that guests will not only participate in shelter life but will participate in the community life of the neighborhoods, towns, and cities to which they move.

It is part of our practice at Wellspring to elect former shelter guests and participants in our other programs to the board of directors. Some former guests take part in our family support programs or take courses at our education center. Some become mentors in various programs, some become volunteers, some are hired as staff. Others give presentations to community groups or speak to the media about their experience of homelessness. When Wellspring wants to plan its next steps we always involve the reflection, feedback, and evaluation of former participants. All of these practices are helping us to live interdependently.

Much of the learning comes from receiving the feedback of formerly homeless women and others who experience or have experienced poverty. Often in their feedback, especially as board members, they tell us they feel "outside," misunderstood, discounted. So, recently, the board of directors spent eight hours over two days in diversity training, with the goal of building a more intentional board community. We focused on several dimensions of diversity that were having an impact on the board's functioning, including the dimension of class. Experiences like this help us to increase the skills that foster appropriate working relationships as a community. We have a long way to go toward being a community, but we are committed to the journey because we know we can do more together than all of us can do singularly and we know from experience the truth of a Celtic saying, "In the shelter of each other the people live."

7

Final Group Reflection

The author and contributors gathered one evening in Boston to share a dinner and to reflect on what we had learned from our writing. A lot of what we worked on together was about the contrasting of two different ways of connecting with people. Throughout the author's study, and the reflections of the contributors it is clear that within the shelter system, services are offered in different ways. Our discussion here focuses on those differences and what we learned in the process of our work. This dialogue is an edited version of a two-hour conversation.

DONNA: What do you feel is the essence of the family support approach we have written about?

NANCY: For me it is acceptance of and respect for the families. I believe it is also acceptance of who we are as shelter providers and of what we are equipped to offer. It involves mutual accountability between staff and families. If a family needs services we cannot offer or if a family does not want to be in a particular shelter, then out of respect for the family we work with them to find more appropriate resources.

MARY: Even if the shelter is not equipped to deal with a particular problem or issue, a family support model offers a means to wrap around beyond the shelter, into the community. Services do not end when a family leaves shelter. The family support model sees all of life as a healing and growing process.

ROSA: When I think back to women that we've had that have been very challenging and they seem not to able to make it in the shelter system, I realize that once I've built a relationship with them, then I am able to understand what makes them so difficult. It is the family support model that encourages us to understand from their point of view, and then we can better work out a balance and how to work together.

DONNA: Paternalism has always been a part of the welfare system in the United States; do you think that today's efforts are different or just more of the same?

MARGARET: I went to graduate school in the mid-sixties. I was struck at that point that there was never a mention of what we received from the so-called clients. What I have come to believe was a critical relational value—that of reciprocity or mutuality—was significantly absent in both the professionals and the curriculum. The helping relationship was very much one-sided: physician/patient, client/professional. There was a giver and a receiver. The movements in the 1960s—civil rights, feminist, war resistance, etc.—began to change that power dynamic in significant ways. Patriarchal structures were radically challenged to be participatory. These and other movements have in the 1990s had their impact upon human service agencies, the best of whom are seeking to create avenues for a consumer/customer voice to shape policies and structures. Some family shelters are seriously engaged in this process.

DEBORAH: I remember hearing stories from my mom who was a single women living in the projects. She would never seek any kind of public assistance because of the way that they operated, like workers coming to your home and looking through closets and searching the house for evidence of a man living there and all that kind of humiliation. I have never experienced that. Maybe some structures, some shelters, and some grassroots organizations have changed, but I am not convinced that there's been a real attitude change from policy makers. Policy makers have not said, "Let's change and make things better for the people getting aid." The people banded together, organized, and they actually forced the policy makers to listen. The policy makers sent in community people to listen and calm things down. That is how my mother began her career as a social worker. I don't think that the people in power said, "Let's give up some power." The change comes from the people who are affected by the situation rising up and saying, "We are not going to take this, we want change," and forcing that change. I think that it is coming around again.

NANCY: I think there is something different going on and it has to do with the fact that here in Massachusetts there is a broad base of people who know the real causes of homelessness and what it takes to end it. We will not settle for paternalism, no matter how benevolent. For a short time in the '80s we had essential resources needed for prevention of homelessness and we had access to affordable housing. Like others, I get discouraged because resources have been cut. But we don't stop working, and we're not going to settle for the crumbs of paternalism.

LISA: How do we get people to really change? The problem is poverty and homelessness is a symptom of poverty like hunger. It is all a symptom of poverty. We keep trying to put Band-Aids here and there, and when the Band-Aids come off, we still have a problem. I think we need to look at the haves and have-nots. Who's poor in this country—women, minorities, women of color, children. It's scapegoating at it's finest, or worst.

DONNA: Is there something that we learned, some insight or lesson that emerged from the research and our work together that you think was surprising and that could add a different dimension to the way these issues are being talked about now?

LISA: I was surprised to learn how other shelters functioned, how bad things can be in shelters.

DEBORAH: For the life of me I can't understand what would motivate staff to treat people as if they weren't worthy.

MARY: I think it's when people, staff, simply don't have the framework in which to do their work. Shelter workers earn low wages, they lack education and/or training, and no one works with them around the systemic cases of homelessness. All they see is families that are under stress, who just endured a major loss and relocation. They lack support to learn ways to support and relate to the families who are in such pain.

ROSA: It seems to me that people in some shelters and the other welfare services don't care about the people. They are just looking for work, there is no motivation. There is no mission, nothing. I wanted to make copies of the book and show it to the entire staff and have some really good discussions together about how do we really make this family support model work. It is a hard thing to do. It takes constant vigilance.

DEBORAH: We need supervision. We need to be able to talk about how heavy this stuff is because this woman is going through the same thing that I went through several years ago. It is hard. The staff are not just workers, but they are human beings in relationship with other human beings and they have needs as well. I also think that the question is how the staff really embrace the mission and how staff help one another.

MICHELLE: When staff treat families poorly, its usually because the system they work in treats them poorly. I always wonder how closely salary and benefit levels, as well as the amount and quality of support and supervision offered to staff, correlate with the relationships between staff and families. It's really a case of the oppressed oppressing the more oppressed. Many of the agencies providing shelter services are systems in which direct service staff have little or no power over their own working conditions, which directly translates to the way they work with families, over whom they do have power.

MARY: When parents are isolated and alone due to poverty, it is very hard to give to their children that which they do not have. I also think that it is very hard for staff to give to guests that which they do not have. It is a flowing waterfall, a whole system that has to be perpetual and go all around. We all need support, safety, and a sense of sharing.

DONNA: The question is: How can you resist being drawn into a paternalistic way of working?

NANCY: For me it is being with the women, sharing a cup of coffee in the morning before anyone else is around. It is about creating spaces where people can move and be together. It is about staff, administration, volunteers, and guests sharing in that space.

LISA: What you are suggesting is a different kind of relationship between staff and guests. It does not follow the accepted model of professional relationships. The boundaries are too close. That is what I liked about connecting with all the people around this table. We can create a model different from the sterile human service model.

DONNA: That leads us to another question. Those professional models come out of disciplines that see people as being dysfunctional. What makes you think a family support model would actually work with homeless families, whom many people see as dysfunctional?

MARY: We have tried to apply short-term models to correct the behavior that has been termed dysfunctional. It has not worked. The family support model brings with it a sense of respect and acceptance that growth is a long-term process and that growth and healing can be achieved in the community not just in the clinic. The community ends up creating a healing, holding environment for all of its members. It is healthier.

DONNA: What would it take to make the Massachusetts family shelter system work? What would you do if you were elected into a position that had the power to make changes?

LISA: It will have to be a cultural movement. People are really into individualism, professional boundaries, and not bringing the family into the work place. That would have to change.

NANCY: Something has to change at a very basic level. If we are going to do this essential community work of sheltering families, then we must demand the resources to do it. Working with homeless families without the resources of affordable housing and jobs that pay a living wage is like trying to be a farmer without land.

DEBORAH: Why can't we restructure the system so that people can get into housing and get what they need rather than continuing to perpetuate taking care of them because they cannot afford housing. Policies need to change so that there is the creation of more housing stock that is affordable.

LISA: There needs to be more community support or centers. Families need to feel connected to their community. They need housing, jobs and day care and places to meet other families as well.

DONNA: What would you do to change it?

MARGARET: It is about education. Education is the key to earning power.

NANCY: If I were in charge I would reaffirm the 1983 state law granting homeless families a right to shelter. I would also organize state government so that the state's housing agency would work with us on a day-to-day basis. Thus, by supplying economic and housing resources, the Commonwealth would be acting as if policy makers believed the problems could be solved. Once families were housed in local communities they would connect with a local network of emotional and educational supports. I would also set a standard of practice for shelter workers, with staff training and support.

MARGARET: I would set up a commission at the state level that looks at integrating services so that families can truly be self-sufficient. We would develop some really meaningful family policies, and we would look at how the different departments, such as education, employment and training, and housing can work to really support families in a meaningful way in the community. I would not look at the provider as the enemy, or a problem to be managed, but rather I'd look at them as a resource. I would bring them together and sit them down and ask what are some of the things we can do within the fiscal constraints that we have.

DEBORAH: Just to add to the recommendations, I would set up a task force to talk to homeless people about their experience and get what it is they went through to get a clearer understanding of what is on the other side. I would then try to bring together the issues brought up by the homeless people and the providers and try to come up with some common guidelines that would work for all people.

MICHELLE: In addition, I would require shelter programs to develop consumer advisory boards, through which former residents provide feedback on program structure, directions, and policies.

MARY: I would want to work with the local community leaders, from churches, schools, and other groups. We would try to figure out the community strengths. Look to how that strength can be used to help all community members, even those in need.

LISA: In addition to what everyone else said, I would look for a way to make the media more friendly.

MARGARET: If we had public policy around the quality of family life, about what every family needed to have, that would help. We've got to have affordable housing. We've got to have jobs that pay a living wage. We've got to have care of the children. We have to allow people to go to school to be trained and educated. We need to reform the system in order to meet the needs of the people, and therefore it seems like presently, the word "reform" is in the wrong place of Welfare Reform. Instead of reforming the system to make it perform, which it hadn't been doing before, we're trying to reform the people to make them conform to the system that needs to be reformed.

8

We Need a Revolution

A true revolution of values will soon cause us to question the fairness and justice of many of our past and present policies.

A true revolution of values will soon cause us to look uneasily on the glaring contrast of poverty and wealth.

—Martin Luther King, April 4, 1967

Is a revolution the only way to realize family support public assistance practices and policies in the United States? Yes, turning full circle in our practices and policies with very low-income families is vital. Is a revolution possible? Yes, I think so. Consider the image of men and women turning full circle in a spiral of collective energy and movement. This kind of revolution can start small and happen anywhere. The revolution, the collective turnabout, that we have proposed throughout this book is one that we characterize as "Power With," not "Power For" nor "Power Over." This perspective is rooted in a deep belief in the importance of mutuality in all relationships and a respect for the potency of knowledge and intelligence gained from lived experience.

A Power For model of connection between families in poverty and helpers is reminiscent of U.S. "almshouse" years, when ladies and gentlemen of middle and higher incomes took care of and were self-appointed moral guides for families whose poverty was assumed to be the result of depravity and low morals.[1] We are not so far from our well-intentioned elder sisters and brothers when we, with more ample incomes and less challenging life circumstances, assume that we know what homeless parents need to do to make their lives better and presume to speak for them in our advocacy and policy-making efforts. In fact, as evidence throughout this book suggests, our condescension and good intentions may not only be off the mark but also may have extremely detrimental effects on the very parents and children we are trying to help.

As we document throughout the book, a Power Over model of helping is particularly demeaning and harmful to those on the receiving end and—as we have shown—to helpers as well. The coercion and intimidation involved in treating parents like children by closely monitoring their behaviors, legislating services, and enforcing strict prohibitions diminishes parents' sense of self and precipitates tremendous resentment. Parents may comply with staff prescriptions, but they and their children ultimately pay the price in increased stress and a desperate sense of isolation. Helpers also suffer. In the words of a staff member I spoke with, "[These controlling interactions] kill something inside you. Something inside you shrinks. You either have to harden or shut down your insides."

The Power With model we have explored here recognizes that parents and helpers are more alike than different; that is, they are human beings with an innate drive to grow and thrive in connection with others. For the moment they are simply in somewhat different life circumstances and could just as easily be thrown into the other's shoes should fate so decide. Helping is synonymous with mutuality; that is, each person gives and takes and holds the other accountable as a responsible adult. The community bonds resulting from this way of working heal and restore parents' self-esteem, strengthen families, enhance helpers' sense of efficacy, and forge alliances that have the potential to precipitate a revolution in our society.

Using a Power With model, a quiet but mighty revolution can happen on the front line when a shelter staff member or welfare worker decides to change her way of working with parents. However, a human service worker does not exist as an island. A not-so-quiet but even more powerful revolution can take place within an organization when an agency head enlists her staff and board in examining their agency mission, organizational climate, physical environment, organi-

ing, staff hiring, training and supervision struc-
·nt of parents in decision making in light of the
ples we describe.

not operate in isolation. They are part of sur-
oods and communities and are profoundly
·, and federal policies and resources. A loud and
·n can happen in the lives of families, human ser-
·munities when federal, state, and local policies
realities of families' lives and transformed to
have real opportunities to work well and par-
ent well and ·   igmatizing connections with government and
private resources. This chapter offers specific recommendations for
revolutionary movements at each of these levels. While I have taken
the lead in writing this chapter, my thoughts draw heavily upon the
insightful reflections of my coauthors.

Revolutions on the Front Line

Frontline workers may have limited power to change the organizations, the neighborhoods, and the public policies that have an impact
on their work with families, at least in the short run. However, they
do have control over what they say and do as they interact with children and parents in the course of day-to-day contacts. These actions
and words can have a profound impact on the ways that parents feel
about themselves, their parenting, and their children. Three key ideas
are important for a frontline worker who wishes to initiate Power
With connections with parents: engage in self-reflective practice;
demonstrate a deep respect for the centrality of children in the lives of
parents who reside in shelters; and de-link parents' personal problems
from their homeless circumstance.

Self-reflective practice.   A frontline worker can initiate regular reflective
conversations with parents with whom she works, conversations in
which they as a two-person team assess how their work together is
progressing: what is working, what is not. Together, they can make
corrections along the way. This process opens the relationship space

that allows each person to hold herself and the other accountable, to learn from their mistakes and move on. The checking-in process also enables a staff member to calibrate her help in a way that is finely tuned to each parent's unique mode of learning, growing, and meeting life's challenges. Standing in parents' shoes, seeking a reality check from trusted colleagues, and maintaining some measure of doubt and humility may help to counteract the natural tendency we all have as human beings to judge and distance ourselves from others under these highly unnatural shelter circumstances.

Respect for the centrality of parenting.   There is no way to care about the long-term well-being of children without respecting and honoring the centrality of the parents in their lives. Validation and strengthening of the parental role is perhaps the most complex aspect of support for families when they live in a shelter. Staff must struggle with walking the thin line between being intrusive and truly helpful. The setting offers unique opportunities for staff to be of considerable assistance to parents. Strong attachments can and do develop between staff and parents who know individual children well, their funny quirks, their habits, food preferences, and so on. Frontline workers, mindful of building upon these bonds, can honor the parental role by resolutely refraining from bypassing parental authority in their noncrisis interactions with children. When a safety crisis occurs and active staff intervention is required, a parent's self-esteem is best protected by handling the situation as discreetly and privately as possible, without judgment. Integral to this process is a recognition of and respect for class, ethnic, and racial differences, especially as they have an impact on differences in parenting norms and values.

Separation of homelessness from parents' personal problems.   Shelter staff are privy to the intimacies of families' lives. They have a very complete knowledge of parents' flaws. When a parent's homeless circumstances and her personal flaws are linked together in a staff member's mind, the propensity to judge, criticize, and become an intrusive, over-responsible helper will be hard to resist. If a staff member can de-link parents' personal flaws and their families' homelessness and become skilled at digging for parents' capacities and strengths, then parents' goals, aspirations, and learning styles will be more recognizable and easier to build upon.

Revolutions Within Sheltering Organizations

Directors and boards of sheltering organizations may not have control over the community resources and public policies that have an impact on the families they serve, but they do have the power to start a close-to-home revolution by initiating processes within their organizations that can maximize supportive, egalitarian connections with these parents. Central to this is leadership that inspires a shared vision created by all who have a stake in the organization, workers and families alike, a dynamic and evolving vision that "moves off the walls and into the corridors, seeking out every employee, every recess of the organization."[2] This way of leading attends more to the processes of relatedness among employees and families that evolve over time than to the building of fixed decision-making structures.[3] In particular, six processes stand out if an agency leader wishes to initiate Power With connections between and among staff and families: instituting organizational reflection; creating substantive decision-making roles for parents; designing family-friendly service environments; fashioning a teamwork environment for staff; building positive connections within the neighboring community; and engaging in the social change process. If an organization has a clarity of purpose and direction that is evident everywhere, "in all its corners,"[4] these processes are the most obvious starting places for the creation of a Power With culture.

Organizational reflectivity.[5] An organization can commit to regular, communitywide self-examination—that is, getting in touch with and critically examining the values that drive program design and helping practices, grappling with value differences, developing a shared vision, and providing safe and regular vehicles for staff and parents to air dilemmas and to influence the ways the program evolves. Because the process of critical self-examination can be messy and uncomfortable, enabling processes need to be in place to foster safe and wise collective reflections. This has leadership and budgetary implications.

Resources are needed for planning sessions and staff/resident retreats, for skillful facilitation, and for putting ongoing, programmatic, reflective evaluation processes into place.

Parent roles in organizational decision making.   The unique vulnerability status of families living in these settings and the inherent imbalance of power between families and providers requires that additional mechanisms for collaborative decision making and for mutual accountability be put into place. Possibilities include parents having a substantial role in devising their own service plan, in crafting and evaluating program rules and enforcement policies, and in providing input on future program design through participation in organizational reflection processes. Parents can also be hired to train staff in sensitive interviewing skills. It is also advisable for programs to establish a variety of family-staff-director vehicles for collaborative review of program operations that have a direct impact on families' lives in shelter settings, in particular shelter rules.

Design of the service environment.   The physical environment speaks louder than words. If the organizational mission includes a belief that families are worthy of respect and are valued members of the community, then this message needs to be "broadcasted" in Wheatley's terms,[6] visible in every corner of the building. That is, the physical space needs to be accommodating to the whole family unit, conducive of community building, accessible for parents and children with disabilities, and attentive to the needs for each family to have its own private spaces and for children to have a space to play. Some of these features have significant resource implications and may require that organizations identify both private and public resources for carrying out site renovations. However, elimination of an institutional look and feel to the space may be easily implemented by ensuring that the physical environment is well cared for and decorated in homey ways. The homier the better for children and parents.

A teamwork environment for staff.   Central to turning full circle at the organizational level is fashioning a team atmosphere that provides staff members with an empowering work experience similar to that being strived for in the relationships between staff and families. If staff members are treated poorly, they will have a hard time resisting the urge to treat families in the same way. The likelihood of instituting a Power With culture in a human service program is greatly enhanced if staff members feel respected and regarded for their insights, their unique skills, and their aspirations, regardless of their degrees or stations in life. This idea, while appealing on the surface, is anything but simple to implement. The approach runs counter to the competitive, hierarchical, and class-based norms prevalent in United States work environments, environments in which the interests of those with higher degrees, more affluence, and greater political influence hold sway. To counter these powerful cultural norms, leaders within organizations will need to find hundreds of ways to ensure that all staff members, no matter what their roles in the organization, are enabled to have an impact on the work environment, including expressing dissatisfactions and contributing to problem solving and visioning for the future. This requires that attention be given to supervisors and their roles. They will need ongoing support to let go of feeling responsible to be the "boss."

The alternative vision here is of a dynamic, spiral of relationships among program managers, supervisors, staff, and families, one in which the locus of control is shared rather than being retained in the hands of directors and supervisors. The locus of control for decision making moves around based upon who is most directly affected by a situation or circumstance. When issues arise, those most directly affected engage in a collective process of unearthing relevant information, considering the options for action, experimenting, and evaluating the effectiveness of the chosen courses of action. Managers and supervisors in such settings are less often the boss and more often the facilitator.

Agency leaders will need to enlist staff members who hold beliefs that reflect the mission of the organization, respect parents and their coworkers, speak their language, understand their cultural values and norms, and are open to personal and organizational self-reflection. Hiring former residents as staff members is a fundamental but incomplete strategy for moving in this direction. Other opportunities for staff are essential that is, they need to participate in creating the organizational vision and they need to receive training and supervision in handling complex parenting situations by being active, nonjudgmental interventionists. Staff need ongoing support for learning how to create opportunities for parents to name their own goals and aspirations, including digging as hard for strengths and capacities as we in the helping professions have become adept in digging for dysfunctions. They need to become skilled in using adult learning models, including the development of individualized, tailored mutual agreements regarding the work parents and staff will be undertaking together, a tool that the staff-parent team can use to guide, assess, and recalibrate their teamwork. Finally, they need training and support for facilitation of group decision-making processes and crisis intervention. Staff members need the same respectful, empowering team atmosphere that is desired in relationships between workers and families. Involvement with families who are at a most desperate part of their journey requires that the organizational climate, structure, and relational processes promote trust and safety both for those who work in and those who are served by the organization.

Positive connections and contributions to the neighboring communities. Having strong positive community roots fuels individual organizations' effectiveness in several ways. First, when sheltering organizations have a strong sense of community at the neighborhood level, the stigmatization of families they serve is reduced. These organizations are contributing to the fabric of the neighborhood, assisting in the development of low-cost housing and of other supports for all families. Second, organizations with deep community roots can facilitate families' linkages, once they leave the shelter, with community services and peer networks in their new home neighborhoods, an essential step for ensuring the continuation of support, as well as their access to low-cost housing, education, and employment opportunities. Third, strong community roots and the leveraging of community resources provide sheltering organizations with some independence, allowing them to resist government pressures to operate in punishing and counterproductive ways with families.

Engagement in the social change process. Sheltering organizations need to be engaged in impacting federal and state policy-making processes with their lived experience. Those families who are directly affected by poverty and those who directly serve them are in a unique position to identify what needs to be done to prevent and address the problems of homelessness and poverty. Organizations can develop educational processes for families and staff to join together in analyzing the causes of and solutions for homelessness and in taking collective action with other community and advocacy partners as a result of their analyses.[7] In addition to their impact on the community, these educational and social change activities heal families' spirits and build solidarity between and among staff and families.

Revolutions in Public Policy

Using a Power With model of engagement in policy making with those who are most directly affected by homelessness and poverty is perhaps the most amorphous revolution or turnabout to grasp. To be effective, policy making at local, state, and federal levels unavoidably must address three dimensions of family homelessness: prevention, amelioration, and escape.[8] That is, ending family homelessness involves finding ways to: increase the likelihood that families with the lowest incomes can keep their housing or obtain alternative low-cost housing; temporarily shelter those who lose their housing; and create realistic avenues for families in shelters to move into their own housing as quickly as possible and to keep it. Determining how government resources are used to balance these three essential needs is the source of tremendous controversy in the policy-making world.[9] What is the proper division of available resources? How much of the limited public dollar pie should go into increasing access to housing assistance? How much should go into building and increasing the capacities of shelters? Given that some families have to live in shelters, what policies should be in place to ensure that they receive quality services? What policy strategies would be most efficient and effective? Using a Power With lens, we propose here that those most directly affected by these policy dilemmas and decisions have valuable perspectives on the issues to offer local, state, and federal policy makers. As the format of this book makes clear, this is a vision that we have long-standing com-

mitments to realizing in the universes in which we carry out our
work to end homelessness.

At the Local Neighborhood and Community Level

Grassroots community activists and leaders, including family and staff
participants from sheltering organizations have a central role to play
in turning the country's public policies around by being present at the
policy-making table and by building neighborhood and community
structures and resources that are conducive for strengthening families,
especially those at high risk of losing their housing and falling into
homelessness. The national family support movement is instructive for
the revolutions that can happen in neighborhoods and local communities and are exemplified by the actions taken by two organizations
already discussed in this book, Project Hope and Wellspring House.
Each of these organizations has invested heavily in building up their
surrounding communities by adding to the stock of low-cost housing, increasing educational and employment opportunities for low-
income parents, and creating multiple avenues for families to make
social connections with each other. They have made conscious organizational decisions, with substantive input from current and former
shelter families, to concentrate the lion's share of their financial and
programmatic resources on these long-term capacity-building priorities rather than on expanding their emergency shelter operations.
They have accomplished these objectives through collaborative partnerships among local, state, and federal governments, the business sector, the nonprofit sector and neighborhood families.

At the State Level

The involvement of families who have been homeless or near-home-
less in state-level legislative and administrative policy decisions is
indeed a revolutionary but highly achievable objective.[10] Within the
last two decades the federal government has increasingly ceded many
public assistance policy and resource decisions to state governments.
This circumstance presents an opportunity for those who wish to
have an impact on state policies and are committed to precipitating a

Power With revolution. State legislators and administrators are close at hand. Evidence presented throughout this book underscores the importance of family and provider perspectives in informing state-level homeless prevention and shelter policies, in particular those having to do with the quality of families' shelter experiences.

Quality assurance standards and quality controls. Quality assurance mechanisms are accepted and integral dimensions of other service systems in our country, including primary health, mental health, education, early childhood, and so on. Why is it that quality standards are absent from our public assistance service arenas? Perhaps the long-standing stigma attached to those who use public assistance provides a partial explanation: outcasts are not in a strong position to ask for high-quality treatment.

It is time to revolt, to turn full circle and raise the quality bar for family shelter life: families who have lived in shelters can help. The evidence in this book strongly suggests that parents, as racially and ethnically diverse as those served in shelters, can and should be hired as partners with state policy makers in creating standards that address the quality of families' experiences in shelter, including: family shelter models; eligibility criteria; the physical environment; service components; service requirements; and shelter rules. They should also be part of review teams regularly sent out by the administering state agency to assist shelter managers and staff in evaluating and improving their programs. In addition, state contracts with shelter organizations should include requirements that their contracted agencies have evaluation mechanisms in place that include parents (former and current residents) as official, and properly compensated, reviewers.

At the Federal Level

As a country, we have always been ambivalent about how big the federal government should be and how much government should impinge upon the private lives of families—a long-standing tension between the opposing poles of individual freedom and community responsibility.[11] The new millennium in the United States is one in which we as a nation have opted for diminished federal resources and public support for those households with the lowest incomes. The role of the federal government in ensuring that all families have enough income to meet basic needs, as well as access to "a decent home and suitable living environment" has devolved to state governments. In turn, state governments have actively abdicated this responsibility to the private market and to local jurisdictions. In effect, government has become more loosely organized at a time when focused, well-targeted public policies are most needed,[12] particularly those having to do with preventing and ameliorating homelessness and poverty. Housing is not a good that an individual family can create for itself. Without publicly subsidized incentives, the private market actively undermines the creation and maintenance of a housing stock adequate to meet the low cost housing demand.[13]

Our public assistance safety net is very shredded. We need to turn full circle on the federal level. Policy makers' distance from the realities of poor families' lives has doomed United States public assistance policies since their inception.[14] With the major revision of social welfare policies that is now underway, we must seize the opportunity to learn from our past and listen to what families say about realistic and non-stigmatizing approaches to income support and housing assistance.

Creating effective avenues for such citizen participation is a complex and challenging enterprise in our current political context. Connecting families directly affected by poverty and homelessness with the career public servants, the "people indoors"[15] who carry out the nuts-and-bolts policy analyses within the executive and legislative branches of government, is a strategy worth pursuing. The following story illustrates one attempt in that direction. A few months ago a senior official within the U.S. Department of Health and Human Services (HHS), two women who had been homeless, and I were involved in an intense series of communications via E-mail, having to do with whether or not "consumers"[16] should be involved in an upcoming federally sponsored conference focused on the use of homeless services data to document the impacts of welfare reform. My "consumer" colleagues and I were vocal advocates for planning a substantive consumer role. The HHS official was skeptical about this idea, given that the substance of the conference discussions was planned to be highly research-oriented and technical. He sent me an E-mail expressing his reluctance to involve consumers and asking for my reaction. My two "consumer" colleagues and I responded swiftly. After impassioned E-mail wrangling, the HHS official agreed to the wisdom of the inclusion of consumers. Subsequently, the two women were invited to share their perspectives as formal conference presenters and their conference expenses were fully covered. The conference was dramatically and positively affected by their ideas and participation. As a result of the substantive contribution of these two women, representatives from each participating city made a public commitment to try to engage consumers in their local homeless services planning efforts.

Revolutions in Poverty Research

The perspectives of parents who are most directly affected by poverty and homelessness are essential to turn around those of us who are engaged in poverty research for a livelihood. I view my own education as a researcher as having two major strands. One was the education I received in a formal doctoral research training program. The other strand is the education I have received in collaborating with my coauthors in the course of writing this book and in carrying out participatory action research over the past seven years. This latter educational pathway has been essential in deepening my understanding of the realities of life for families struggling with poverty and its devastating effects. Working as a teammate with men and women who have been homeless or near homeless has deepened my commitment to using a Power With orientation as a researcher.

The following two examples are illustrative of the ways in which I have found this participatory research approach so useful. First, I worked on a research project designed to inform the state's redesign of the family shelter system.[17] The core research team consisted of myself and four women who had been homeless with their children in Massachusetts. Together we designed the survey instrument they used to interview parents who were on the brink of becoming homeless. They and I co-led focus groups across the state to solicit input from shelter and homeless prevention service providers. They assisted in making sense of the data we collected and in developing the final recommendations. They participated as presenters with me when we met with state policy makers over a six-month period to brief them on the findings and to move forward in using the findings for the development of the state's plan for redesign of the system. Their contributions to this project were innumerable. Their insights from having been homeless greatly informed the content of the survey questions, the wording of questions, strategies for recruiting families, and the interpretation of parents' responses. In addition, they were able to go below the surface in the sessions with providers. They had lived in the shelters. They asked extremely insightful questions of providers having to do with the quality dimension of service provision. The presence of these women lent an atmosphere to the focus group gatherings that raised the bar with providers. Consumers had to be talked about in respectful ways, without being objectified as a defective group of people.

Second, we have involved men and women who have been homeless in our implementation of a statewide homeless services data system. During our first year of implementation, they were paid participants in a time-limited working group that developed the privacy protection policies, including informed consent procedures, information security procedures, and our client code approach. We have a consumer panel of four persons whom we hire to help us plan and conduct training workshops for case managers in programs using this data system, focused on sensitive interviewing skills and privacy protections. Our belief is that the accuracy and reliability of the information is greatly enhanced if case managers interview homeless persons with sensitivity and respect for their right to privacy. Three consumers also hold official seats on this project's steering committee. One of these persons is heading up a new effort to conduct focus groups in shelters who are using the data system, for the purpose of promoting awareness and self-advocacy among consumers in shelters. We hired another one of these persons as a part-time staff member. She works as a research assistant on a number of our studies that have to do with housing, homelessness, and welfare reform.

In my experience, those directly affected by poverty and homelessness bring a certain lens to research findings that differs from the lens used by researchers, service providers, and policy makers, simply because they have inside experience of the issues being studied. Their views are a critical reality check for those of us well-intentioned researchers and policy makers who are looking at the numbers with empathy for those we are studying, but from a cool distance nonetheless. This way of working is built upon a long international (and local) participatory action research tradition.[18] In this bottom-up approach to research, the systematic gathering of information about the realities of disempowered and disenfranchised people's lives is carried out for the expressed purpose of having an impact on public consciousness in an effort to bring about positive social change—that is, an end to oppressive societal structures and conditions.

We need a revolution within helping relationships, within our human service organizations, within neighborhoods, within public policy making and research circles. A transformation of oppressive practices and structures is possible. These issues matter if we want to be a society in which children hold their heads high, think of themselves as competent, are eager to meet a new day, and have a sense of respect and pride for their parents. These issues are important if we want to be a society in which we treat each other—the haves, the have-some, and the have-nots—as equals. If this is how we want our society to be, then we need to understand the ways in which the human service sector and our government policies support and fail to support those children and parents who have no other option but to ask for government assistance. And then we need to act on that informed understanding.

Notes: Text

Prologue

1. U.S. Dept. of Housing and Urban Development 1998.

2. U.S. Dept. of Housing and Urban Development 1998.

3. In 1998 Congress approved funding for fifty thousand new housing vouchers, an important step forward but clearly inadequate for meeting the high demand for rental housing assistance.

4. Bassuk et al. 1997; Rog, Holupka, and McCombs-Thorton 1995; Shinn et al. 1998; Stretch and Kreuger 1993.

5. U.S. Dept. of Housing and Urban Development 1998.

6. U.S. Dept. of Housing and Urban Development 1999

7. U.S. Dept. of Housing and Urban Development 1998.

8. U.S. Dept. of Housing and Urban Development 1998.

9. U.S. Dept. of Housing and Urban Development 1998.

10. Stevenson and Donovan 1996.

11. Wolff 1998.

12. Hochschild 1989, 1997; Nippert-Eng 1996; Perlow 1997.

13. Allard et al. 1997.

14. Gordon 1994.

15. Harris 1997; Dunst, Trivette, and Deal 1994; Dunst et al. 1993.

1. Parenting and Public Assistance

1. Massachusetts Organization of State-Funded Shelter Providers 1986.

2. Dunst, Trivette, and Deal 1988; Weinreb and Buckner 1993. See Family

Resource Coalition of America's principles of family support practice, www.frca.org.; and K. E. Harris 1997.

3. D. A. Stone 1999.

4. Mead 1997. Mead's treatment of paternalism in the context of the current welfare reform debates is closely aligned with the most negative assumptions regarding the personal characteristics of those who rely upon public assistance. He advocates the use of paternalistic policies and practices involving "close supervision of the dependents" (p. 1). "Merely helping people has not removed pervasive poverty. Government's priority should not be to keep its hands clean but to do what is necessary to integrate the seriously poor into larger society. The assumptions of paternalism no doubt are demeaning, but the problem the poor have with working and other civilities are far more damaging to them" (p. 27).

5. U.S. Conference of Mayors 1998.

6. Bassuk et al. 1997; Jencks 1994; Nunez 1994; Rosenheck, Bassuk, and Saloman 1998; Rossi 1994; U.S. Conference of Mayors 1998.

7. Feins and Fosburg 1998; Jacobs, Little, and Almeida 1993; Rossi 1994.

8. Rossi 1994, p. 382.

9. Menzies 1992; Tiernan 1992.

10. Argeriou 1992.

11. Hartman 1989; Lovell 1992; Rivlin 1986.

12. Marsh 1992.

13. DeParle 1997.

14. Bassuk et al. 1997.

15. Bassuk et al. 1997.

16. DuBus and Buckner 1998; Koblinsky, Morgan, and Anderson 1997; Zima et al. 1999.

17. Bassuk et al. 1997; Goodman 1991; Rosenheck et al. 1998; Zima et al. 1999.

18. Koch, Lewis, and Quinones 1998; Roofless Women's Action Research Mobilization 1997.

19. Koch et al. 1998.

20. Banyard and Graham-Bermann 1998; Hausman and Hammen 1993.

21. Berck 1992; Boxhill and Beaty 1990; Kozol 1988; Molnar 1988; Roofless Women's Action Research Mobilization 1997; Walsh 1992.

22. Feins and Fosburg 1998; Jacobs et al. 1993; Rossi 1994.

23. Feins and Fosburg 1998.

24. Allard et al. 1997.

25. Feins and Fosburg 1998; Rossi 1994.

26. At the time I carried out this study, some families unable to be accommodated in other programs were sheltered on a temporary basis in hotels/motels. Between 1994–1998, hotel/motel shelter wss no longer an official sheltering option in the state; however, many family shelter programs used private funds to temporarily shelter homeless families who are denied shelter by the local welfare office. Due to recent increases in family homelessness in Massachusetts, the state is once again placing families in hotels/motels.

27. Massachusetts Dept. of Transitional Assistance and Dept. of Social Services 1997 data.

28. M. Stone et al. 1998.

29. Macro Systems, Inc. 1991.

30. Jacobs et al. 1993.

31. In 1997, one-third of families who found housing through the state's homeless prevention services and 63 percent of those who left family shelters programs were able to obtain a housing subsidy. Massachusetts Dept. of Transitional Assistance and Dept. of Housing and Community Development 1997 data.

32. I asked each director in the mailed survey to indicate how many parents or parent substitutes and children they were actually serving on a particular day of the year, March 31, 1994. I also asked them to describe several demographic characteristics of those family members (gender, age, educational attainment, and race/ethnicity). Because single mothers with preschoolers was the most common family type in these shelters, the case studies and interviews I carried out focused on understanding parenting issues for mothers of infant, toddler, and preschool children; they did not focus on fathers or parents who were only with older children.

33. Albelda, R. 1996; Torres and Chavez 1998.

34. Blau 1967.

35. Blau 1967; Cook 1977; Wallace and Wolf 1991.

36. Wallace and Wolf 1991.

37. Blau 1967; Cook 1977; Scott 1985.

38. Blau 1967.

39. Blau 1967; Dunst et al. 1988; Wallace and Wolf 1991.

40. D. Stone 1997.

41. Dunst et al. 1991.

42. Hemminger and Quinones 1991; Jacobs et al. 1993; Walsh 1992.

2. Family Shelter Environments

1. In order to protect their anonymity, I have disguised the identities of mothers, staff, directors and shelter agencies throughout the book.

2. Berck 1992; Feins and Fosburg 1998; Jacobs, Little, and Almeida 1993; Rossi 1994.

3. Rossi 1994.

4. Kozol 1988.

5. Grant 1991.

6. Berck 1992; Walsh 1992.

7. Walsh 1992.

8. Walsh 1992, pp. 60–61.

9. Molnar 1988, p. 91.

10. Hausman and Hammen 1993.

11. Boxhill and Beaty 1990.

12. Boxhill 1989.

13. Hemminger and Quinones 1991.

14. Hemminger and Quinones 1991, p. v.

15. Hemminger and Quinones 1991, p. 30.

16. Hemminger and Quinones 1991, p. 30.

17. Jacobs et al. 1993; Rossi 1994

18. These figures are considerably lower than those reported from Jacobs et al.'s 1993 survey of family shelters across the nation (mean=17 families, range=2 to 200).

19. Liebow 1993.

20. Rossi 1994.

21. Similar experiences have been noted by victims of natural disasters who are the recipients of a flood of donations. While givers are well intentioned, recipients are in the best position to know which specific donation would be most functional and useful (Grove 1999).

22. By 1999 families in these circumstances no longer had priority for this type of housing.

3. Parental Rights and the Protection of Children

1. The range varied from a low of five to a high of thirty-eight children in residence on any given night in the shelters participating in this study.

2. This finding is based upon the research of Ellen Bassuk and her colleagues, who carried out extensive interviews as part of a longitudinal research study with 216 poor housed and 220 homeless women living in Worcester, Massachusetts.

3. Boxhill and Beaty 1990; Hausman and Hammen 1993; Koblinsky, Morgan, and Anderson 1997; Walsh 1992; Weinreb and Buckner 1993.

4. Dunst et al. 1993; Halpern 1993; Krauss and Jacobs 1990; Lightburn and

Kemp 1994; Rounds, Weil, and Bishop 1994; Trivette and Dunst (1994); Trivette, Johns, and Harvey 1994.

5. Brofenbrenner 1979.

6. I asked all mothers and staff members to describe both successful and unsuccessful interactions in relation to each of six family support principles (Dunst et al. 1991). Specifically, I asked them to describe examples of successful and unsuccessful help giving related to: (1) building relationships among parents in the shelter; (2) increasing the number of people they could count on when they needed support with their children; (3) working as a team; (4) resolving differences between staff and mothers related to child-rearing norms; (5) affirming mothers' strengths and primary decision-making role as parents; and (6) attending to concerns mothers had regarding caring for their children in the presence of others.

7. Sixty-three percent of the 126 homeless women interviewed by formerly homeless researchers of the Roofless Women's Action Research Mobilization (RWARM) project expressed self-blame for their homeless circumstance.

8. Berck 1992; Walsh 1992.

9. Bassuk, Browne, and Buckner 1996; Bassuk et al. 1996; Bassuk et al. 1997.

10. Friedman et al. 1996; Friedman et al. 1997.

11. Straus 1994. Straus argues that any form of hitting a child is child abuse and should be illegal, on the grounds that, although spanking is common practice in the United States, corporal punishment is associated with delinquency, aggression, and other serious social problems. Lazelere (1994) disagrees with Straus, citing evidence from Sweden that a ban on all forms of corporal punishment (including mild spanking) is associated with higher rates of child abuse. He suggests that when parents have some sense of control with their children, escalation of negative behaviors may be interrupted, thus preventing the tendency for parents to dispense harsher discipline to their children.

12. Boston Foundation 1999. In 1999 the average rental fee for a two-bedroom apartment in Boston was $1,350 per month, out of reach for even a single person earning as much as $41,000 per year.

13. Dunst, Trivette, and Deal 1988.

4. Shelter Rules

1. Walsh 1992; Hemminger and Quinones 1991; Molnar 1988.

2. Betsy Santiago in particular was extremely influential in helping me to

craft questions covering shelter rules for my interviews with managers, staff, and mothers.

3. Customarily in Massachusetts, personnel in local welfare offices operate as gatekeepers for families' entry into publicly funded shelters and direct families to shelters with openings who (on paper) can accommodate their needs, taking into consideration such factors as family size, family constellation, and location of families' home communities. At times parents receive information from other parents or staff in human service agencies regarding which shelters to avoid and which shelters to try to enter. If the state is paying for a family's shelter, there is no guarantee that a family's wish or preference will or can be honored.

4. Grant 1991.

5. To analyze mothers' responses regarding shelter rules, I coded responses in support of or neutral to the rule as indicators of satisfaction. Examples of responses coded in this manner were: "It's okay"; "It's good"; "I have no comment"; "I may not like it, but it's necessary." I coded responses expressing negativity regarding the rule as indicators of dissatisfaction. Examples include: "It's ridiculous"; "It's a problem"; "It's humiliating"; "It's not good."

6. Kubler-Ross 1997.

5. Individualized and Standardized Service

1. Trivette and Dunst 1994.

2. Dunst et al. 1993.

3. Dunst, Trivette, and Deal 1988; Dunst, Trivette, and Deal 1994; Dunst et al. 1993; Trivette and Dunst 1994; Trivette et al 1994.

4. Mead 1997.

5. Payne 1997.

6. Payne 1997; Dunst et al. 1988

7. Dunst et al. 1988.

8. Liebow 1993.

9. Feins and Fosburg 1998.

10. Feins and Fosburg 1998.

11. Jacobs, Little, and Almeida 1993.

12. Jacobs, Little, and Almeida 1993.

13. I modeled the questions on those used by Jacobs, Little, and Almeida 1993.

14. Jacobs, Little, and Almeida 1993; Molnar 1988.

15. The third meeting has already been described in detail in chapter 2.

These descriptions are based upon detailed field notes I wrote to chronicle my observations and reactions immediately after each meeting.

6. The Paradox of Self-Sufficiency: Building Community and Interdependence

1. Morone 1990.
2. Stack 1974; Edin and Lein 1997.
3. Coontz 1992; Jones 1995.
4. Hochschild 1989.
5. Handler 1995.
6. Albelda and Tilly 1996; Handler 1995.
7. Bassuk and Rosenberg 1990; Dunst, Trivette, and Hamby 1991; Dunst, Trivette, and Deal 1988; Dunst, Trivette, and Deal 1994; Jacobs, Little, and Almeida 1993.
8. Rog, Holupka, and McCombs-Thorton 1995.
9. Bassuk et. al 1996.
10. One part of this research involved asking mother-staff pairs about examples of both successful and unsuccessful help giving that had occurred in their relationship. I met with each mother and staff member separately to hear these stories. Each mother signed a consent form that spelled out this research method prior to my interview with the staff member who had worked with her.
11. Freeman and Robbins 1998.
12. I did not ask managers to provide me with information regarding the incomes of staff members. Rather, as a way of understanding class differences between staff and mothers, I asked for information regarding the educational attainment of staff and of mothers.
13. I asked managers to indicate the percentages of families who left their shelters within the past twelve months with respect to the primary reasons that led to their departure, including: moving into permanent housing; moving into a transitional housing program; leaving voluntarily prior to accessing permanent or transitional housing; leaving due to expressed dissatisfaction with the program; or leaving voluntarily due to rule violations. I asked them to select the category that best described families' primary reasons for leaving, with the total percentages equaling 100 percent.
14. This finding is somewhat misleading. It does not reflect within-program variability. For example, some families may have stayed for only a few days while others may have stayed for over a year. In addition, this information is not reflective of the time individual families spent being homeless. Whether families have spent time in other shelters, or on the street, or dou-

bled up with friends or relatives was not captured in this survey of shelter directors.

15. Transitional housing programs are designed as long-term treatment programs in which families have their own apartment but agree to an intensive service plan focused on personal and social change and growth.

16. In 1997, 63 percent of families in Massachusetts, who moved from a DTA-funded emergency shelter into their own home, did so with a housing subsidy, while only 33 percent of families on the brink of becoming homeless, served by homeless prevention programs in the state, were able to secure subsidized housing. See Stone et al. 1998.

17. See Stretch and Kreuger 1993. Based on their findings, having a Section 8 certificate was significantly associated with prevention of repeated incidences of homelessness.

18. Positive reasons included leaving for permanent or transitional housing. I considered any other category to be a negative reason for leaving because all of those reasons implied that families leaving under those circumstances continued to be in an unstable and transient housing situation. To test hypotheses regarding associations between managers' espoused helping practices and specific program features, the study sample was divided into three groups, according to the same methodology used to select case study sites. That is, the first step involved calculating the four helping practices subscale scores for each program. Respondents' subscale scores for the helping practices scale were collapsed into two groups: family-centered and family-focused into one group (referred to as family support); family-allied and professional-centered (referred to as prescriptive). The programs with the highest scores on the combined family support subscale (highest fifth) were designated as the family support group (n=9). The programs with the highest scores on the combined prescriptive subscale (highest fifth) were designated as the prescriptive group (n=10). All other programs were designated as mixed (n=28).

19. Sarah Haig Friedman, who reviewed an earlier version of this chapter, greatly influenced my thoughts on these issues. I am most grateful for her insights on the themes in this chapter.

8. We Need a Revolution

1. Gordon 1994.
2. Wheatley 1994, pp. 55–56
3. Wheatley 1994.
4. Wheatley 1994, pp. 55–56.

5. Schall 1995.
6. Wheatley 1994.
7. Friere 1970.
8. Rosenthal forthcoming.
9. Jencks 1994; Rossi 1994; Rosenthal forthcoming.
10. The Boston Foundation, an influential philanthropic organization in Massachusetts, through the Fund for the Homeless, currently the Fund for Self-Reliance, has provided leadership through its long-standing commitment to a Power With orientation; this has precipitated the growth and expansion of homeless-led service and advocacy organizations in the Greater Boston area. My coauthors and I are working to realize this objective as members of Homes For Families, a statewide organization committed to a partnership among those families directly affected by and those working to end family homelessness in Massachusetts. In this organization, parents who have been homeless hold leadership positions, hold half of the seats on the board, and regularly inform the organization's actions regarding state homeless prevention and shelter policies.
11. Jacobs 1994; Stone 1997.
12. Morone 1990.
13. Stone 1993.
14. Gordon 1994.
15. Morone 1990.
16. "Consumer" is the best term we have been able to come up with as yet to designate official positions for persons who have been homeless on steering committees and other official decision-making bodies. This term, while not ideal, is preferable to "homeless" or "formerly homeless," which have a negative and totalizing connotation.
17. This project was funded by the Boston Foundation and was a collaboration between the Center for Social Policy within the McCormack Institute and Homes For Families, Inc.
18. Hall 1993; Roofless Women's Action Research Mobilization 1997.

Notes: Reflections

1. Parenting and Public Assistance

1. Friere 1970.
2. Koch, Lewis, and Quinones 1998.
3. Koch et al. 1998.
4. Koch et al. 1998.
5. Jordan 1991.

5. Individualized and Standardized Services

1. Better Homes Fund 1990; Weinreb and Buckner 1993; Weinreb and Rossi 1991; Welch 1985.

Bibliography

Abramovitz, M. 1996. *Regulating the Lives of Women: Social Welfare Policy from Colonial Times to the Present*. Rev. ed. Boston: South End Press.

Albelda, R. 1996. *An Economic Profile of Women in Massachusetts*. Boston: McCormack Institute for Public Affairs, Center for Women in Politics, University of Massachusetts, Boston.

Albelda, R. and C. Tilly. 1996. It's a Family Affair: Women, Poverty, and Welfare. In D. Dijon and A. A. Withorn, eds., *For Crying Out Loud: Women's Poverty in the United States*. Boston: South End Press.

Allard, M. A., R. Albelda, M. E. Colten, and C. Cosenza. 1997, February. *In Harm's Way? Domestic Violence, AFDC Receipt, and Welfare Reform in Massachusetts*. Boston: University of Massachusetts.

Allard, M. A., R. Bucci, D. H. Friedman, J. Green, M. Hayes, T. Mason, M. Spade, V. Steinitz, M. Stone, and E. Werby. 1997. *Over the Edge: Cuts and Changes in Housing, Income Support, and Homeless Assistance Programs in Massachusetts*. Boston: McCormack Institute for Public Affairs, Center for Social Policy, and College of Public and Community Service, University of Massachusetts, Boston.

Argeriou, M. 1992. Perception, Policy, and Progress. *New England Journal of Public Policy* 8: 455–470.

Banyard, V. L. and S. A. Graham-Bermann. 1998. Surviving Poverty: Stress and Coping in the Lives of Housed and Homeless Mothers. *American Journal of Orthopsychiatry* 68: 479–489.

Bassuk, E. L. 1986. Homeless Families: Single Mothers and Their Children in Boston Shelters. In E. L. Bassuk, ed., *The Mental Health Needs of Homeless Per-*

sons: New Directions for Mental Health Services, no. 30. San Francisco: Jossey-Bass.

Bassuk, E. L. 1992. Women and Children Without Shelter: The characteristics of Homeless Families. In M. J. Robertson and M. Greenblatt, eds., *Homelessness: A National Perspective.* Topics in Social Psychiatry, E. L. Bassuk, series editor. New York: Plenum Press.

Bassuk, E. L. 1993a. Homeless Women: Economic and Social Issues: Introduction. *American Journal of Orthopsychiatry* 63: 337–339.

Bassuk, E. L. 1993b. Social and Economic Hardships of Homeless and Other Poor Women. *American Journal of Orthopsychiatry* 63: 340–347.

Bassuk, E. L. and L. Rosenberg. 1990. Psychosocial Characteristics of Homeless Children and Children with Homes. *Pediatrics* 85: 257–261.

Bassuk, E. L., A. Browne, and J. C. Buckner. 1996. Families Living in Poverty. *Scientific American* 275: 60–67.

Bassuk, E. L., L. Rubin, and A. S. Lauriat. 1986. Characteristics of Sheltered Homeless Families. *American Journal of Public Health* 76: 1097–1101.

Bassuk, E. L., L. F. Weinreb, J. C. Buckner, A. Browne, A. Salomon, and S. S. Bassuk. 1996. The Characteristics and Needs of Sheltered and Low-Income Housed Mothers. *Journal of the American Medical Association* 276: 640–646.

Bassuk, E. L., J. C. Buckner, L. F. Weinreb, A. Browne, S. S. Bassuk, R. Dawson, and J. N. Perloff. 1997. Homelessness in Female-Headed Families: Childhood and Adult Risk and Protective Factors. *American Journal of Public Health* 87: 241–248.

Berck, J. 1992. *No Place to Be: Voices of Homeless Children.* Boston: Houghton-Mifflin.

Better Homes Fund. 1990. *Final Report: Evaluation of Programs for Homeless Families.* Newton, Mass.

Better Homes Fund. 1999. *Homeless Children: America's New Outcasts.* A Public Policy Report from the Better Homes Fund. Newton, Mass.

Blau, P. M. 1967. *Exchange and Power in Social Life.* New York: Wiley.

Boston Foundation. 1999. *Boston's Indicators of Progress, Change, and Sustainability.* Boston.

Boxhill, N. 1989. Forming Human Connections in Shelters for Homeless Women and Children. *Zero to Three* 9: 19–21.

Boxhill, N. A. and A. L. Beaty. 1990. Mother/Child Interaction Among Homeless Women and Their Children Using a Public Night Shelter in Atlanta, Georgia. In N. A. Boxhill, ed., *Homeless Children: The Watchers and the Waiters.* Atlanta: Atlanta Task Force for the Homeless.

Brofenbrenner, U. 1979. *The Ecology of Human Development.* Cambridge: Harvard University Press.

Browne, A. and S. S. Bassuk. 1997. Intimate Violence in the Lives of Homeless and Poor Housed Women: Prevalence and Patterns in an Ethnically Diverse Sample. *American Journal of Orthopsychiatry* 67: 261–278.

Caton, C. L. M. 1990. *Homeless in America.* New York: Oxford University Press.

Cook, K. 1977. Exchange and Power in Networks of Interorganizational Relations. *The Sociological Quarterly* 18: 62–82.

Coontz, S. 1992. *The Way We Never Were: American Families and the Nostalgia Trap.* New York: Basic Books.

Dehavenon, A. L. 1997. *Charles Dickens Meets Franz Kafka: How the Giuliani Administration Flouted Court Orders and Abused Homeless Families and Children.* New York: The Action Research Project on Hunger, Homelessness, and Family Health.

DeParle, J. 1997, August 24. It Takes a Village to Reform Welfare. *New York Times Magazine,* pp. Cover, 33–37, 47, 54, 59–61.

DuBus, P. and J. C. Buckner. 1998. A Shelter Is Not a Home: Homeless Urban Mothers and Their Children. *Bulletin of Zero To Three, National Center for Infants, Toddlers, and Families* 19: 18–23.

Dulwich Centre. 1996. Speaking Out and Being Heard. *Dulwich Centre Newsletter* 4: 3–56. Adelaide, South Australia.

Dunst, C. J., C. M. Trivette, and A. G. Deal. 1988. *Enabling and Empowering Families: Principles and Guidelines for Practice.* Cambridge: Brookline Books.

Dunst, C. J., C. Johanson, C. M. Trivette, and D. Hamby. 1991. Family-Oriented Early Intervention Policies and Practices: Family-Centered or Not? *Exceptional Children* 58: 115–126.

Dunst, C. J., C. M. Trivette, A. L. Starnes, D. Hamby, and N. J. Gordon. 1993. *Building and Evaluating Family Support Initiatives: A National Study of Programs for Persons with Developmental Disabilities.* Baltimore, Md.: Paul Brookes.

Dunst, C. J., C. M. Trivette, and A. G. Deal. 1994. *Supporting and Strengthening Families:* vol. 1, *Methods, Strategies, and Practices.* Cambridge: Brookline Books.

Edin, K. and L. Lein 1997. *Making Ends Meet: How Single Mothers Survive Welfare and Low-Wage Work.* New York: Russell Sage Foundation.

Embry-Nimmer, Z. 1995, September. Definitions and Historical Context of U.S. Homelessness. In *Women and Homelessness: Many Things Gone Wrong.* A Report on the Activities of Women of Color on Homelessness and Housing and the Women of Color Resource Center at the UN Fourth World Conference on Women/NGO Forum, Beijing and Huairou, China.

Feins, J. D., L. B. Fosburg, C. Barron, N. Kay, and D. Baker. 1994. *Evaluation of the Emergency Shelter Grants Program:* vol. 2, *Site Profiles.* Washington, D.C.: U.S. Dept. of Housing and Urban Development, Office of Policy Development and Research, Contract: H-5882.

Feins, J. D. and L. B. Fosburg. 1998. Emergency Shelter and Services: Opening the Front Door to the Continuum of Care. *Proceedings of the National Symposium on Homelessness Research: What Works*. U.S. Dept. of Housing and Urban Development and U.S. Dept. of Health and Human Services, Washington, D.C.

Freeman, P. and A. Robbins. 1998, March. The Health Data Privacy Debate: Can We Achieve Comprehension Before Closure? An Occasional Paper of the J. W. McCormack Institute of Public Affairs. Boston: University of Massachusetts, Boston.

Friedman, D. H., D. Anthony, D. DeFreitas, B. Farrell, B. Santiago, M. Hayes, and R. Bucci. 1996. *Families at Risk: Final Report*. Boston: McCormack Institute for Public Affairs, Center for Social Policy, University of Massachusetts, Boston.

Friedman, D. H., M. Hayes, J. McGah, A. Roman. 1997. *A Snapshot of Individuals and Families in Boston's Emergency Homeless Shelters*. Boston: McCormack Institute for Public Affairs, Center for Social Policy, University of Massachusetts, Boston.

Friere, P. 1970. *Pedagogy of the Oppressed*. New York: Continuum Books.

Goodman, L. A. 1991. The Relationship Between Social Support and Homelessness: A Comparison Study of Homeless and Housed Mothers. *Journal of Community Psychology* 19: 321–332.

Gordon, L. 1994. *Pitied, But Not Entitled*. New York: Basic Books.

Grant, R. 1991. The Special Needs of Homeless Children : Early Intervention at a Welfare Hotel. *Topics in Early Childhood Special Education* 10, no. 4: 76–91.

Grove, F. 1999, March 12. Flood of Donations Another Disaster for Victims. *Boston Globe*.

Halpern, R. 1993. The Societal Context of Home Visiting and Related Services for Families in Poverty. *The Future of Children* 3: 158–171.

Handler, J. F. 1995. *The Poverty of Welfare Reform*. New Haven: Yale University Press.

Harris, D., P. Baker, L. Lee, and D. Roher. 1997. *TAFDC Advocacy Guide: An Advocate's Guide to the New Welfare Rules in Massachusetts for Parents with Dependent Children*. Boston: Massachusetts Law Reform Institute and Massachusetts Continuing Legal Education, Inc.

Harris, K. E. 1997. Integrating Community Development and Family Support. *Family Resource Coalition Report* 16: 4–7.

Hartman, A. 1989. Homelessness: Public Issue and Private Trouble. *Social Work* 34: 483–484.

Hausman, B. and C. Hammen. 1993. Parenting in Homeless Families: The Double Crisis. *American Journal of Orthopsychiatry* 63: 358–369.

Hemminger, H. and W. Quinones. 1991. "We Are Like You": The Lives and
    Hopes of 79 Formerly Homeless Women. Proceedings of a Symposium:
    Choosing the Future. Gloucester, Mass.: Wellspring House.

Hochschild, A. R. 1989. *The Second Shift: Working Parents and the Revolution at
    Home*. New York: Viking Press.

Hochschild, A. R. 1997. *The Time Bind: When Work Becomes Home and Home
    Becomes Work*. New York: Henry Holt.

Hodnicki, D. R. and S. D. Horner. 1993. Homeless Mothers' Caring for Chil-
    dren in a Shelter. *Issues in Mental Health Nursing* 14: 349–356.

Jacobs, F. 1994. Child and Family Policy: Framing the Issues. In F. Jacobs and M.
    W. Davies, eds., *More than Kissing Babies: Current Child and Family Policy in the
    United States*. Westport, Conn: Auburn House.

Jacobs, F. H., P. M. D. Little, and C. Almeida. 1993. Supporting Family Life: A
    Survey of Homeless Shelters. *Journal of Social Distress and the Homeless* 2:
    269–288.

Jencks, C. 1994. *The Homeless*. Cambridge: Harvard University Press.

Jones, J. 1995. *Labor of Love, Labor of Sorrow*. New York: Vintage.

Jordan, J. V. 1991. The Meaning of Mutuality. In J. V. Jordan, A. G. Kaplan, J. B.
    Miller, I. P. Stiver, and J. L. Surrey, eds., *Women's Growth in Connection: Writings
    from the Stone Center*. New York: Guilford Press.

Keigher, S. M. 1992. Rediscovering the Asylum. *Journal of Sociology and Social
    Welfare* 19: 177–197.

Koblinsky, S. A., K. M. Morgan, and E. A. Anderson. 1997. African American
    Homeless and Low-Income Housed Mothers: Comparison of Parenting
    Practices. *American Journal of Orthopsychiatry* 67: 37–47.

Koch, R., M. T. Lewis, and W. Quinones. 1998. Homeless: Mothering at Rock
    Bottom. In C. Garcia-Coll, J. L. Surrey, and K. Weingarten, eds., *Mothering
    Against the Odds: Diverse Voices of Contemporary Mothers*. New York: Guilford
    Press.

Kozol, J. 1988. *Rachel and Her Children*. New York: Ballantine.

Krauss, M. W. and F. H. Jacobs. 1990. Family Assessment: Purposes and Tech-
    niques. In S. J. Meisels and J. P. Shonkoff, eds., *Handbook of Early Childhood
    Intervention*. New York: Cambridge University Press.

Kubler-Ross, E. 1997. *On Death and Dying*. New York: Collier.

Larzelere, R. E. 1994. Debate 12: Corporal Punishment by Parents. In M. A.
    Mason and E. Gambrill, eds., *Debating Children's Lives: Current Controversies
    on Children and Adolescents*. Thousand Oaks, Calif.: Sage.

Lassiter, A. 1997, July/August. The New Social Architects. *Policy Review*: 52–57.

Liebow, E. 1993. *Tell Them Who I Am*. New York: Free Press.

Lightburn, A. and S. Kemp. 1994. Family Support Programs: Opportunities for

Community-Based Practice. *Families in Society: The Journal of Contemporary Human Services* 75: 16–26.

Lovell, A. M. 1992. Classification and Its Risks: How Psychiatric Status Contributes to Homelessness Policy. *New England Journal of Public Policy* 8: 247–263.

Macro Systems, Inc. 1991. *Homeless Families with Children: Programmatic Responses for Five Communities*, vols. 1 and 2. Washington, D.C.: U.S. Dept. of Health and Human Services.

Marris, P. 1996. The Trouble with Sharing. In G. C. Hemmems, C. J. Hoch, and J. Carp, eds., *Under One Roof: Issues and Innovations in Shared Housing*. Albany: State University of New York Press.

Marsh, S. 1992. Making the Homeless Disappear: Redefining Homelessness in Massachusetts. *New England Journal of Public Policy* 8: 511–521.

Massachusetts Department of Public Welfare. 1993. *Congregate Shelter Service Contract*.

Massachusetts Institute for a New Commonwealth. 1996. *The State of the American Dream in New England*. Boston.

Massachusetts Organization of State-Funded Shelter Providers. 1986. *A Service Model for Homeless Families*. Boston.

McKnight, J. 1995. *The Careless Society: Community and Its Counterfeits*. New York: Basic Books.

Meade, L. M. 1997. *The New Paternalism: Supervisory Approaches to Poverty*. Washington, D.C.: Brookings Institute.

Menzies, I. 1992. Homelessness in Boston: The Media Wake Up. *New England Journal of Public Policy* 8: 695–702.

Michlitsch, J. N. and S. Frankel. 1989. Helping Orientations: Four Dimensions. *Perceptual and Motor Skills* 69: 1371–1378.

Miles, M. B. and A. M. Huberman. 1994. *Qualitative Data Analysis*. 2d ed. Thousand Oaks, Calif.: Sage.

Miller, D. S. and E. H. B. Lin. 1988. Children in Sheltered Homeless Families: Reported Health Status and Use of Health Services. *Pediatrics* 81: 5, 668–673.

Mills, C. and H. Ota. 1989. Homeless Women with Minor Children in the Detroit Metropolitan Area. *Social Work* 34: 485–489.

Mishel, L., J. Bernstein, and J. Schmitt. 1997. *The State of Working America: 1996–1997*. Economic Policy Institute. Armonk, N.Y.: M. E. Sharpe.

Molnar, J. M. 1988. *Home Is Where the Heart Is: The Crisis of Homeless Children and Families in New York City*. New York: Bank Street College of Education ERIC Document Reproduction Service, No. ED 304 228.

Morone, J. A. 1990. *The Democratic Wish: Popular Participation and the Limits of American Government*. New York: Basic Books.

Nippert-Eng, C. E. 1996. *Home and Work: Negotiating Boundaries Through Everyday Life*. Chicago: University of Chicago Press.

Nunez, R. D. 1994. *Hopes, Dreams, and Promise: The Future of Homeless Children in America*. New York: Homes for the Homeless.

Nunez, R. D. 1996. *The New Poverty: Homeless Families in America*. New York: Plenum.

Payne, J. L. 1997, May/June. The Smart Samaritan. *Policy Review* : 48–53.

Perlow, L. A. 1997. *Finding Time: How Corporations, Individuals, and Families Can Benefit from New Work Practices*. Ithaca: Cornell University Press.

Porter, T. Winter. 1992/1993. Partners for Success: Family Support for Formerly Homeless. *Family Resource Coalition Report* 11: 6–7.

Powell, W. E. 1994. The Relationship Between Feelings of Alienation and Burnout in Social Work. *Families in Society: Journal of Contemporary Human Services* 75: 229–235.

Rivlin, L. 1986. A New Look at the Homeless. *Social Policy* 16: 3–10.

Rog, D. J., C. S. Holupka, and K. L. McCombs-Thorton. 1995. Implementation of the Homeless Families Program: Service Models and Preliminary Outcomes. *American Journal of Orthopsychiatry* 65: 502–513.

Roofless Women's Action Research Mobilization. 1997, April. *Lifting the Voices of Homeless Women: Summary of Findings and Recommendations*. Boston: Women's Institute for Housing and Economic Development and Center for Community Planning, University of Massachusetts, Boston.

Rosenheck, R., E. Bassuk, and A. Salomon. 1998, October. Special Populations of Homeless Americans. *Proceedings of the National Symposium on Homelessness Research: What Works*. U.S. Dept. of Housing and Urban Development and U.S. Dept. of Health and Human Services, Washington, D.C.

Rosenthal, R. Forthcoming. Responses to Homelessness: Past Policies and Future Directions. In R. Bratt, C. Hartman, and M. E. Stone. *Housing: Foundation for a New Social Agenda*. Philadelphia: Temple University Press.

Rossi, P. H. 1994. Troubling Families: Family Homelessness in America. *American Behavioral Scientist* 37: 342–395.

Rounds, K. A., M. Weil, and K. K. Bishop. 1994. Practice with Culturally Diverse Families of Young Children with Disabilities. *Families in Society: Journal of Contemporary Human Services* 75: 3–15.

Ruddick, S. 1989. *Maternal thinking: Toward a Politic of Peace*. Boston: Beacon Press.

Schall, E. 1995. Learning to Love the Swamp: Reshaping Education for Public Service. *Journal of Policy Analysis and Management* 14: 202–220.

Scott, J. C. 1985 . *Weapons of the Weak: Everyday Forms of Peasant Resistance*. New Haven: Yale University Press.

Shinn, M. B., B. C. Weitzman, D. Stojanovic, J. A. Knickman, L. Jimemez,
L. Duchon, S. James, and D. H. Krantz. 1998. Predictors of Homelessness
Among Families in New York City. *American Journal of Public Health* 88:
1651–1657.

Stack, C. B. 1974. *All Our Kin: Strategies for Survival in a Black Community*. New
York: Harper and Row.

Stevenson, M. H. and E. Donovan. 1996. How the U.S. Economy Creates
Poverty and Inequality. In D. Dijon and A. A. Withorn, eds., *For Crying Out
Loud: Women's Poverty in the United States*. Boston: South End Press.

Stone, M. 1993. *Shelter Poverty: New Ideas on Housing Affordability*. Philadelphia:
Temple University Press.

Stone, D. 1999, March/April. Care and Trembling. *American Prospect*, 61–67.

Stone, M., D. H. Friedman, M. Spade, K. Armenoff, E. Werby, E. Douglas, and
E. Ward. 1998. Housing Affordability. In *A Profile of Housing in Massachusetts*.
Boston: University of Massachusetts, Boston..

Straus, M. A. 1994. Debate 12: Corporal Punishment by Parents. In M. A. Mason
and E. Gambrill, eds., *Debating Children's Lives: Current Controversies on Children and Adolescents*. Thousand Oaks, Calif.: Sage.

Stretch, J. J. and L. W. Kreuger. 1993. Five-Year Cohort Study of Homeless Families: Coordinated Case-Managed Services. In C. J. Morton, D. Wilkinson,
and D. Patterson, eds., *Promoting Family Health in the 1990s: Strategies for Public
Health Social Work*. Berkeley: School of Public Health, University of Califor-
nia at Berkeley.

Tiernan, K. 1992. The Politics of Accommodation. *New England Journal of Public
Policy* 8: 647–667.

Torres, A. and L. Chavez. 1998, November. *Latinos in Massachusetts: An Update*.
Boston: Maurico Gaston Institute for Latino Community Development and
Public Policy, University of Massachusetts, Boston.

Trivette, C. M. and C. J. Dunst. 1994. *Characteristics and Consequences of Help-Giving Practices in Human Service Programs*. Morganton, N.C.: Center for Family
Studies.

Trivette, C. M., C. J. Dunst, N. Johns, and K. Harvey. 1994. *Family-Centered
Maternity Care: Fact or Fantasy*. Morganton, N.C.: Center for Family Studies.

U.S. Conference of Mayors. 1998. *A Status Report on Hunger and Homelessness in
America's Cities, 1998: A Thirty-City Survey, December 1998*. Washington, D.C.

U.S. Department of Housing and Urban Development. 1998. *Rental Housing
Assistance—The Crisis Continues: The 1997 Report to Congress on Worst-Case
Housing Needs*. Washington, D.C.

U.S. Department of Housing and Urban Development. 1999. *Waiting in Vain: An
Update on America's Rental Housing Crisis*. Washington, D.C.

Wallace, R. A. and A. Wolf, eds. 1991. *Contemporary Sociological Theory: Continuing the Classical Tradition*. 3d ed. Englewood, N.J.: Prentice Hall.

Walsh, M. E. 1992. *"Moving to Nowhere": Children's Stories of Homelessness*. Westport, Conn: Auburn House.

Weinreb, L. and J. Buckner. 1993. Homeless Families: Program Responses and Public Policies. *American Journal of Orthopsychiatry* 63: 400–409.

Weinreb, L. and P. Rossi. 1991. Homeless Families: Public Policies, Program Responses and Evaluation Strategies. In E. Bassuk, ed., *Homeless Families with Children: Research Perspectives*. Rockville, Md.: U.S. Dept. of Health and Human Services.

Welch, S. 1985. *Communities of Resistance and Solidarity: A Feminist Theology of Liberation*. New York: Orbis Books.

Wheatley, M. J. 1994. *Leadership and the New Science: Learning About Organization from an Orderly Universe*. San Francisco: Berret-Koehler.

Wolff, E. 1998. Recent Trends in the Size Distribution of Household Wealth. *Journal of Economic Perspectives* 12: 131–150.

Zima, B. T., R. Bussing, M. Bystritsky, M. H. Widawski, T. R. Belin, and B. Benjamin. 1999. Psychosocial Stressors Among Sheltered Homeless Children: Relationship to Behavior Problems and Depressive Symptoms. *American Journal of Orthopsychiatry* 69: 127–133.

About the Authors

Rosa Clark currently provides follow-up support services to families who have moved from the Project Hope family shelter to their own homes. Prior to this position, she directed the agency's family shelter program for seven years. She became acquainted with the agency when she and her son were homeless and lived at Project Hope in 1984. Rosa had a starring role in Project Hope's video production, "Women of Strength." She also led a reflection process with women in the Project Hope shelter that resulted in a written account of their stories, *Women in the Struggle*. Rosa was born in Honduras and moved to the United States when she was fourteen years old.

Brenda Farrell responds to families on the brink of losing their housing who are seeking help from a homeless prevention agency in Worcester, Massachusetts. Prior to this position, she was the director of membership for Homes for Families, a statewide advocacy organization committed to ending family homelessness in Massachusetts. Brenda shares her insights on public policy responses to family homelessness through frequent speaking engagements at local and national conferences. Within the past five years she has conducted participatory action research as a University of Massachusetts Boston family researcher with the Roofless Women's Action Research Mobilization (RWARM) project and the Families At Risk project. Brenda had a starring role in a video produced by Project Hope, "Women of Strength." Brenda's courage in speaking out is grounded in her family's tragic loss of housing and devastating experience with shelter life in 1990.

Donna Haig Friedman, Director of the Center for Social Policy within the McCormack Institute, University of Massachusetts, Boston, carries out participatory action research focused on public policy issues affecting the lives of low income families. She teaches graduate courses in family policy, program evaluation, and qualitative research design at the university.

Deborah Gray is currently the education coordinator for the Family Nurturing Center of Massachusetts. Using a family support approach, she organizes and facilitates self-help groups around parenting and communication skills, focusing on getting parents the services and information they need. In the past year she has conducted workshops and trainings on parent involvement and parent leadership development in Asheville, North Carolina, and Aspen, Colorado, as well as Lynn and Sturbridge, Massachusetts. For the past six years Deborah has been on the board of Parents United For Child Care, a position that has helped her to develop advocacy, organizational, and public-speaking skills. For the past two summers Deborah has been a Primary Source Scholar presenting at Simmons College and the National Educational Research Center. In this capacity she has presented in two courses: Black Yankees: The African American Experience in New England for 1609 to 1910 and Literacy in the Nineteenth Century. She has traveled twice to Africa as part of her journey of personal enlightenment. She is working on a masters degree in Human Services at the University of Massachusetts, Boston, where she discovered the Roofless Women's Action Research Mobilization (RWARM) project, became a participatory action researcher, and currently participates in Women and Community Development. She found that through these professional activities, including the creation of the Family Nurturing Center, she could use her life experiences, including being homeless and in temporary need of welfare, to help other women and families who are in need of services.

Michelle Kahan, a senior research associate with the Center for Social Policy, McCormack Institute, University of Massachusetts, Boston, and nonprofit management consultant, works with nonprofit and public organizations on issues of homelessness and family violence. She provides leadership, technical expertise, and training in the areas of program planning, development, and evaluation; project management; capacity building; organizational development; and grant writing and administration. Michelle has held executive director and staff positions with family shelter and battered women's service organizations and currently evaluates and provides technical assistance to supportive housing programs for the city of Boston. As a board member of Homes for Families (HFF), Michelle also works to formulate and advocate for statewide policies to address the needs of homeless families and, ultimately, to break the cycle of homelessness and poverty in Massachusetts. Through her work with HFF, Michelle has learned a great deal about the experience of homeless families and has intensified her commitment to improving the access, delivery, and quality of homeless services. She is committed to taking action toward these goals in partnership with families who have experienced homelessness and to developing program and administrative policies that are based upon the collective wisdom of families' experiences.

Margaret Leonard has worked with impoverished families in East Harlem, New York, and Dorchester, Massachusetts, for over thirty years. As executive director of a family-based neighborhood development organization since 1985, she has developed and continues to oversee on-site social service and economic empowerment programs (e.g., shelter, child care, adult education, economic literacy, transition to work) serving low-income families in crisis. She has been a catalyst in forging strategic alliances, partnerships, and collaborations at local, city, and state levels that create a continuum of care and support for low income families in the move from crisis to stability. Under her leadership, Project Hope has become an active partner with the Dudley Street Neighborhood Initiative in rebuilding the infrastructure of one of Boston's poorest inner-city neighborhoods to help transform it into a vibrant urban village.

Mary T. Lewis has been a professional social worker for over twenty-five years. For the past five and a half years, she worked as a family life advocate at the Wellspring House Inc. in Gloucester, Massachusetts. She coauthored a chapter in a book edited by Surrey and Weingarten and published by Guilford Press, *Mothering Against the Odds*. In her chapter, "Mothering at Rock Bottom," she and her coauthors explore the impact of homelessness on mothers' sense of themselves as parents. She has worked and lectured both in Asia and within the United States. Mary developed her framework for help giving from her professional work and her personal experience as the adoptive parent of one son and the birth parent of three sons. Committed to lifelong learning, Mary recently left her position at Wellspring House to return to graduate school.

Nancy Schwoyer is a founder and Executive Director of Wellspring House, Inc., an eighteen-year-old community-based organization in Gloucester, Massachusetts. Her practice comes out of a lifelong commitment to social justice, which was awakened as a result of her participation in the civil rights and peace movements of the 1960s. Fundamentally, she views herself as an educator, one who uses an action–reflection model, rooted in the experience of local community. The mutual learning experience inspires and energizes Nancy.

Elisabeth Ward, a single mother, is a full-time student at the University of Massachusetts, Boston, and a part-time research assistant at the university's McCormack Institute of Public Affairs. She and her son spent seven weeks in a family shelter in 1989. She has also worked on the staff at the same shelter where she was a guest.

Index